THE BOOK OF
MODERN JEWISH ETIQUETTE

THE
BOOK
OF
MODERN JEWISH
ETIQUETTE

A GUIDE FOR ALL OCCASIONS

Helen Latner

Harper & Row, Publishers, New York
Cambridge, Philadelphia, San Francisco, Washington
London, Mexico City, São Paulo, Singapore, Sydney

First PERENNIAL LIBRARY edition published 1986

Library of Congress Cataloging-in-Publication Data

Latner, Helen.
   The book of modern Jewish etiquette.

   Includes index.
   1. Jewish etiquette. 2. Judaism—Customs and practices. I. Title.
[BJ2019.5.J4L37   1986]   395′.089924   86-45124
ISBN 0-06-097054-5 (pbk.)

86 87 88 89 90 MPC 10 9 8 7 6 5 4 3 2 1

To B.S. (ז״ל),
My parents, my husband, and my children—
links in the living chain of Judaism

CONTENTS

JEWISH PRACTICE: THE BASICS OF OBSERVANCE

KASHRUT: DIETARY LAWS

TABLE CEREMONIES AND BLESSINGS

THE SABBATH

HOSPITALITY: *HAKHNASAT OREHIM*

LIVING IN A PLURALISTIC WORLD

HAPPY OCCASIONS

BIRTH

BAR/BAT MITZVAH

TWO OTHER HAPPY OCCASIONS

FUNERALS AND MOURNING

INTRODUCTION

When I told people I was writing a book of Jewish etiquette I was almost invariably asked, "What is *Jewish* etiquette?" The question is natural, for although there are translations of the Talmudic tract Derekh Eretz (Proper Behavior), there is no single comprehensive work for the layman that deals with Jewish social practice, custom, and rule. There is more to our way of life than is set forth in the few pages devoted by conventional etiquette books to weddings and bar mitzvahs. In the Jewish view, the concept of "proper conduct" implies a total lifestyle, encompassing the details of daily living as well as the formal occasions and important events of life.

There was a time when the knowledge of this lifestyle was passed from one generation to another within a tightly structured, close community. But, alas, the Jewish community in our time is fragmented and spread far and wide over the world. Many modern Jews, brought up with little or no traditional training, very often have no one to turn to for information. They seek a way to affirm their Judaism with dignity and conduct a graciously ordered Jewish life in the midst of a largely non-Jewish world.

This book is an attempt to present in one reference volume a guide to the Jewish way to celebrate a marriage, the birth of a child, a bar or bat mitzvah, to cope with difficult times in life brought on by old age, illness, death, or divorce. It suggests many felicitous occasions often overlooked or unknown today, among them ceremonies for the naming of girls, housewarmings, *oyfruf* (calling a bridegroom to the Torah), reaffirmation of marriage vows, minor holidays, and newly created celebrations.

Women will find a discussion of their changing roles in religious, business, and social life, but the book is addressed to men as well, for both share equally in these areas of Jewish life.

Family life is examined and a guide set forth for parents who wish to train their children in good manners based on Jewish ideals, even though their way of life may be very different from that of their grandparents.

Relations with the community and with non-Jewish neighbors are also discussed, including questions that arise out of invitations to a church wedding or funeral, tours to Christian sites, Christmas customs, and the like.

The non-Jew, seeking to understand his Jewish friends and business associates, will also find this a useful guide. Through an understanding of each other's cultures, both Jew and non-Jew can achieve ease in their social and business contacts and avoid embarrassment or inadvertent rudeness.

Jewish practice has its own innate refinement and distinction, stemming basically from Judaic ethics, from an affirmation of life, from the kindness, consideration, grace, and seemliness that are the essence of good taste. Maintaining his own customs and lifeways, whether from cultural, ethnic, or religious motives, need not condemn a Jew to the ghetto. Ethnic self-expression, exploration, and affirmation of one's traditions are today enthusiastically accepted for all the diverse peoples that make up America. We are free to search for our right way, instead of rigidly conforming to the behavioral standards of another culture.

Of course, there is no *one* right way for a Jew. There is an old adage that if you pose a procedural question (a *shayleh*) to two Jews you will get at least three answers! I have presented Orthodox, Conservative, and Reform practices wherever they differ in matters of ritual; the nonobservant person's viewpoint is also considered. The answers to many problems are multiple, because even within one Jewish group the usage has many variations. The consideration of a seemingly simple query "When must one wear a hat?" provides an insight into this fascinating variety of attitudes.

While I have touched on the philosophic and religious rationale underlying ritual and custom, I have tried to avoid pressing for religious conformity. The choice of lifestyle remains a decision for the individual.

Minhag—what people *do* in certain life situations—is the subject of this book. In matters of *halakhah* (rabbinic law) it points out areas in which difficulties or questions may arise, without venturing to offer an authoritative solution. These are problems which should be taken up with a qualified rabbi.

Yes, there is a note of nostalgia in the description of some of the customs now almost vanished from the life of the less observant. But with knowledge, they can be revitalized and enjoyed in a modern, liberal setting. My aim is to point the way to a synthesis of ancient traditions and contemporary life that will be a link to the centuries-old chain of a noble heritage.

If you want to get an answer, you have to ask a question. To my many friends and relatives, whom I have badgered with unexpected queries, and who have never failed to give a thoughtful response, I offer a heartfelt *"Todah Rabbah!"* I must especially thank Rabbi Abraham Lopes Cardozo of the Spanish and Portuguese Synagogue (Shearith Israel) in New York, and his wife, Irma; Rabbi Arthur Rulnik, of Congregation Knesses Israel in Pittsfield, Massachusetts, and his wife, Adrienne; and Rabbi Harold I. Salzman of Temple Anshe Amunim in Pittsfield, for their patience and kindness in reading portions of the manuscript, making many suggestions, and giving me the freedom of their congregational libraries. My gratitude goes also to the gracious and helpful reference staff at the Berkshire Athenaeum; to Dina Abramowicz and the Archives librarians at the YIVO Institute in New York; to Leon and Esther Cohen, Dr. Saul Hofstein and his wife Isabel, Dr.

Lester Mark and his wife Muriel, Drs. Harold and Lillian Ratner, Norman and Belle Goldklang, Doris and Perry Bloom for letting me rummage through their libraries and their minds; and to Barbara Wilson, bridal consultant at Bergdorf Goodman, George Raymond of Cartier's, and Grace Kahn of the American Jewish Congress Overseas Department for their professional assistance. More personally, I wish I could adequately reward my husband David, and my children, for encouraging me, believing in my project, and leaving me free to work. Credit for creating and developing the illustrations goes to my daughter, Abigail S. Bordeleau. For using his "beautiful" lens to make the cover photo I thank my stepson, Peter A. Latner. And if there is somewhere a glowing, golden "good friend" award, it must go to Julia Weissman, whose devoted listening, gentle confidence, and practical suggestions showed me the way to begin.

The transliteration system used in this book is based on the one used in the *Encyclopedia Judaica* for Hebrew words, and the YIVO system for Yiddish words, with a few exceptions for words that have passed into common usage with a varying transliteration, as for example, matzos and lehayim. The definition of each Hebrew or Yiddish word in the text can be found on the pages printed in boldface in the index.

Helen Stambler Latner

Becket, Massachusetts, 1981

EVERYDAY GOOD MANNERS

Who is worthy of honor? He who respects his fellow men.

—PIRKE AVOT

In contemporary Jewish thought, *menshlikhkayt*, the essential quality of the *human* being, as opposed to mere being, is the foundation of everyday good manners, and knowing how "to be a *mensh*" is the concern of etiquette. Certain patterns of conduct are regarded as fine, *sheyn*—that is, admirable. It is almost impossible to consider the full meaning of *sheyn* or *menshlikh* actions without going back into traditional thought, which either consciously or subliminally influences the behavioral modes of all Jews, even those who consider themselves emancipated from some ritual requirements because they follow modernist or assimilationist thinking.

Judaism concerns itself as much with behavior as with belief. Long before worldly etiquette books were first compiled, a concept of "right" or "fitting" conduct permeated Jewish thinking about relationships between people. There are not only many scattered axioms, but also an entire minor tractate of the Talmud (Derekh Eretz, or Proper Conduct) dealing with good manners and rules of etiquette. Almost every aspect of a person's life is covered in these works.

What is the foundation of this behavior structure? Not mere courtesy, but the idea that good manners are the tangible embodiment of the precept to love one's neighbor as oneself. The early writers on good manners gave exquisite consideration to every daily action. With keen insight they set down rules that are still operative today concerning relations between host and guests, parents and children, master and servant, husband, wife, and family.

Respect for parents, the learned, and one's elders was considered a hallmark of refinement; embarrassing any person, in public or in private, was held to be a sin, as grievous as shedding his blood.

Table manners, cleanliness, seemly clothing, food, and drink, manner of walking, proper bearing in an argument, even proper conduct in the toilet are considered in these tracts. Remarkably, although their specific content may refer to an obsolete way of life, the underlying maxims still apply to the proper conduct of life today.

1. Family Life

SHOLEM BAYIS: *THE PEACEFUL HOUSEHOLD*

Life within the family circle comes under special rabbinical scrutiny. Still most effective as principles for ordering the life of the household are the maxims relating to *shalom habayit* (Yiddish: *sholem bayis*)—peace in the house.

The responsibility for his family's conduct once rested squarely on the husband and father. He was supposed to train and guide wife, children, and servants, and merit the deference due him as head of the house by his own exemplary behavior. Nowadays, women often carry a great deal of the burden of childrearing or share the duties with the father. The precepts originally addressed to the *pater familias* now apply to both father and mother.

In the old tracts a man is told to show honor and respect to his wife, for "blessings rest on a man's home only on account of his wife." He must not cause her to weep, for "God counts her tears" (Ketuboth 62a), and he is enjoined to consult her on all household matters. An affecting guide to family harmony is found in Baba Mitziah 59a, which tells a husband: "If your wife is short, bend down and listen to her."

Moreover, a family head is urged to show forbearance, to be slow to take offence, and to avoid terrorizing the household so as to limit contentious confrontation. A man was not even supposed to enter his own home without knocking (Midrash Lev 21:81; Nid 16b), so as not to alarm those within (a reflection of the harshness of Jewish life in the Middle Ages, and a custom, alas, that is even apropos today).

Servants and employees were to be treated with the courtesy one would expect for oneself. The laws of Sabbath and holiday rest applied to them as well as to the family members.

BEING A PARENT

The Children. Jewish ethics postulate that consideration must be given to the essential human dignity of one's children. The Talmud tells parents and teachers alike, "Let the honor of your pupil be as dear to you as your own." Thus even the youngest members of the family should not be embarrassed or demeaned.

Parents, certainly, should represent authority. They rightly make and enforce the rules of the home and shape the child's life. But that authority must be blended with love and a positive recognition that children have the same emotions as adults.

Sarcasm, disdainful comments, disrespect, and unnecessary harshness from adults, especially parents, cause the powerless child to regard the world as unresponsive to his needs and feelings. An overpermissive home, on the other hand, often conveys the idea that no one cares enough about the child to limit and order his world. Children have a right to privacy, to having their wishes taken into consideration, to an explanation why their wishes cannot be granted, and to a gradual acceptance into maturity and independence as they grow into their teenage years. The ideal home will create a serene, regulated environment in which a child feels secure and loved.

Jewish Education. The practical duty of parents toward their children is for their well-being, of course, and also for their future. In addition to his duty to arrange marriages for his daughters, a father has always been expected to provide his sons with an education (originally, in Torah), and to teach them a trade or profession so that they could support themselves. The Talmud even suggests that a child should be taught to swim. And thus we progress to the sports, music, and dancing lessons of today.

Parents who would not think of neglecting their children's secular training are sometimes uncritically indulgent about their Jewish education. To bring a child up without some knowledge of and social ease in Jewish practice is as negligent as to fail to teach him proper table manners or polite conversation. Since social demands will be made on every individual in areas of Jewish observance, some Jewish education can be regarded as a necessary social grace.

Every Jewish child should learn about his heritage through training in a religious or cultural school. The family should choose an affiliation closest to their own traditions and see to it that the child attends. At the very least, a child should be given some training in the history and meaning of Judaism; he or she should learn enough about the ritual to know how to conduct himself in a synagogue and what observances are required on the Sabbath and the holidays.

It is a mistaken kindness to spare the child this "extra" training. To give a child no training at all, perhaps on the ground that the parents do not attend services and consider themselves free of religious obligations, makes the child the neighborhood exception. Moreover it implies that Jews really have no religion or culture worth transmitting today. Ultimately, the vacuum created leaves the child prey to any attractive sect that seems to have the answers to life's problems. The very child who complains about having to attend services and go to Hebrew school often grows up to reproach his parents for their failure to transmit to him any understanding of his background.

There are times when the demands of business or profession cause a Jewish family to live in a community where there is little or no organized Jewish life. In such a situation, thoughtful parents take upon themselves the responsibility to teach their children as much as they can about cultural values and traditional ideas. There are many books and records available; mail-order services are offered by the dealers in religious objects in many urban Jewish communities.

Children and Home Ritual. As soon as they can eat by themselves, children should be given a place at the holiday and Sabbath table. If they cannot sit through the whole meal, especially if it will run on to a late hour, as the Seder usually does, they should be given their own little supper earlier and be present for the Kiddush and Hamotzi (blessing the wine, the hallah or matzo), and perhaps the first course as well. The holiday and Sabbath meal rituals are followed with some small variations by Orthodox, Conservative, and Reform.

As they grow up, children should be taught to stand for and respond to these blessings, and to say the short Grace after meals if they are to be excused from the table early.

Parents who are not observant themselves but celebrate the holidays or have occasional Sabbath dinners with more traditional family members or friends should plan to take their children along on such occasions and make opportunities for the youngsters to practice "company manners" at the home dinner table beforehand. They may quite properly ask that their children be included in a holiday invitation, for it robs a family celebration of much of its warmth and significance to leave the children at home with a babysitter. It also cuts off an unparalleled opportunity to teach the meaning of Judaism in a life experience instead of in a textbook.

The Passover Seder, in particular, is an event that requires the presence of a child. Hanukkah, Purim, and Sukkot are other festive holidays made for youngsters' participation.

BETWEEN THE GENERATIONS

Respect. The deference and respect that must be shown to one's parents, to the old in general, and to teachers and scholars have never changed in Jewish thinking.

To honor one's parents is one of the Ten Commandments, not a mere tradition. When asked which of the Commandments was the most important, the rabbis pointed to this one, the Fifth, for, they reasoned, if a child follows the precepts of his parents, they will teach him all the others.

Ideally, one must respect the ideas, opinions, and orders of one's parents, and live so that one does not bring shame upon them. No sacrifice is too great if it enables parents to live in comfort and honor.

Practically speaking, children should show deference not only in heroic ways, but in the small change of daily living. From a Jewish point of view, the emphasis is wrong in the kind of television commercial that shows a mother who "really cares" rushing out to buy the "right" muffins or cereal for her children just before breakfast—it is the child who should be dashing out to the store to show her proper respect.

When Elderly Parents Live in a Nursing Home.   Whether elderly parents reside in a home for the aged or are still able to maintain their own ménages, it is an important part of the duty of respect to visit or write them frequently, and to show them honor on such occasions as birthdays and religious holidays.

Grandchildren should be taken on such visits when they are old enough, and in this way taught the duty of filial courtesy. Cards, letters, and little gifts do not take very much time, but they bespeak continuing love and thoughtfulness.

When Aging Parents Live Alone.   When grandparents live nearby, a grandchild's offer to do some marketing, bring a daily newspaper to a shut-in, or accompany a frail older person to the bank, the stores, or the library, is most welcome. To assign such chores to one's children on a regular basis is to school them in caring.

When distance makes this impractical, regular letter-writing by children can bring great joy to grandparents. They are always interested to hear of a child's progress in school and see his completed handiwork. Many a wall in a retirement village apartment is covered with framed clippings, children's drawings, and family photos.

A cassette recorder is another unparalleled way to bridge distance and keep the family close. Exchanging tapes makes it possible to share all kinds of experiences, from the baby's first words to his graduation speech. It is also a good way to preserve the grandparents' reminiscences as a form of oral autobiography.

Couples who sometimes feel irked by their duty to their parents should reflect on the example they set their own children, and on the harvest of loneliness they may reap in their own old age in turn.

When Aging Parents Live with Their Children.   The minor inconveniences of having a healthy elderly parent reside with the family must be balanced against the alternative of sending him or her off to spend his remaining days alone in a home for the aged; neither decision is an easy one to make. Difficult as the adjustment between the generations may be, an understanding of the true meaning of respect points the way.

The child should strive to make the parent feel like a welcome member of the family and not like an undesired guest given grudging shelter. The elderly parent must accept, as far as possible, household standards rather different from his own, and must especially avoid deprecating the way that children order their lives. Each person in the household must respect the privacy of the others, no matter what their ages.

The younger members of the household must remember that they are here because of the nurturing, and often the sacrifices, of the old, and the old should cherish the love and affection of a caring family. This, in essence, is the secret of living amicably together across the generations.

Problems of Observance. Observance of *kashrut* (dietary laws), the Sabbath, and the holidays sometimes poses problems between generations. These are matters of conscience that each family must resolve in its own way. Often conflicts can be avoided by arranging separate kitchen facilities and private entrances to living quarters.

The less observant family members should recognize that, to the observant, following Orthodox law is a paramount obligation. To flaunt one's nonobservance, or to scoff at pious practices, is rude and inconsiderate.

2. Personal Interaction: Men and Women

JEWISH ATTITUDES TOWARD SEX

The pleasures of love and sex within the framework of marriage are regarded positively by Judaism. The commandment to be fruitful and multiply is considered binding upon men, and early marriage, as close to the age of eighteen as possible, was thought to be most desirable, even though it often entailed financial support of the newlyweds by the parents.

The nature of proper marital relationships is studied in many Talmudic tractates and spelled out in the Shulhan Arukh. It is very clear that sexual satisfaction is a duty owed by the husband to the wife (*mitzvat onah*). Refusal of sexual relationship by either is grounds for a divorce, although a husband may not force his wife if she is unwilling, nor can she be compelled to live with a man who is repulsive to her.

Enjoyment of sex is considered one of the delights of the Sabbath. Any sexual actions and positions that give pleasure, even intercourse in the nude, if the wife insists on it, are permitted in various writings. However, extramarital sex, incest, adultery, and any relationships other than the usual heterosexual are severely condemned.

Modesty and reserve are urged. Because of the rules forbidding sexual intercourse in public, the sages forbade it in the presence of a child who could talk, even if the child was asleep. And they required that the shades be drawn.

The sex drive of a woman is recognized and regarded as normal. She may express her desire to her husband by various hints, and if he notices that she is making an effort to be attractive to him, he must satisfy her. The regularity with which a wife may expect her husband to have marital relations with her is set forth as an essential part of the marriage contract in the Mishnah (Ketubot 5:6). It sets that duty as every day for taxpayers, twice a week for laborers, once a week for ass drivers, once a month for camel drivers, and once every six months for sailors. Occupational determinism even goes so far as to indicate that scholars engaged in Torah study may reserve Friday nights for their marital duties. Frequency is further limited by the prohibition of contact with a menstruous woman.

In modern Jewish thinking, many varied attitudes toward traditional rules can be discovered. What unifies them all is the underlying positive recognition of sex life as the fulfillment of a positive commandment and a pleasure that both persons have a right to enjoy. We have come a long way from the superstition and naïvete of some of the rabbinic writings, but our responses to this fundamental life drive have been shaped by this centuries-old attitude—*gam zu l'tovah*—this, too, is good!

TRADITIONAL PROPRIETY

Propriety between the sexes is very carefully spelled out among the Orthodox. A man is expected to be most deferential and careful in his dealings with women. He is not supposed to spend time alone with any woman other than his wife or daughters, and never to engage in idle talk with them. A woman's voice is regarded as so seductive that a man is forbidden to listen to a strange woman singing. In fact, women generally are regarded as so dangerously attractive that very strict Hasidim avoid looking directly at them, face to face, unless they are closely related.

CONVENTIONS OF SEPARATION

Among the strictly observant, women are required to separate themselves physically from men during their menstrual periods. One may not touch the menstruous woman (*niddah*), or anything she sits or lies upon until she has been to the *mikveh* (ritual bath) after her period.

Since one cannot very well inquire into the physical status of the women outside of the family, the idea of total physical separation developed among the strictly observant. The separation is expressed in many ways, the most obvious being the women's gallery in the synagogue. At Hasidic and Orthodox formal dinners and receptions, separate seating is arranged for men and women, sometimes in different banquet rooms, or on opposite sides of the same large hall, often with a divider screen down the middle. There is no mixed dancing. At all social gatherings men and women tend to form separate groups, although in an informal setting men and women do greet each other, mingle, and converse.

Physical contact is avoided in many small ways as well. An Orthodox woman does not offer to shake hands with a man. She does not directly hand something into his hands, but puts it down before him, so that he may pick it up from "neutral territory," as it were. She does not sit in her husband's chair, out of respect for his status as head of the house, as well as out of regard for separation.

In business and professional circles, these Orthodox conventions are easily observed. Private professional consultations are, of course, permitted; as for ordinary working arrangements, men and women have since time immemorial shared the same office, store, or marketplace. It is only necessary, for propriety's sake, that they not be exclusively alone together.

Among Conservative and Reform Jews the conventions of separation are not observed.

WHEN TO SHAKE HANDS

The controversial handshake is perhaps best avoided between the sexes if one of the people meeting or being introduced is Orthodox. A nonobservant man may safely shake hands with a woman who offers her hand; the nonobservant woman need not extend her hand at all, if in doubt, but content herself with a pleasant smile and a nod of recognition.

One may freely shake hands with a person of the same sex. Although it may seem awkward to the nonobservant, it is perfectly correct, upon being introduced to an Orthodox man and his wife, for a man to shake hands with the husband but not with the wife, and vice versa.

One may also simply not offer to shake hands at all, but acknowledge the introduction with a warm smile and a cordial greeting. This is probably the most gracious resolution of this minor problem. However, no one should leave another with his hand extended and ignored. It constitutes a rebuff that is almost unforgivable.

COURTESY BETWEEN THE SEXES

What some authorities are today bruiting about as the "etiquette of equality between the sexes" has always been the norm in Orthodox circles. Good sense, courtesy, and consideration now dictate, for non-Orthodox and Orthodox alike, that the person closest to the door opens it, the person passing through holds it open for the one following, that unless real danger from the street threatens, a man need not keep changing sides as they cross the road when he is walking with a woman. A person, male or female, who needs help getting in or out of a car should be given it by whoever is already out of the car; those who are hale and hearty can manage on their own. Respect is shown to persons of distinction or marked age by men and women alike.

A NOTE ABOUT THE MIKVEH (RITUAL BATH)

In Orthodox practice the *mikveh* is used for prescribed ritual immersions not only by women after their menstrual periods, but also by brides before their weddings, by converts to Judaism, by men who have had a nocturnal emission, and, among Hasidim, by men on the eve of the Sabbath and holidays. The immersion is not performed for cleanliness but to achieve ritual purity.

How does using the *mikveh* differ from taking a bath at home? The Orthodox answer is that, following careful preliminary ablutions, one must perform the immersion in a body of "living waters"—a brook, lake, or sea—or a traditional *mikveh*, a bath specially built to contain such water flowing directly from a spring. The *mikveh* must be constructed according to exact rabbinical specifications governing size, water content, and flow.

A modern *mikveh* is usually a spotlessly clean, tiled establishment not unlike a small swimming pool, complete with lockers, dressing rooms, private bathing rooms, hair dryers, and sometimes a small hairdressing and manicure salon.

Procedure.   The proper procedure is to undo the hair, shampoo it completely, remove all nail polish and clean under the fingernails and toenails (some cut the nails), take a complete bath, and then enter the *mikveh* pool itself. There one follows the immersion ritual and says the prescribed prayers. One must submerge the body so completely that the hair floats on the surface of the water. The only witness actually present at a woman's immersion is the female attendant; sometimes another woman who has accompanied a convert may also be present. The rabbi in charge accepts the statement of the female witnesses that the immersion has been properly carried out.

There are separate hours for men and women, naturally, and there is always an attendant of the same sex who is happy to assist a person unfamiliar with the routine.

It is customary to bring a fresh change of clothes to dress in after the ceremonial immersion.

Fees and Tips.   Most *mikvehs* are supported by contributions from people in the community who use them regularly. The occasional visitor should leave a donation if there is no entrance fee and use her own judgment about tipping the attendant. If services similar to those of a beauty salon are used, a comparable tip should be given. The same would apply to aides who provide towels and clean the bathing and dressing areas. When there is an older woman in charge of the whole operation, it is more gracious to offer her a small "donation" for the upkeep of the *mikveh* (apart from any fee charged) in lieu of a tip.

Men should follow the same procedure with male attendants.

Reform Practice.   Reform groups have done away with all forms of immersion.

3. Social Interaction: People to People

DEALING WITH CONFLICTING MORES

At one extreme of the Jewish social spectrum is traditional Orthodox behavior, based on complete, scrupulous observance of Jewish law; at the other is that of the modernist, who has freed himself from all these restrictions and may have adopted many non-Jewish customs. For both, understanding and respecting differing lifeways is important for pleasant social and business relationships.

A person trained in the traditional outlook may find social life, student life, or work in a freer environment troublesome at first. Quietly maintaining one's standards, explaining simply, "I do not eat . . ." or "do . . ." whatever is against your principles should be sufficient to establish your lifeway among thoughtful associates. A lengthy explanation will only lead to an inconclusive, perhaps alienating discussion.

The prohibition against embarrassing another, since it is common to all standards of etiquette, applies also to less observant persons. They must therefore be understanding of the difference in lifeways of the more orthodox, and better yet, follow them when entering a traditional milieu—attending religious services, festivities or funerals, teaching, studying, or working with Orthodox people. Some very obvious instances are refraining from smoking and riding on the Sabbath, wearing a hat, and dressing properly. It is, at the very least, rude to tease or cajole someone into "just tasting the ham—[or lobster]" or to ride or shop on the Sabbath. Such attempts to persuade others to bend the rules by which they must live, although often couched as a joke, are anything but funny. The more observant person rightly resents them.

The reverse is true also. If an Orthodox person feels moved to correct the behavior of a less observant relative or friend, he should do so quietly and privately. A stranger visiting a synagogue and asked to put out a cigarette, for instance, should be addressed politely and calmly. The visitor should accept the correction with good grace, realizing that in this milieu he or she is the person behaving improperly, whatever his personal code of conduct may be.

SABBATH AND HOLIDAY
RESTRICTIONS ON SMOKING

Among the observant, one does not smoke during the twenty-five hours from a half hour before sundown on Friday to a half hour after sunset on Saturday.

One does not smoke on Yom Kippur, in all groups—Orthodox, Conservative, and Reform.

On holidays one may smoke, according to Orthodox practice, but may not ignite a match or lighter. A light must be procured either from another smoker's lit cigarette, from a special candle kept burning for this purpose in some homes and synagogue lobbies (never the actual holiday candles), or from some other already-burning flame, such as the pilot light of the kitchen stove.

Conservative and Reform Jews do not observe these holiday restrictions.

TRADITIONAL GREETINGS AND SALUTATIONS

Cordiality in greeting the people you encounter is ingrained in Jewish tradition. Rabbi Johanon ben Zakkai, a great sage, was reputed to be so punctilious in proffering his greetings to people that no one was ever able to salute him first. The careful attention to the expression of cordiality has given rise to a series of Yiddish and Hebrew ceremonious phrases of greeting for every occasion. The languages are interchangeable; one may respond in Hebrew or Yiddish to a greeting in English (or the vernacular of the community), and vice versa. Examples are given in Table 1, "What to Say When."

It is customary, in traditional correspondence, articles, and books, to use certain acronyms for polite salutations or interjections. A letter may have not only the customary acronyms shown in Table 2, "Traditional Written Greetings," but also one for the Torah portion of the week (Sedra) preceding the date. The polite expressions are added after the names of the persons mentioned, as indicated in Table 2.

SOCIAL KISSING

In some nontraditional circles friends and relatives kiss when they meet. If, among couples, a male acquaintance greets his friend's wife with a kiss, the husband must return the courtesy. One who does not care for indiscriminate kissing usually finds it difficult to avoid it without seeming cold. One may

Table 1. What to Say When *

Occasion	Greeting	Response	Notes
Everyday greetings	*Shalom*—[Peace] Hello or goodbye	*Shalom* or *Shalom lekha*—[Peace to you] Hello or goodbye	Used to answer the telephone or conclude a conversation in Israel, and in some world Jewish organizations.
	Shalom aleykhem—[Peace to you] Hello or goodbye	*Aleykhem shalom*—Same	Sometimes used by Jews to identify one another in strange surroundings, especially when traveling.
Welcome to a visitor or returning traveler	*Barukh haba*—[Blessed be he who comes in] Welcome	*Barukh hanimtza*—[Blessed be the one present] Thanks	Also a ceremonial welcome to bride and groom, or an infant presented for circumcision; no response is given.
		Barukh hayoshev—[Blessed be the one who is seated (at the table)] Thanks	Response to a host who is seated at the table.
Polite inquiries (Hebrew)	*Ma shlomeykh?* (fem.)/ *shlomkha* (masc.)—How are you?	*Barukh hashem!*—[Praise God!] Things are good.	All are formal responses. One is not supposed to recount specific good or bad things, lest they worsen, nor is one supposed to arouse bad feelings, either of envy or sorrow.
(Yiddish)	*Vos hert zikh?*—What's new? *Vos makhst du?* (familiar) or *Vos makht ir?* (formal)—How are you?	*Nisht koshe!*—[Not difficult] Fine, A-OK *Azoy, azoy!*—So-so!	

Occasion	Expression	Response	Notes
Visiting the sick (Hebrew)	... *refuah shelemah*—... a complete recovery	*Amen!* *Todah* or *Todah rabbah*—Thank you very much	For leave-taking—may be combined with English, Yiddish, or Hebrew expressions for "May you have . . ." or "I (we) wish you. . . ."
To a convalescent (Yiddish) (Hebrew) (Aramaic)	*Tsu gezunt!*—To good health! *L'veriut!* (Same) *Asuta!*—(Same)	*Amen!* *Todah rabbah!*—Thank you	Appropriate for leave-taking.
To one who sneezes	Same as above		
Birthday—especially of an older person (Yiddish)	*Biz hundert un tsvantsik*—[To one hundred and twenty] May you live to . . . *Tsu lange yohren*—To long years (of life)	*Amen!*—Thank you	A wish for long life. Especially suitable for a birthday toast.
Congratulations—general	*Mazal tov*—[Good fortune] Congratulations	*Barukh tihyeh*—[Be you blessed too] The same to you, thank you	Response to all good news, especially on hearing of family events, as weddings, births, etc.
	Kol hakovod—[All honors (to you)] Congratulations	*Todah rabbah*—thank you	Israeli felicitations on successful accomplishment.

• The literal English translation, when different from the colloquial meaning, is shown in brackets.

Table 1. What to Say When* (cont'd)

Occasion	Greeting	Response	Notes
Synagogue (Hebrew) (Yiddish)	*Yishar kohakha Yasher koakh*—[May you be strengthened] Congratulations	Thank you	Greeting to a person who has been called up for a Torah reading or other synagogue function; also, congratulations on a major accomplishment in general.
	Hazak u'varukh or *Hazak barukh*—[Be strong and blessed] Congratulations	Thank you	Sephardic greeting used as above.
	Hazak v'ematz—[Be strong and of good courage] Congratulations	Thank you	Used as above—especially for a bar mitzvah boy upon conclusion of his Torah reading.
Sabbath day (Hebrew) (Yiddish)	*Shabbat shalom Gut Shabbos*—Good Sabbath	Same, or *Shabbat shalom u'mvorakh*—A good Sabbath and a blessed week	
Close of Sabbath (Hebrew)	*Shavua tov*	Same, or *Shavua tov u'mvorakh*	Greeting at the close of the Sabbath day, after Havdalah prayer, or on Saturday night.

Category	Greeting	Response	Usage
(Yiddish)	Gut vokh or a gute vokh—A good week	Same, or Gut vokh, gut yohr—A good week and a good year	
Rosh Hodosh—New Moon (Yiddish)	Gut khoydesh	Same, or . . . gut yohr	A greeting after blessing the new moon, or on Sabbaths when the date of the new month is announced, and during the week in which it starts.
Holidays—general (Yiddish)	Gut yontev (Yiddish form of Hebrew Yom tov)—A good holiday	Same	Used for all holidays and festivals.
(Hebrew)	Hag same'ah or Moadim l'simhah—A joyous holiday(s)	Same, or Haggim u'zmannim l'sason—[Holidays and festivals for joy and gladness]	Used on festivals.
(Yiddish)	A gut'n mo'ed	Same, or any Hebrew variants above	Variant used on intermediate days of festivals.
Holidays—specific Rosh Hashanah—New Year	L'shanah tovah (1) Shanah tovah—A good year Tizku l'shanim rabot (Sephardic)	L'shanah tovah tikkatevu (2)—May you be inscribed for a good year (in the Book of Life) Gam atem—The same to you	Either phrase (1) or (2) may be used interchangeably as greeting or response during the Days of Penitence preceding Rosh Hashanah and on the day.

• The literal English translation, when different from the colloquial meaning, is shown in brackets.

Table 1. What to Say When° (cont'd)

Occasion	Greeting	Response	Notes
Yom Kippur	*L'shanah tovah tikha-temu* (1)—May you be sealed for a good year (in the Book of Life)	*G'mar hatimah tovah* (2)—A felicitous sealing (in the Book of Life)	Phrases (1) and (2) may be used interchangeably, as above, on Yom Kippur and until the end of the Sukkot festival (Hoshana Rabba)
		G'mar tov—A good seal	Shortened form of (2), used as a response only.
Sukkot	*V'hayita akh same'ah*—May you have only joy	Thank you, or *Gam atem (l'ha)*—The same to you	To the host and hostess when visiting the *sukkah*.
Passover	*L'shanah haba'ah b'Yirushalayim*—Next year in Jerusalem!	*Amen!*	Said at the conclusion of the Haggadah reading and at the end of services in synagogue.
General rejoicing	*Mazel tov!* *B'siman tov!* (Sephardic)—Congratulations	*Amen!* or Thank you, or *Barukh tihyeh*—[Blessings to you, too]	On hearing good news, and on joyous occasions, especially family events, as engagements, weddings, births, bar mitzvahs.
	Lehayim—To life!	*Lehayim tovim u'l'shalom*—To a good life and peace	Toast upon taking a drink, usually wine or whiskey. To "make a *lehayim*," "*makhen . . .*" (Yiddish)—is to seal a bargain, celebrate an event, express congratulations or good wishes.
(Yiddish)	*Zol zayn mit glick!*—Here's luck (good fortune)!	*Amen!* or *B'siman tov,* or *Mazel tov,* or *Lehayim*	Used as a toast, as above.

Occasion	Phrase	Response	Notes
During mourning	*Hamakom yenahem etkhem b'tokh avelei Tziyyon v'Yirusha-layim*—May the Lord comfort you among all mourners for Zion and Jerusalem	No response is customary.	Addressed to the mourner during the week of mourning (*shivah*, which see).
(Yiddish)	*. . . nor af simkhes*—May we meet on happier occasions	From a mourner, no response is necessary. From others, *Amen!* or the same.	Addressed to other visitors in a house of mourning, especially on leave-taking. The English is frequently used also.
Sad occasions Upon hearing of a death (Hebrew)	*Barukh Attah Adonai, Eloheynu Melekh Ha'olam, dayyan ha'emet.*—Blessed art Thou, O Lord our God, King of the Universe, the true judge.		
Leave-taking (Yiddish)	*. . . nor af simkhes*—May we meet on happier occasions	*Amen!*, or the same	Appropriate at unveilings, when visiting the critically ill (to other visitors), etc.

• The literal English translation, when different from the colloquial meaning, is shown in brackets.

Table 2. Traditional Written Greetings

Abbreviation		Means	When and how abbreviation is used
Transliteration	**Hebrew**		
B'ezrat Hashem	בעזרת השם (ב"ה)	With the help of God	Written in the upper right-hand corner of a letter
Ad me'ah shanah	עד מאה שנה (עמ"ש)	Until a hundred years	Written after the addressee's name in the heading of a letter
Natreih Rahamana u'varkhei	נטריה רחמנא וברכיה (נר"ו)	May God guard and bless him (you)	Formal address after salutation
Sheyihyeh l'orekh yamim tovim amen*	שיחיה לאורך ימים טובים אמן (שליט"א)	May he (you) live for many good days, amen.	As above
Zekhuto yagen aleinu	זכותו יגן עלינו (זי"ע)	May his merit protect us	After the name of a deceased distinguished person (Hasidic)
Zikhrono l'verakhah	זכרונו לברכה (ז"ל)	May his memory be for a blessing	After the name of the deceased (also in speech)
Zekher tzaddik l'v'rakhah*	זכר צדיק לברכה (זצ"ל)	May the memory of the pious be for (us) a blessing	As above

* The abbreviations are sometimes used as words, as *shlita* or *zeytzel*, in conversation.

make some joking remark about not wanting to spread the latest "bug" and offer only a cheek to be kissed.

Among the traditionally observant, men and women do not kiss socially, except for the very old greeting the very young, parents kissing children, or siblings kissing one another.

One may sometimes see Hasidic men greet each other with the formal kiss on both cheeks, the gesture of respect and cordiality, which is also extended to the older generation. Women, of course, greet each other with a social kiss quite usually.

4. Dress

TRADITIONAL PROPER DRESS

Dressing neatly and as well as one can afford is urged in the Talmud, where a man is advised to spend more on his clothing than on his food, and more on his wife and children than on himself.

Spotless cleanliness, in these tracts, is considered essential to personal dignity, and slovenliness a disgrace. Modesty of dress is also important, especially in women, because of their great powers of attraction. Neither sex is to dress outlandishly.

Among traditionalists today, modest dress for women means long sleeves (at least three-quarter length), a neckline that is cut no deeper than a hand's-breadth, and a conservative hemline. Stockings or tights are always worn, even by little girls. "See-through" styles and sometimes even sheer stockings are not acceptable.

Slacks and shorts for women are still controversial: pants because they are thought by some to be "men's attire"; shorts, immodest. Most observant women will accept shorts only for active sports, and preferably only among women or members of their family. Pants, however, have become an integral part of an active life, and are obviously more modest than shorter dresses, so that traditionalist opposition has slowly crumbled. The more conservative woman wears pants only for sports, very occasionally to work, and never to the synagogue.

The traditional woman has always covered her hair in public, with a hat, scarf or wig, once she married.

THE HAT QUESTION

The one distinctively Jewish habit of dress that almost every non-Jew recognizes is the skullcap or the Hasidic "beaver" hat. Many a battle has been fought over the right of the Orthodox man to cover his head, and conversely, of the rebellious to go bareheaded.

The origin of the custom is obscure; covering the head is not ordered in the Bible or the Talmud, and still was not universal among Jews in the eighth century. Yet the practice, copied, some say, from the custom of Babylonian scholars, became widespread enough by the twelfth century for Maimonides to declare that it was not proper for a scholar to study or teach bareheaded. Although by the eighteenth century the Vilna Gaon permitted it, traditional Jewry eventually came to equate bareheadedness with frivolous behavior.

Pragmatists claim that the custom of covering the head originally made sense under the burning sun of the desert and persisted in the Diaspora as a sign of unity, identity, and even ethnic freedom.

As for women, head covering, especially covering of the hair, is an offshoot of the Middle Eastern custom of the veiling of women, a practice of modesty and seclusion. In the late eighteenth century wigs became "modern" among Hungarian and Polish women; others wore caps, bonnets, and headdresses similar to those worn by the matrons and widows in non-Jewish society.

Now that wigs have become high fashion again, there has been some discussion among Orthodox women of the propriety of wearing wigs, as following a custom of non-Jews (*derekh hagoyim*). At very elegant Orthodox functions one can observe many women wearing both the most modish of wigs and an evening headdress as well. Even in some Reform congregations women cover their hair at services, and in some Sephardic communities unmarried girls do so as well.

Modern Practice. There is today a wide disparity in the practice of head covering, even within traditional groups. Orthodox men and women never go bareheaded, except for young unmarried girls. Males in such groups, including babies, wear yarmulkes even when sleeping; married women always wear either a wig or a kerchief, even inside their own homes. But there are other traditional groups where the women do not wear wigs, only hats or kerchiefs; some do not cover their hair when at home. At the other extreme are some Reform congregations that have attempted to outlaw men's wearing hats in the synagogue.

In general, Conservative and Reform men do not wear a street hat except to keep warm. Conservative practice mandates a head covering in the sanctuary. In Reform circles it is optional.

Some authorities have held that the skullcap is necessary only when teaching or studying religious subjects, reciting a blessing, or praying. If wearing a hat or skullcap will cause loss of livelihood or bring Judaism into scorn, they hold that one need not wear any headcovering while at work or engaged in the study or practice of one's profession (nonreligious).

On college campuses and in communities where there are large modern Orthodox groups one can see many young men wearing a very small crocheted or embroidered yarmulke (*kippah*) perched on the back of their heads, almost as a symbol of their religious and cultural alliance and their ethnic liberation. In such groups, crocheting a *kippah* for one's current young man is a young woman's early gift of affection. Other words for a yarmulke are *kappel* (*Yiddish*) or skullcap (English).

When in Doubt. A woman wondering whether to wear a hat to a social or religious function will always be correct if she adds a hat or scarf to her costume. Properly chosen, it complements and finishes her outfit; if, after she arrives, she feels the hat is not necessary, she can always remove it. As for men who do not habitually wear hats or skullcaps, they might perhaps be guided by the epigram that defines an Orthodox Jew as one who never takes his yarmulke off, a Reform Jew as one who never puts one on, and a Conservative Jew as one who carries a yarmulke in his pocket, "just in case"! Most politicians, Jewish or not, have learned to carry a yarmulke and don it when appearing before traditional Jewish groups.

To Sum Up: When a Hat Is Necessary. A yarmulke (or a head covering for a married woman) is worn in traditional practice whenever one recites or hears a blessing or prayer, partakes of meals where benedictions are recited, enters a sanctuary, or studies a religious text.

A traditional host should provide yarmulkes for less observant or non-Jewish guests. Offering one to a guest is a tactful way to suggest the need to wear it. At elaborate Orthodox functions lace scarves are provided for women: white or bright colors at festivities, black at funerals.

A guest should follow the practice of the host or hostess to avoid offending; refusing or neglecting to use a proffered head covering becomes a rude disregard of a custom important to the host.

Removing One's Hat. The custom of a man's removing his hat as a gesture of respect causes some problems for Orthodox men. A skullcap is always correct and may be kept on at all times, but the street hat should be removed inside buildings such as courthouses, theaters, churches, places of public assembly, restaurants, and the like.

Elevators are no longer a problem, as modern practice in crowded buildings now allows all men to keep their hats on when in transit.

The street hat is always removed when the national anthem is played or the flag is carried past in a parade or public assembly, while the skullcap may be left on.

SOME SPECIAL NOTES FOR WOMEN

Self-improvement/charm books are legion. Their authors might be surprised to find that the enduring part of their contents goes back to the Talmud. Poise, as expressed in a well-modulated speaking voice, a reposeful attitude, and attentive listening are all praised in rabbinical works as admirable qualities in a woman, who is further advised to use cosmetics and scents, and to adorn herself to maintain her attractiveness to her husband. A modern woman would add that this applies to men as well.

Makeup. Traditional customs do not permit the actual application of makeup on the Sabbath, although it may be used before sundown. Many "twenty-four-hour" lipsticks, rouges, and eyeshadows are available to last through the Sabbath day. Mascara should be carefully checked to be sure it does not run while one is asleep.

A guest at a traditional Sabbath bar mitzvah or kiddush should not touch up her makeup publicly. Even the dap of lipstick that convention permits at the table after dining is not correct in this setting.

Perfume. Perfume has been a highly favored adornment since the days of the Queen of Sheba. Sweet scent was worn to greet the Sabbath and the *neshamah yeterah* (added soul) one was granted for the day.

There are hundreds of modern fragrances to choose from, and the problem is only in deciding which are suitable for you, and using them with discretion, so that a cloud of overpowering scent does not precede your entrance or linger on after you leave. Now that men use perfumes freely, the same principles apply to their choices.

Jewelry. For jewelry the artistic rule that "less is more" is particularly apropos. A complete set—necklace, earrings, brooch, bracelet, and rings—even of the finest gems, is too much. Leaving off one or two items to wear at another time is always wise.

The fortunate woman who owns a magnificent bracelet or necklace ought to give it the proper elegant display by wearing it with an uncluttered outfit, with special attention to the relationship between neckline and necklace.

Taste and discretion would indicate that elaborate display should be confined to dress occasions. To wear conspicuous pieces of gold and gem jewelry to work, especially when using public conveyances to travel there, is an invitation to thieves and muggers. One should at least follow the precaution of covering the jewelry with gloves, scarf, or coat. It is not unheard of to be mugged for a convincing-looking "fake."

An ornate gold and diamond wristwatch should be thought of as a bracelet in planning an ensemble. Only a minimum of other pieces should be worn with it. Certainly no additional bracelets should be worn on the watch wrist, although some slim bangles or a charm bracelet may go on the other if the occasion is very dressy.

Gloves. Although gloves are no longer absolutely required for a ladylike appearance, they add a finishing touch to any ensemble. A well-dressed woman still wears or carries harmonizing gloves for every costume.

For evening wear long gloves add elegance, and, in observant circles, must be worn if the gown has short sleeves. Long gloves are kept on unless one is eating, when they are taken off. The practice of slipping the hands out of the lower part and tucking that into the wrist of a long glove is rather unattractive, but is the only choice at an Orthodox gathering.

For informal dress, gloves may be kept on indoors or not, as you choose. You may remove the right glove and carry it at a reception or religious service, where you will be needing a hand free to turn the pages of a prayerbook, or to shake hands upon meeting people.

In Orthodox circles, try to avoid carrying both gloves outdoors on the Sabbath. They may be carried about inside the house or synagogue.

Handbags. Handbags are not carried by Orthodox women on the Sabbath and holidays. Some less observant traditionalists set aside a small purse especially for these days, one in which they have never carried money, so that they may have a place for their keys, eyeglasses, medications, and other essentials. A purse that may be worn on a shoulder strap or belt, making it part of the costume instead of an object one carries, is favored by some.

In Conservative and Reform circles, which are less strict about carrying things on the Sabbath and holidays, good taste would indicate the use of a small dressy handbag that is obviously not part of one's workaday attire.

Furs. Furs, at one time relegated to "evening only" wear, are now considered proper for any time of day—out-of-doors. Furs have a function—to keep the wearer warm—and it is ostentatious, if not silly, to wear a small fur indoors at a formal social occasion, especially during the warmer spring and fall months, as one so often sees women doing at bar mitzvahs, wedding ceremonies, and in hotels and restaurants. Unless the sanctuary or dining room is frigidly air-conditioned, a small fur should not be worn indoors. If, as happens frequently nowadays, a checkroom will not accept a fine fur, the wearer should drape it over the back of her chair, or hold it in her lap.

Shoes for Holidays and Sabbaths.   On the High Holidays, some women leave a pair of comfortable slippers in the synagogue cloakroom or in the drawer under their seats, to wear during the long periods of standing during the services. Other observant women leave their dress shoes in the synagogue and don walking shoes to go to and from services, if a long trek on foot is involved. You may carry the spare pair to synagogue on the eve of the holiday.

In some congregations, leather shoes are not worn on Yom Kippur. Now that so many shoes are made of various synthetic materials, you no longer need wear sneakers at services, although the custom may still be seen among the very observant.

Festive Sabbath occasions among the Orthodox, which involve a good deal of walking, may also be dealt with by leaving your dress shoes at the synagogue before the Sabbath. You may not take them home until after Havdalah—the conclusion of the Sabbath.

A Basic Dress Wardrobe.   A basic dressy day wardrobe for synagogues and festivities that will cover all types of services would include a dress or suit, conservatively cut, but in the latest, most attractive fashion, one or two superb hats to harmonize with it (for Orthodox events), beautiful shoes and gloves, and a suitable coat or fur. A dress handbag is suitable for Conservative and Reform services. Fine style is important, for most Orthodox women, despite the restrictions they must meet, dress in the height of fashion and luxe for festive occasions and holiday services. Such ensembles are also suitable for wear at a church wedding.

Formal Dress.   A woman may wear a long skirt to any dressy function that starts after 6:00 P.M. One may make an exception for weddings that start at the fashionable hour of 4:00 P.M. and go on to cocktails, dinner, and dancing in the evening, although a street or ballerina-length cocktail dress is a better choice than a long evening gown for this late-afternoon hour.

Unless she is certain that the party is being given by people with a Conservative or Reform outlook, a woman would be best advised to select a formal gown with a modest décolletage or one that has its own jacket or stole to cover the shoulders. An extreme décolletage is always out of place in the sanctuary during bar mitzvah or wedding services, in all groups.

Fashions in long dresses for day wear come and go. Unless the tailored "long look" is really in vogue for day, it is not correct to wear a long skirt to a morning or midday function, although one sometimes sees women doing it at bar mitzvahs and weddings. No matter what the fashion, an obvious formal gown or dinner dress is out of place and in poor taste in the daytime.

SOME SPECIAL NOTES FOR MEN

The customs governing correct dress have changed so much in recent years that men now have as great a choice of styles and colors as women do; however, the basic principles of good fit, fine quality, and appropriateness to figure, age, and occasion always apply.

In recent years there has been an increasing relaxation of formality in social life, and many men report that they now find the dark business suit with white shirt and elegant tie acceptable for most functions at which they would once have appeared in a full black-tie outfit.

For summer wear, the conventional choice would be a fine tropical tan, beige, or white suit, or a black-and-white combination. For an original look, summer formal wear may be as varied as one's imagination

Basic Dress Wear. For a basic synagogue and festive wardrobe a man needs a fine dark suit for dress occasions, a coordinating hat (usually a felt fedora, although for summer one might want to add a straw or panama), appropriate dress shoes, a suitable dress topcoat, and a few handsome skullcaps for those occasions when he does not wish or need to wear a hat, but will need a head covering.

The Tallit. Every man who attends services regularly should have his own *tallit* (Yiddish: *tallis*) or prayer shawl, and a proper velvet or silk bag in which to carry it. A good *tallit* is made of fine wool, pure silk, or an acceptable synthetic, and has an elaborate front border with the blessing woven or embroidered in.

The *tallit* may vary in size from a small scarf, usually worn by young boys, to a very large cloaklike affair worn by older men, sometimes with an ornate silver frontpiece. At the very least, the *tallit* should be large enough to cover the shoulders.

"Black Tie." An invitation reading "Black Tie" requires that a man wear a tuxedo or a dark dress suit, black dress shoes, evening shirt, and black bowtie. Pumps, a matching cummerbund, or a fancy vest of velvet, brocade, or silk may also be worn. Jewelry should be restrained, but real.

Black tie attire is correct for any occasion after 6:00 P.M., except that it may be worn to a wedding starting at four o'clock, especially if the woman a man is escorting will be wearing a formal gown.

Men who wear "black tie" regalia infrequently will do best to rent their outfits from a fashionable quality supplier. If a man must appear frequently at formal dinners, gala dances, and other evening affairs tendered by organizations, he might want to invest in his own dinner suit and accessories. An all-year-weight fabric in a conservative style is a wise choice. It should be purchased at a fine store where the fitting will be impeccable.

Pockets and Carrying. Many men use a briefcase or man's handbag with modern, almost pocketless suits; it is important to remember that one does not carry objects to synagogue services or a traditional Sabbath bar mitzvah. Moreover, since a man may put things into his pockets where they are theoretically unseen, he should be careful, on such occasions, to avoid unseemly pocket bulges, jingling change and keys.

A man who habitually keeps a pencil or a pen in his outside coat pocket should remember to remove it. Some men make an exception for an eyeglass case for reading glasses that always remains in the pocket, if the glasses are essential to the man's participation in the services.

BUSINESS DRESS FOR MEN AND WOMEN

There is a great latitude and variety in clothing considered appropriate for work today. People just starting out in their careers should observe how others in their field dress, and be guided accordingly. In the advertising, fashion, theater, publishing, and music world a more highly styled look prevails. Other circles, such as law, banking, or teaching are more conservative. In some offices, pants for women and dungarees for both sexes are acceptable; in others, not. Settling on a look that is smart but not wildly avant-garde will make for a wardrobe that remains in style and appropriate longer.

Women like to be noticed, of course, but regard for modesty of neckline and hemline, especially when bending over files and work tables, is sensible. Regardless of one's religious outlook, avoiding bareness, sheerness, and a provocative no-bra look is a good way to prevent annoying attentions and comments from the men with whom one associates, not to mention malicious gossip from the women.

Men's business dress may run the gamut from the wildly new to the garb of the Hasid, in frockcoat and a dark hat (always on) who often has *peyot* (ear curls) in addition to a beard.

A man dealing with Orthodox associates may feel he should dress more traditionally, but among young observant men highly styled clothing is very much in vogue. In some circles, as long as the tiny yarmulke is worn, "anything goes."

5. Table Manners

Rabbi Akiva felt that good manners were such an essential part of a person's education that he would have his pupils take dinner with him so that he could himself instruct them in proper table manners.

Training in modern table manners begins at home. An early start is the best way to develop ease not only in the correct use of silverware but also in habits of deference and consideration for others at the table, and in familiarity with Jewish table ceremonies.

A GUEST AT DINNER

As one moves out into the social world and confronts unfamiliar situations, it helps to remember that one can always watch the host or hostess for a clue to unfamiliar rituals, elaborate table settings, or exotic foods.

Seating. The hostess at a home dinner party indicates where she wants her guests to sit. It is usual to alternate men and women; in fashionable circles husbands and wives are not seated together, on the theory that an unfamiliar dinner partner makes for more stimulating conversation, but in traditional groups couples are not separated. A hostess may try to introduce some variety in the seating by alternating both sides of the table so that a man and a woman not married to each other at least face each other across the table.

In an informal setting, such as a dinner party among close friends or relatives, the guests may be asked to seat themselves. The women, who will be seated first, should see to it that alternate seats are left for the men, unless, as some Orthodox people do, they seat all the women on one side and all the men on the other.

The places of honor at a home dinner table are to right of the host and hostess. When a rabbi, cantor, or an elected official and spouse are invited to dinner, the couple should be given the honor places, the man to the right of the hostess and the woman to the right of the host. It is gracious to recognize the importance of a former mayor, senator, or judge in the same way. Others deserving the places of honor are any persons occupying positions of prestige in the community or the person in whose honor the dinner party is being given.

Within the family such honored places should go to the oldest members present, usually the grandparents. If both sets of parents are visiting a married child, it is most tactful to seat the couples across the table from each other and next to the in-law of the opposite sex, with the husband's mother and father seated on each side of the hostess and the wife's mother and father on each side of the host.

If the seating is segregated according to the Orthodox tradition, the male guest of honor would be seated on the host's right and the female guest of honor at the hostess's right. At such dinners a woman is usually accorded precedence at the women's tables in accordance with her husband's rank.

When to Start Eating.   At home dinners, when no blessings have been said, one watches the hostess. As soon as she unfolds her napkin and places it in her lap, all the others at the table may do so and begin to eat.

If there is no maid and the hostess is serving the meal herself, she may ask the guests not to wait but to start eating while she brings in the food and serves it. But it is more gracious in such situations for the hostess to plan a first course that may be set out beforehand at each place and to serve the following courses on platters that may be passed while she is seated, so that all may start to eat together at her signal, and the guests are not left awkwardly waiting for her, or alternatively, feeling that they have accorded her second-class status by ignoring her absence from the table.

Children eating with the family should wait for their parents to start before they begin eating, and an attentive husband should wait for his wife to be served before beginning.

At formal dinners, one may begin as soon as most at the table and on the dais are seated, if it is clear that the blessings will not be said. Otherwise one must wait for the Hamotzi (Grace, or blessing over the bread). At a very large banquet, it is permissible to say the blessing for all at one's table and begin.

At weddings and bar mitzvahs, it is customary to wait for the ceremonial entrance of the bride and groom or the bar mitzvah boy, or, when their entrance will be delayed, to wait for someone at the bridal or honor table to say the Hamotzi.

SAVOIR-FAIRE AT TABLE

Enjoying Company Meals.   The key to enjoying a social meal is ease at the table, and that comes from relaxation as much as from knowledge of the fine points of table manners. Many people eat their everyday meals under intolerable tension, then find it a strain to slow down at a social occasion, take the time to cut food small, chew it slowly, sip liquids slowly instead of gulping them, and intersperse the courses with pleasant conversation.

The rationale of proper table manners is to avoid unsightly eating practices that will make dining with you unpleasant for your companions and to converse only about agreeable and, it is to be hoped, amusing topics. Quarrels, embarrassing reproofs, and corrections (whether of children or an unfortunate spouse), and tedious, unpleasant accounts of health, financial, or emotional problems are all in poor taste and to be avoided.

It is easy to slip into gross ways when eating on the run—lunch at your desk, dinner in front of the TV set, or a snack while reading. It makes good sense to practice relaxed, refined eating habits all the time as a foundation for poised good table manners in public.

Which Fork?   At a properly set table, the silver is arranged so that the utensils farthest from the plate (on either side) are used for the first course, with the next piece laid for the second course, and so on. When in doubt as to the proper implement to use at an elaborately set table, one should watch the hostess for a clue.

Using Knife and Fork.   Readers of spy novels are well aware of the difference between American and continental styles of handling knife and fork, since it is one of the clues to the nationality of a mysterious figure! Either style is correct—the "zigzag" American habit of transferring fork from right to left hand and back when cutting and eating fork foods, or the continental "two-handed" system, where the fork stays in the left hand, the knife in the right.

Helping Yourself from a Serving Dish.   When a platter is passed with both a serving spoon and fork on it, you use both—the fork to spear the food, the spoon to support it securely. Always use the serving silver to take a helping from the dish, and take care to put it back on the platter. You never use the silver from the place setting to help yourself.

When a platter contains a number of different garnishes surrounding the entree, take a serving of the main course, then help yourself to the other items, such as a broiled tomato half or a stuffed mushroom, parsley, watercress, or a slice of lemon.

That Last Drop.   A soup plate may be tipped to get the last spoonful, but tilt the plate away from yourself. Soup served in a cup is eaten with a spoon, but the last part may be drunk from the cup. A bit of bread or roll on the end of the fork may be used to sop up the last bit of a sauce or gravy.

Unfamiliar Foods.   If you are uncertain whether to use a spoon or a fork (or fingers) on an unfamiliar dish, you may often solve the problem by watching the host or hostess. If the dish is a food you have never encountered before and the way to eat it is not fairly obvious, you may very correctly ask, making a casual remark such as, "I've never had prickly pears [or whatever the food is] before. Just how does one eat this?"

A person who observes *kashrut* or has food allergies may ask how a dish has been prepared, or whether there are certain ingredients in it that he must avoid, but never in such a way as to call attention to his food problems or embarrass the hostess.

Accidents at the Table. Who has not had some mishap, such as tipping over a full glass, while dining? The important thing to remember is that it is not a major disaster and is best passed over lightly, with a minimum of fuss. One apology should be enough. The hostess should do her best to make light of the accident.

Spilled water or wine should be mopped up quickly with paper towels. If there is no pad under the tablecloth, a dish or wad of paper towels should be put under the wet spot to protect the tabletop. After the excess wine has been mopped up, the wine stain may be covered with salt rubbed into the spot. The wet spot should then be covered with a clean napkin, and the mishap forgotten about. After the guests leave, the hostess should immediately soak the wine-stained linens in cold water overnight. This will usually rescue both tablecloth and tabletop.

If there has been a real spill of food from a platter, immediate action must be taken to prevent permanent damage to the rug or floor and to avoid leaving a slippery patch which may cause others to fall.

Both guest and hosts must minimize such problems in the interest of not spoiling the party for all the others present. At the embarrassing moment of such episodes they always loom larger than they really are.

Praise and Thank You. Ideal dinner guests always praise the efforts of host and hostess to entertain them. A good dinner deserves favorable comment, as do table decorations, good wine, and good company. An especially gracious touch is to write a thank-you note a day or two after the dinner party. Although one may express thanks by telephone, a written note actually takes less time, is less obtrusive on another's free time, and is expressive of true social elegance.

6. Hosting a Dinner

TABLE SETTING

An attractive table makes good food taste better and shows guests and family that special efforts have been made in honor of their valued company. Holiday rejoicing, Sabbath rest, celebration of happy days, birthdays, anniversaries, and important family events can all be themes of table settings.

Sabbath and Holiday Table Setting. Styles of table decoration have become so free and informal that almost any pleasing combination of colors and materials may be used. The dishes, silver, glassware, cloth, and ornamental objects must, however, harmonize in style and texture. One should not, for example, use sterling silver with earthenware pottery, or fine crystal and china with rough straw mats.

The traditional cloth for Jewish holidays and Sabbaths is white damask or lace, with the *hallahs*, covered by a special cloth, as the centerpiece. If the table is large enough, an elaborate candelabrum or two Sabbath candlesticks may be set on the table as well; however, the ceremonial candles may not be moved, once lit, or snuffed out after dinner, and for this reason many prefer to place the candles on the sideboard, where they may be left to burn down to the end, out of the way of the dinner service. Short Sabbath candles are used, not dinner tapers. (See Chapter 17.)

A floral centerpiece is also appropriate for Sabbath and holiday use, with the hallahs placed at the head of the table before the host. The floral arrangement should be low, so that diners may see each other.

When a buffet table is set against the wall, the centerpiece may be as tall and full as the table permits, since guests will be looking at, not over, it.

Flowers, fruit, and greenery should be real, not plastic, although for some striking nonnatural effects, silk or bead flowers, wooden fruits, or huge paper blooms work very well.

Dishes and Silver. It is customary to use the finest dishes, crystal, and silver for the Sabbath and holidays. For other meals you may be as formal or informal as you please, always suiting the decor to the occasion and the guests.

Paper napkins and dishes and disposable glasses should be used only at the most informal of family meals, or when a very large group of guests is to be served at a cocktail party or buffet, although it is much more elegant to

SOME TYPICAL PLACE SETTINGS

Figure 1. First Course on the Table. No soup spoon or bread-and-butter dish used; water glass only.

Figure 2. Dessert Silver on the Table. A place setting with a soup spoon and bread-and-butter dish; the dessert spoon is between the soup spoon and knife. Both wine and water glasses are used.

Figure 3. Dessert Silver on the Table. In this setting, the salad knife and fork are placed on either side of the dinner plate for a separate salad course served after the main course. The dessert spoon and fork are set above the dinner plate. A herring or fish fork may be placed to left of the meat fork or to the left of the knife. For setting with a fish knife, see Figure 4.

Figure 4. Formal Dinner with Several Wines. The large goblet is for water; then come glasses on a diagonal from right to left for these courses: soup (sherry); fish (white wine); meat (red wine); and dessert (champagne). Glasses may also be set in a straight line. Champagne only may be served throughout, necessitating only one wine glass. Note the fish knife and fork. For gefilte fish, only a fish fork is necessary.

rent glasses and plates for a really important occasion if the home supply is not large enough.

Disposable plates should be of the finest quality so they do not buckle when filled with food, or disintegrate when the food is cut or a hot sauce is ladled on.

Individual Place Settings.   Individual places are arranged to be equidistant and opposite each other. Silver and napkins are placed about an inch from the edge. The usual arrangement for the flatware is in the order of use from the outside (away from the plate) in, forks and napkin on the left, spoons and knives on the right. The napkin may be placed on the service or dinner plate if a first course is not set out on the table.

Dessert silver may be put on the table or served with the dessert later. Spoons for coffee or tea are served on the saucer with the beverage.

For a festive holiday or Sabbath gathering, the host may set out ornamental skullcaps at each man's place, on top of the napkin.

A child's place might be set on a special plastic placemat to eliminate messes caused by spilled wine or the traditional holiday apple and honey. With new kits available you can plasticize a mat the child has designed and drawn himself. There will be less wine spilled if the child has his own special small wine glass. If there are many children at the table, the best choice is probably one of the good plastic lace cloths. It also helps to remember the Old Country saying that it isn't Passover until someone spills some wine on the tablecloth!

SERVING A DINNER AT HOME

The Serving Necessities.   A salt cellar and a ceremonial hallah knife are placed alongside the hallah for Sabbath or holiday meals. Additional salt and pepper may be set in individual shakers at each place or in larger ones at each end of the table.

Butter or margarine may be set out on the table with a server, to be passed and used by all, with bread or sliced hallah served from a basket or tray. Alternatively, one may set a pat of spread and a dinner roll at each place on the bread and "butter" plate.

The serving utensils needed for each dish to be passed at the table should be placed on the platter with it, or set before the host or hostess who will be carving or serving it up.

Wines.   Red wines should be opened about half an hour before serving and left to "breathe" at room temperature; white and rosé wines should be chilled thoroughly before serving. The bottles may be brought to the table if they are fifths or liter sizes. Wine from larger bottles (half gallon, 1.75 liters, or larger) should be poured into smaller decanters for table service and kept at the proper temperature for the variety.

Champagne, rosé, and white wines should be kept cold in ice in a cooler if the bottle will not be emptied in the first round of the table.

Much interesting information about serving and storing wines and liquors can be found in the booklets distributed by the major producers and available at all good liquor stores.

Dessert, Coffee Service.   Dessert service varies. The dessert may be set out on individual plates and served to the guests by the maid or the hostess, or brought in on a platter or in a bowl, together with a stack of dessert plates. The hostess then fills the plates and the maid serves them, or the filled plates are passed down the table.

Coffee may be served at the table from a service set before the hostess. If liqueurs are served, the bottle and glasses are placed before the host.

If space permits, it is far more gracious to have coffee and liqueurs in the living room. This is the time for relaxed conversations and perhaps listening to music, away from the remains of dinner and the sounds of kitchen clean-up activities.

A hostess who has no maid may discreetly slip away for a brief turn in the kitchen after the coffee is served, perhaps to put perishable foods away or set the pots and pans to soaking, but she should not spoil her own pleasure in the party and her guests' enjoyment of her company by washing up and cleaning the kitchen while her guests are present.

Enough Is Enough.   The Jewish tradition of hospitality is one of abundance, of urging guests to eat and drink copiously, sometimes more than they really want to consume. With half the world on one special diet or other, and the other half "on the wagon," it is not gracious, but rude, to force food and drink on diners. First helpings should be of a reasonable size. Second helpings should be offered, but not "pushed." No comment should be made about foods not eaten.

As for alcoholic beverages, a host who jovially insists upon his guests' drinking more than they want is no friend; he may, indeed, be helping to set up a serious accident on the trip home. If a guest really is not sober enough to drive home, the host should be prepared to drive him home or call a cab for him.

BUFFET SERVICE

Meals for a large party are most easily served buffet style. In a traditional setting, a large hallah (two for the Sabbath) may be part of the table decor, and a guest or the host may recite the Hamotzi and cut the hallah into slices to begin the repast.

When this is not done, the hostess usually invites her guests to help themselves. Many people are reluctant to be the first to plunge a fork into a beautifully arranged platter, creating a frustrating situation for the hostess. She may break the ice by filling a plate and offering it to the guest of honor.

When there is a great deal of coming and going, as at an "at home," the formal concluding Grace may be dispensed with because all have not eaten together. Some will say the opening Hamotzi and the concluding Grace formally to include all present, leaving it up to the individual arriving at odd times to say any necessary benedictions privately.

SETTING A SIMPLE BUFFET TABLE

Silver, napkins, and glassware for Figure 5 may be arranged on a separate table, or at places already set at small tables. Alternatively, place settings of fork and spoon, individually wrapped in a dinner napkin, may be set out on the buffet table alongside the stack of plates. Glassware may then be set up in the bar or soft-drink area, coffee and dessert service prepared separately in another area.

The table should be arranged in the order in which the food should be picked up: napkin, plate, hot dishes, cold dishes, salad, bread, relishes, fork. Serving pieces should be placed alongside each food platter.

Foods should be kept properly hot by using candle warmers, chafing dishes, or electric hot trays. In very warm weather, chilled foods should be set out in pans of crushed ice to keep them cold. The table should be protected from the heat or the dampness with trivets or mats under each dish.

ACCOMMODATING THE OBSERVANT GUEST

When your home is not kosher, problems arise from time to time when an invitation is extended to a guest about whose dietary observance you are not certain.

The tactful way to handle this is either to ask, at the time of the invitation, whether the guest "eats everything" or has any special food needs (this would cover allergies and diets as well), or alternatively, to plan a *parve* (neutral) or dairy menu that all may partake of without problems of *kashrut*. The host and hostess have an obligation both to inform their guests that

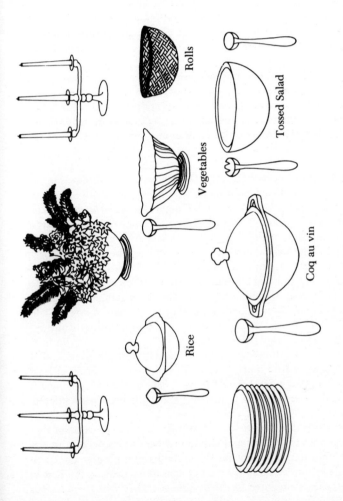

Rolls

Vegetables

Tossed Salad

Coq au vin

Rice

Figure 5. Simple Buffet Table. (One main dish)

their home is not kosher, and to be clear about the acceptable food that will be served, such as fish or dairy dishes.

In cities with large Jewish communities one may also make special provisions for guests by ordering a prepared meal from kosher or *glatt kosher* caterers. These usually come with complete plastic cutlery and dishes. The guest should be told that this will be provided for him.

Some *glatt-kosher* (ultraobservant) people do not eat anything but fruit or cold salads away from home; some do not accept invitations to dine in households or restaurants where they feel any question about the dietary observance.

Both host and guest must accept graciously the meeting of two very different lifestyles, and be tolerant and understanding of the other's attitudes. To take offense because a guest does not eat everything served, when it is a matter of principle for him, or conversely, to expect an entire social event to be revised to meet the religious standards of one visitor, is rather unrealistic—and perhaps even selfish.

When You Are the Observant Guest.

A guest who is uncertain as to the *kashrut* of the home should not ask directly whether the food will be kosher, as this may embarrass the host. Instead, he might say, when invited, "You know, I eat only kosher food. Perhaps I had better come only for dessert." This allows the hostess to offer whatever accommodation she wishes, without the guest's making special demands or questioning the *kashrut*.

When you are visiting family members or close friends in an informal setting, you may offer to bring a kosher-prepared dish as a contribution to the refreshments; using aluminum-foil throwaway containers eliminates any problem of contaminating your own kosher pot or pan. A kosher delicacy, such as gefilte fish or noodle pudding, is often enthusiastically received—best to make a large batch!

In a less intimate situation you may bring as a hostess gift some kosher crackers and cheese, or fruit, nuts, or cake, so as to be sure there is at least one dish to feast on. But a guest should be very careful not to imply by gift or manner that there is anything insufficient about the hospitality offered.

When the Parents Are Observant.

Kashrut is a frequent cause of friction between in-laws or parents and children, where elements of a power ploy may also enter into the problem. When the parents observe the traditional dietary laws, the children have an obligation to provide the best in kosher food, especially prepared for their parents, if they wish them to visit for meals. But parents, especially in-laws, must be reasonable in their demands, and accept with good grace the special arrangements made for them. Certainly, it is not tactful to grumble, while taking part in a specially prepared meal, about other observances that are not being kept up.

7. Dining Out

When taking guests out to dinner in a restaurant, a host should check both the dietary needs of his guests and the *kashrut* of the eating place.

It is tactful to let the most observant member of the party name the place in which it is comfortable for him to dine, since some will not patronize an establishment that is not Sabbath observing, some do not eat meat outside their own homes, and so on. (See Chapter 9.)

WHAT NOT TO ASK FOR

A Jewish guest who does not observe the dietary laws and the non-Jewish guest should know that at a kosher meat meal no butter, cream, or other dairy products will be served. Therefore he should not ask for butter for his bread or vegetables, or cream for his coffee.

One may see kosher-*parve* margarine or nondairy creamers on the table. These are always served in their original kosher-labeled containers so that there may be no mistake as to what they are.

No shellfish or pork products will be served.

PREPAYING A SABBATH MEAL

Many kosher eating places have special arrangements for prepayment that make it possible to dine out without handling money on the Sabbath. One generally pays a set dinner charge on the eve of the Sabbath for the Friday meal and can sometimes also prepay a midday dinner for the next day. This accommodation is readily available in kosher student dining halls and in restaurants and pensions in Jewish communities all over Europe as well.

Those not wishing to sign a Sabbath restaurant check in a hotel where they are staying on a long-term basis can usually make the same arrangement with the management even if the place is not Orthodox.

This is very helpful, also, for a host and hostess entertaining many Orthodox weekend guests for a wedding or bar mitzvah.

WHEN A RESTAURANT IS UNSATISFACTORY

Sooner or later, everyone has a dining-out experience that is unpleasant, if not a disaster. What to do if the service is extremely poor, the food borders on the inedible, or the menu offers nothing you can safely eat?

There is no need to suffer in fuming silence through a ruined evening. If you are headed for the theater or have some other time deadline to meet, you should inform the waiter as soon as you are seated. If after an unreasonable wait your order has not been taken, or it has not been served, it is correct and eminently sensible for the party to get up and leave. Although you should certainly make your dissatisfaction known to the person in charge, a noisy altercation should be avoided.

No tip is necessary if no food at all has been brought to the table. If any of the courses have been served, you pay for what you have eaten and no more. When there is a cover charge, you may have to pay it, if bread, water, and so on were set out for you.

When the waiter is rude, inefficient, or inept, there is no need to slavishly tip the usual 15 or 20 percent. You may quite properly reduce the tip, and in extreme cases, make a controlled, quiet complaint to the management.

When the service is adequate but the drinks or food are unsatisfactory, it is correct to make a courteous complaint, to send a dish back to the kitchen to be done to your satisfaction or changed for the proper order if a mistake has been made. If the problem is not caused by the waiter, he should be tipped properly. It is unfair to take it out on the serving staff when it is the kitchen, the bar, or the management that is at fault.

By the same token, if you are pleased, if the cooking and the service have been excellent, let the management know. Tip the waiter generously and also convey your compliments to the chef. You will find that a little judicious praise makes everyone glow.

If you have special food needs, it makes sense to ask to see the menu before you are seated. Should there not be a suitable choice, you will be able to leave without causing any problems.

"DOGGIE BAGS"

The high cost of dining out and the extravagant size of main-course portions have between them ended the snobbism that once attached to "doggie bags." Although the name has entered the popular lexicon, it is no longer necessary to pretend that the food is being taken home for a pet.

It is perfectly proper, even in the most elegant restaurant, to ask a waiter to wrap up a leftover portion of a main dish or dessert. And, at last, some caterers are attempting to end some of the criticism of ostentatious waste by providing "doggie bags" at the Viennese dessert table, so that guests may take home the usually superfluous but gorgeous pastries.

8. Forms of Address

Rank has not only privileges, but also titles. On those occasions when you must introduce a person of distinction at a meeting or banquet, or are presented to one, it is important to know how to address him or her correctly, to avoid embarrassment, and sometimes even giving offense where honor was intended.

There are many permutations of title and variations in protocol in forms of address, introduction, and social usage. The paragraphs following cover the situations most common to people active in political, religious education, organization, and international business circles.

A dignitary's exact title and full name (and the correct spelling) should be carefully checked when you are preparing programs and publicity releases. Some names in government, politics, and education can be verified in almanacs, or *Who's Who*. *Who's Who* is also a good source of spouse's names. You may inquire also of the person's secretary, or the organization he or she represents. Other good sources of information are the White House Social Office or the State Department in Washington, the consulate or the embassy of the foreign country involved, and the protocol division of the U.N.

CORRESPONDENCE

Writing to public figures to express your ideas or comments on controversial public issues is a right you may wish to exercise. It is also necessary from time to time to write such personages on business matters, to extend invitations to various functions, to enlist support or express thanks for their interest in various causes.

For such correspondence you use the formal letter form, more commonly referred to as the "business letter," although the contents of the letter may not, strictly speaking, deal with matters of business. The form reflects the importance and ceremony attached to the correspondence because the subject is a formal one and the person addressed is a dignitary in his or her field, perhaps in the world.

Meticulous care should be taken for correct spelling of names and correct initials; people are easily offended when the writer gets their names wrong.

Salutations. The salutation is always punctuated with a colon; in American usage the comma is incorrect in the salutation of any formal letter.

As for wording, the standard "Dear . . . :" is always correct. The salutation "Sir:" may be used instead when writing to most political and diplomatic figures, but it has begun to seem rather stuffily old-fashioned.

In American usage "My dear . . . :" is considered correct for a slightly less formal usage, while in British correspondence "My dear . . . :" is only correct for informal correspondence with close friends. Note the lowercase "d."

Closings. Formal closings may vary. "Yours very truly," is the most common closing, but one may also choose from among "Sincerely yours," "Respectfully yours," and "Yours faithfully," plus all the permutations of these forms, depending on their appropriateness to the contents and the person addressed.

"Respectfully yours," should be used sparingly: only for the president of the United States, persons of high religious office, and the chief governing officers of educational institutions, governors, and heads of state.

All closings are punctuated with a comma.

Social Usage. When a dignitary is married, social invitations are addressed to him or her and spouse. Placecards, menus, programs, and the like are inscribed without the given name.

When a Married Woman Is the Dignitary. Now that more and more women hold public office, army, religious, and educational posts of prominence, the manner of addressing them and their husbands in social correspondence has changed. A woman retains her title with her name, and her husband is addressed second, as "Mr." or by his own title, as in "The Honorable Bella Abzug and Mr. Martin M. Abzug" (for a member of Congress).

Professionally, a woman is addressed by her title and the name under which she has chosen to carry on her career. In diplomatic or cabinet circles, she may be addressed as "Madam Secretary," "Madam Minister," or "Madam Ambassador" (note that there is no "e" on "Madam"), but never by a concocted feminine term, as "ambassadress" or "mayoress." Women military officers are addressed by the title pertaining to their rank.

TITLES

Doctoral Degrees.   If a person has the degree of D.D., L.L.D., or Ph.D., he or she may be addressed either as "Dr. So-and-so" or by the title pertaining to the position, as rabbi, dean, or professor. If one is not sure of the doctoral degree, it may be more gracious to call the person Dr., although there are many Ph.D.s who do not use the title professionally. The use of the official title is probably the best compromise.

Use of Esquire.   Lawyers may have the title "Esquire" added after the name, as "David J. Cohen, Esq." (note: no "Mr."). A woman lawyer may also use this title after her name, but it seems rather incongruous as the word is specifically masculine in gender. The use of the title in general is waning, especially since the State Department has begun to phase it out in official correspondence. If a lawyer has received the degree of J.D. and uses it professionally, he or she is referred to as "Marian Brenner, J.D.," and "Esq." is omitted.

In the salutation of a letter or in indirect address, a lawyer is referred to as "Mr.," "Mrs.," or "Ms."

The Use of the Word "Reverend."   "Reverend" in a title is an adjective, not a noun, and is properly preceded by "the" in formal usage, as "the Reverend Dr. Wise." Variant forms without "the," such as "Rev. Mr. [or Dr.] Holmes" are considered incorrect, as either a first or subsequent reference, by a majority of usage experts. The expression "the Reverend" without a name is also considered incorrect, while the use of "Reverend" as a form of direct address, unaccompanied by a name, is considered impolite. Hence, such expressions as "Let us ask the Reverend his opinion," or "Reverend, will you lead us in the Grace?" are uncouth and should not be used.

One may use the expression "Reverend Sir" when speaking to a Christian clergyman who does not have a doctoral degree.

Foreign Diplomats and Rulers.   The presidents, ambassadors, and cabinet ministers of foreign countries are referred to as "His Excellency." If they have titles of military rank, the title is included after, as in "His Excellency, General Charles de Gaulle."

Wives of Foreign Dignitaries.   It has become the custom to refer (in English) to the wives of foreign dignitaries as "Madame," after the French usage, regardless of the country they serve. Thus one would refer to the wife of the Italian ambassador as "Madame," not "Signora" (or "Mrs."!). In speaking the language of the country, of course, the usage appropriate to the language would pertain.

Hebrew Honorifics.   In Hebrew, *"adon"* equals "Mr.," and *"geveret,"* "Mrs."

Formal Introductions.   When making a formal presentation at a dinner, meeting, TV program, or the like, one always uses the full title: "Ladies and Gentlemen, the President of the United States"; "the Chief Rabbi of Edinburgh, Dr. Hayyim Levy"; "the Right Reverend Peter O'Brien, the Bishop of Chicago"; etc.

"The Honorable."   It is customary in the United States to give the title "The Honorable" to many high state and federal officials. The title is always used with "the," with or without any other title, as "The Honorable Ella T. Grasso, Governor of Connecticut," or "The Honorable Abraham A. Ribicoff." The person never uses the title in referring to himself; it is an honorific entirely for others to use. Once a person has been entitled "The Honorable," he may be referred to by this appellation even after he has retired from office.

JEWISH PRACTICE: THE BASICS OF OBSERVANCE

"I give thee good doctrine. It is a tree of life for them that hold fast to it."

—FROM THE SABBATH LITURGY

KASHRUT: DIETARY LAWS

The concept of *kashrut* originates in the Bible itself—Leviticus 2 and Deuteronomy 14 outline the permitted (kosher) and forbidden (*treyf* in Yiddish, *terefah* in Hebrew) foods, the ritually fit and unfit. A complicated system of laws relating to the slaughter, preparation, and consumption of kosher foods was in time developed by rabbinic masters.

In contemporary traditional thinking the observance of *kashrut* is regarded both as a spiritually refining act of self-discipline and as an instrument of community survival and ethnic identity.

Orthodox Judaism scrupulously follows all these laws. Reform Judaism does not adhere to the dietary laws, although many of its members do not eat pork or shellfish for symbolic reasons. Among Conservatives, the dietary laws are kept in principle, but in personal practice many have adopted the Reform position. Some keep the home kosher but "eat everything" when dining out.

Non-observant Jews and non-Jews alike should be aware of the general outlines of *kashrut* to avoid embarrassment at Orthodox functions, or when extending hospitality to the observant.

9. *What Is Kosher?*

Complete manuals on keeping a kosher home are readily available from Orthodox and Conservative women's organizations. In brief, only certain meats, fowl, and fish may be eaten; meat and milk foods may not be cooked or eaten together. Moreover, two sets of dishes, pots, utensils, cutlery, and so on must be used to avoid mixing meat and milk (*fleyshig* and *milkhig*) foods in preparation and serving. Fish, eggs, vegetables, and fruits are *parve* (neutral) and may be used with either meat or milk foods.

PERMITTED FOODS

Among meats, the permitted animals are those that have a cloven hoof and chew their cud. All fowl are permitted except birds of prey. The animals also must be ritually slaughtered by a qualified *shohet* (ritual slaughterer) and the meat prepared for cooking by soaking and salting to drain all the blood from the flesh. Fish, to be kosher, must have scales and fins.

KOSHER WINES AND CHEESES

All wines served in traditional homes must be kosher, that is, bottled under rabbinical supervision. Conservative practice now permits the use of non-kosher wines at the table, but kosher wine is still used for Kiddush, the blessing said over wine. Reform practice permits the use of any wine for all purposes, but many still cling to kosher wine for Kiddush out of respect for tradition.

There are no restrictions on the use of grain alcohols except on Passover. (See Chapter 17.)

In strictly traditional homes only cheese labeled kosher is served, because of the use of rennet and other animal substances in its manufacture. Recently, the Conservative rabbinate issued a ruling allowing the use of any cheese made from the milk of "clean animals." There has never been any restriction in Reform groups.

FORBIDDEN FOODS

Pork, wild birds, and wild game are *treyf,* as are oysters, lobsters, crabs, shrimp, snails, eels, insects (except for certain locusts), and reptiles.

TWO SETS OF EVERYTHING

The two sets of dishes, pots, silver, and so on, are kept completely separate by a system of marking, separated storage and washing.

In many homes, meat dishes and pots are marked with red, and milk dishes and pots with blue. Any other consistent color scheme may be used. Two distinctly different silver patterns are used. Tablecloths, dish towels, racks, and brushes are similarly keyed and cabinets and drawers marked. Some Orthodox housewives even separate the uses of the two sides of a double-bowl sink. In large households, camps, hotels, and restaurants there are often two complete, separate kitchens.

Servants and children should be carefully trained in the use of the separate sets of utensils. A guest offering to help the hostess in a kosher kitchen should always ask which dishes, silver, or towel to use.

10. Special Problems of Kashrut

"WAITING TIME"

Among the Orthodox, the separation of meat and milk foods is carried even further by observing a waiting period between the consumption of a meat meal and the later eating of dairy foods. The time can vary from one hour to six, depending on the group. The waiting time observed between eating dairy foods and a later meat meal is usually shorter; some do not wait at all.

In offering light refreshments or a buffet, it is thoughtful to have only *parve* (neutral) salads, cakes, and sherbets, or if a whipped-cream confection or ice cream is on the menu, to offer also fresh fruit, so that all may partake, no matter what they may have eaten before their arrival.

PREPACKAGED KOSHER MEALS

Frozen kosher dinners (often referred to as "airline meals") or fresh-prepared takeout foods are available in cities with large Orthodox communities. A host providing such a meal for a kosher guest should keep the food in its sealed wrappings while heating it, and keep the plastic cutlery usually supplied sealed in the wrapper it comes in, leaving it for the guest to break the seals when the meal is served. A paper plate should be used. In that way, there can be no question about the complete *kashrut*.

Some ultra-Orthodox people will accept only the supervision of their own rabbinical authorities. It is best to ask directly which supplier the guest would prefer. This also makes it clear that a kosher repast will be provided and eases any doubts the observant person may have about accepting the invitation.

CAKE AND BREAD

Many packaged breads and cakes contain milk or milk by-products (such as casein). These, of course, cannot be served at a meat meal. Breads and cakes made with lard are altogether *treyf*.

Kosher and *parve* breads and cakes may be obtained in Jewish bakeries. Some commercial bakers mark their packages with both a kosher seal and the word *parve* to indicate their acceptability.

Most French and Italian breads are made without either shortening or milk and so can be used as *parve*-kosher, but labels should be carefully checked or inquiries made of the bakery.

KOSHER LABELS

Food processed under rabbinical supervision should carry the Ⓤ seal of the Union of Orthodox Jewish Congregations, the most widely distributed label, or the symbol, name, and address of the organization certifying the *kashrut* of the product.

"KOSHER-STYLE"

Restaurants calling themselves "Jewish style" or "kosher stylè" are not necessarily kosher. The same is true of delicatessen meats labeled "Jewish" or "New York" style. A restaurant, to be truly kosher, must be under the supervision of an Orthodox rabbinical organization and also be under the eye of a *mashgiah*, a supervisor of *kashrut*. A delicatessen product must be similarly guarded and carry the seal of local rabbinical approval or the Ⓤ of the Union of Orthodox Jewish Congregations on its wrapper. (See Chapter 9.)

"IMITATION" PRODUCTS

There are many synthetic cream products now available as desserts, including even a new cheeseless cheesecake. The non-Jewish guest should not assume that the rules are being bent in order to permit an elaborate dessert. The same is true of new "nonmeat" breakfast products that resemble bacon, ham, or sausage. These are of such recent introduction that their acceptance in traditional Jewish menus is rare.

To some traditionalists there is something offensive about all of these products, which although "legal," give the appearance of a violation of a centuries-old tradition (called *mipney marit ha'ayin*). Others have no objection to moving with the times and modern chemistry. The decision to use or not use such products is an individual matter.

TABLE CEREMONIES AND BLESSINGS

11. Table Ceremonies

Ritual Handwashing. In strictly Orthodox tradition, ritual handwashing is done before partaking of bread. The men all don skullcaps first. In some homes, especially on the Sabbath, the handwashing is done by passing a pitcher and basin around at the table; each person pours a few drops of water over the fingertips of each hand (the right hand first), then silently recites the blessing:

Barukh Attah Adonai, Eloheynu Melekh Ha'olam, asher kiddeshanu b'mitzvotav v'tzivanu al netilat yadayim.
Blessed art Thou, O Lord our God, King of the Universe, who has sanctified us by His commandments and commanded us concerning the washing of hands.

As soon as the hands are dried, the blessing is said over the bread, without further talk or interruption.

In less observant homes the ceremonial washing is dispensed with, but the blessing is said over the bread before the meal is served.

BLESSING THE BREAD: HAMOTZI

Unless one is familiar with the custom of the household, one should wait to see whether and how the blessing over the bread will be said before touching anything on the table. In some families it is said before every meal, in others only on the Sabbath and holidays (when it will be preceded by Kiddush, the blessing over wine). (See Chapter 26 for the section on the Sabbath.)

In a traditional household all the men wear yarmulkes at table through the entire meal; others put them on only for the blessing over bread and wine.

A dinner guest asked to say the blessing over the bread may defer to his host or one of the children present, but it is such a simple ritual that one should learn the blessing and graciously accept the honor. The text is:

Barukh Attah Adonai Eloheynu Melekh Ha'olam hamotzi lekhem min ha'aretz.
Blessed art Thou, O Lord our God, King of the Universe, who brings forth bread from the earth.

The company respond "Amen."

In some households this is said standing. All are then seated, if they have been standing. The bread or hallah is cut, and portions distributed to all at the table. The diners need not repeat the blessing if they responded with "Amen." Sometimes the bread is sprinkled with salt, or dipped into the salt cellar before tasting. One may begin to eat the bread as soon as it has been passed to all. The meal service then proceeds as usual.

The blessing over the bread (and the wine, if on the Sabbath) makes it unnecessary to say any of the other blessings for various kinds of food before partaking of them during the meal. (See Chapter 12.)

All branches of Judaism use the same blessings.

GRACE AFTER MEALS: BIRKAT HAMAZON

When the meal is concluded, the host may ask one of the guests to lead in saying Grace. If there are more than three men present, the full Grace is said, including the appropriate psalms and blessings. At a smaller party, a shorter Grace may be said.

The recitation of the formal Grace may be announced by the leader in Hebrew as *"Rabotay nivorekh,"* or in Yiddish as *"Rabosay, mir vellen bentshn,"* both of which mean, "Gentlemen, let us say Grace."

Because of these rituals, a certain sanctity attaches to any repast, and a yarmulke is worn by the men at the table either during the entire meal (among the Orthodox) or during the recitation of the benedictions only (among the Conservative and Reform).

Women join in the recitation of Grace, although they do not lead it in traditional groups.

It is customary, at large Orthodox dinners, to provide booklets containing the text of the Grace and other blessings for the guests to use and keep as souvenirs of the occasion. Some households also pass out these pamphlets (called *bentshers* in Yiddish) to be used at the table at home.

A person who is eating alone or is pressed for time may use the short forms noted below.

Children are sometimes excused early from the table after saying a simple one-sentence Grace:

> *Barukh Attah Adonai Eloheynu Melekh Ha'olam hazan et hakol.*
> Blessed art Thou, O Lord our God, King of the Universe, who provides food for all.

There is also an Aramaic short form. (See Chapter 12.)

When Hamotzi and Grace Are Not Said.   A traditionalist may find himself at a less observant table where these rituals are not observed. He may carry them out for himself unobtrusively by washing his hands just before dinner and saying the blessing silently. He may conclude his repast with the short Grace said silently.

A sensitive host, noting this, will wait for his guest to finish the blessing before starting the meal service or rising from the table after the meal.

Knowing that one has an Orthodox guest, one may wish to honor his practices by asking him to say the blessings at the meal, even though one does not usually observe this custom.

12. Blessings for Various Occasions

Benedictions (*berakhot* in Hebrew, *brokhes* in Yiddish) or blessings have been set by tradition for practically every act and occurrence in life. In the Orthodox view, the world and all it holds is the creation and property of God. If a person is permitted to enjoy or take part in any aspect of it, he is called upon to thank God for it; even in adversity he recites benedictions that recognize the sovereignty and majesty of the Lord.

A long list of blessings for every act and occasion will be found in daily prayerbooks. There are also small pamphlets (in Yiddish, *bentshers*) containing the text of Grace after meals and other frequently recited blessings.

Anyone moving in Jewish circles should be conversant with these blessings. The same texts are used in the three major groups of Judaism.

To those who practice saying them, blessings serve many spiritual functions, preventing mere routine performance of commandments and good deeds (*mitzvot*) and sanctifying common physical acts. In heightening awareness of the "miracles that are daily with us" the blessings intensify appreciation and enjoyment of the world and of life itself. The practice becomes a continuing affirmation of Jewish identity.

Parents seeking to instill habits of thankfulness and wonder in their children may wish to teach them some of the blessings which follow. Training them in the habit of saying such *berakhot* as the blessing of food before eating it, the Grace after meals, and the Sheheheyanu, the blessing of thanks for many happy occasions is an objective way of teaching them gratitude for the good they have received; it may help to erase some of the unthinking complacency with which children accept as their due all the efforts parents and society make on their behalf.

RESPONSE TO A BLESSING

On hearing someone say a blessing, one responds "Amen," meaning "May it come to pass." One does not say "Amen" after a blessing he has said himself, unless it is part of the actual text.

BLESSINGS OF ENJOYMENT

All of the blessings in this category begin with the same opening phrases affirming the kingship of God. They are usually referred to by the phrases that follow this introduction—as *Hamotzi* (blessing over bread) or *Shehakol* (blessing over most other foods).

Opening Phrase.

Barukh Attah Adonai Eloheynu Melekh Ha'olam . . .
Blessed art Thou, O Lord our God, King of the Universe . . .

Blessing.   On breaking bread:

. . . *hamotzi lekhem min ha'aretz.*
. . . who brings forth bread from the earth.

Before eating cakes, cookies, or other foods prepared from grain:

... *borey miney m'zonot.*
... who creates various kinds of foods.

Before eating other foods (meat, fish, eggs) or drinking any other liquid
except wine:

... *shehakol niyeh bidvaro.*
... by whose word all things come into being.

Before drinking wine:

... *borey p'ri hagofen.*
... who created the fruit of the vine.

Before eating fruit:

... *borey p'ri ha'etz.*
... who created the fruit of the tree.

On seeing the wonders of nature (lightning, shooting stars, sunrise,
great deserts, high mountains):

... *oseh ma'aseh bereshit.*
... who has made the works of Creation.

On first seeing an ocean or sea:

... *she'asa et hayom hagadol.*
... who has made the great sea.

BLESSINGS ASSOCIATED WITH COMMANDMENTS

In this category are the *berakhot* recited during ritual observances, such as
putting on the *tallit* (prayer shawl), ritual washing of the hands, lighting
Sabbath and holiday candles, reading from the Torah, and the like. Texts of
berakhot are in the daily or holiday prayerbooks.

BLESSINGS OF PRAISE

These are benedictions to be uttered during personal prayer or other occasions for expression of praise. The Eighteen Benedictions of the morning

prayers, and Birkat Hagomel (thanksgiving) and Sheheheyanu, are in this category.

Grace after meals (short forms, especially suitable for children):

... *hazan et hakol.*
... who provides food for all.

Aramaic (known as the "Shepherd's Grace"; note that this benediction does not follow the usual form):

... *Brikh Rakhamana Malka d'Alma mara de hay pita.*
Blessed be the Merciful One, King of the Universe, the master of this bread.

On any joyous occasion—for birthdays, anniversaries, wearing a new garment or enjoying a new possession, hearing good news, tasting a new fruit (or the first of the season), and the like; also after blessing candles and saying Kiddush on festivals and other holidays:

... *sheheheyanu v'kiyemanu, v'higgianu, lazman hazeh.*
... who has kept us in life, and sustained us, and enabled us to reach this season.

BLESSING OF THANKSGIVING: HAGOMEL

Hagomel, referred to in Yiddish as *bentshn Gomel,* is a blessing of thanksgiving, customarily said in synagogue upon safe return from a long journey, recovery from a serious illness, or escape from other perils. The text of the blessing and the response to it will be found in the daily prayerbook.

SYNAGOGUES AND SERVICES

Know before Whom thou standest. . . .

13. *The Synagogue*

In the Hebrew names for a synagogue one may discern some of its many functions in the life of the Jewish community. It may be referred to as the *bet hatefilah* (house of prayer), *bet haknesset* (house of assembly), *bet hamidrash* (in Yiddish *besmedresh*, house of study). From ancient times on, perhaps even before the Babylonian exile, the synagogue and its courtyards served as a meeting place, court of law, educational institution, library, communal social center, and even the site of the *mikveh* (ritual bath). The most important ceremonial occasions of life, from the naming of a child to a memorial service for the dead, still take place there.

Synagogues are independent institutions, even though they may belong to central organizations within their particular branch of Judaism; thus, many small variations in structure, custom, ritual, and liturgy can be observed in visiting them. Although their congregants may refer to them by different names (among the Orthodox the word most commonly used is the Yiddish *shul;* among the Conservatives, synagogue; and in Reform groups, temple), and the buildings may exhibit striking architectural differences, perhaps the most interesting fact is that throughout the entire Diaspora and over the many centuries of Jewish history, the basic features of synagogue worship have remained the same.

PHYSICAL STRUCTURE

Every synagogue must contain a Torah (Scroll of the Law), handwritten on parchment and wound on wooden rollers. The Torahs are the most sacred objects in the synagogue, elaborately adorned with traditional velvet or brocade "dresses," silver crowns, bells, and breastplates.

The Torah is kept in an Aron Kodesh (the Holy Ark), which may be a freestanding cabinet or a built-in recess, also elaborately ornamented. It is usually on the eastern side of the building, so that congregants will be facing east as they turn toward it in prayer. In Israel the Ark will be on the wall that faces toward Jerusalem. It is customary to stand whenever the Ark is open during the prayer service.

The *parokhet* (curtain) is a brightly colored drapery that hangs between the doors of the Ark and the scrolls to separate this "holy of holies" from the synagogue proper. Many synagogues also have a set of white draperies used for the High Holidays. Some drape the Ark in black on Tishah b'Av to symbolize mourning for the Temple.

The Ner Tamid is the Eternal Light, a lamp kept perpetually lit, hanging before the Ark as a symbol of eternal faith. The lamps are finely wrought and often works of art in themselves.

The menorah is a candelabrum symbolic of the Temple, a reminder of the seven-branched candelabrum that stood there in ancient times. It is usually six- or eight-branched so as not to duplicate the Temple exactly.

The reader's desk (*bimah* or *almemar;* Sephardic, *tebah*) and the lectern (the *amud*) occupy differing positions in different synagogues. To emphasize the centrality of Torah study, the Orthodox, both Ashkenazic and Sephardic, place the *almemar* in the center of the room, opposite the Ark, with the pews built around it, while the *amud* stands directly before the Ark, on a slightly lower level.

In Reform and Conservative congregations, where the sermon is emphasized, the reader's desk is placed on a platform in front, alongside the speaker's lectern. Here the word *bimah* refers to the entire platform-pulpit area. On this platform are seats for rabbi, cantor, synagogue officials, and honored participants.

By the very nature of the services conducted in it, a synagogue cannot have an "altar." Through careless adoption of a Christian term, however, the area at the front of the sanctuary is sometimes referred to as the "altar." This is incorrect and offensive. You stand "on the *bimah* (platform)" or "before the Ark," or speak "from the pulpit or lectern." Similarly, a *huppah* (wedding canopy) is set up "before the Ark" in a sanctuary. There cannot, properly speaking, be an altar in a Jewish house of worship until the Temple is rebuilt in Jerusalem and sacrifices are offered there once more.

In Orthodox synagogues, there is a separate women's section, the *ezrat nashim,* either a balcony or a section along one side or the rear of the room, screened and separated from the men. Some Conservative congregations have both mixed seating in the center sections and segregated men's and women's seating on the sides; Reform congregations have mixed seating only.

USE OF LANGUAGE AND MUSIC

The language used in the services may vary from the almost entirely Ashkenazic Hebrew (as in older Orthodox *shuls*), the Sephardic Hebrew and some English or the vernacular of the congregants in more modern Orthodox and Conservative congregations, to the largely English service typical of Reform temples.

Music varies from the traditional unaccompanied chant, when the service is led by a layman in Orthodox and Conservative synagogues, to elaborate set pieces delivered by a full choir (male) and cantor. There is no instrumental music during services, a continuing sign of mourning for the destruction of the ancient Temple.

In Reform temples, instrumental music and women's voices are permitted, and so one may hear an organ and a mixed choir, even a woman *hazzan* (cantor). Reform Judaism also encourages innovation in musical composition, while the others maintain traditional Hebrew modes, with some Hasidic and Israeli melodies added for responsive singing.

In general, there is much more active participation by the congregants in Orthodox and Conservative services.

14. Visiting a Synagogue

SYNAGOGUE DRESS AND DECORUM

Many a social occasion brings a guest to a synagogue where he is unfamiliar with the service. Such visitors sometimes find themselves hesitant to participate fully because of the superficial, but very obvious differences in practice. There are certain basic guidelines that can make this experience more comfortable and meaningful. As long as he is conversant with these basic rules, a guest should not feel awkward; the "regulars" are happy to help a visitor feel at ease.

Proper Attire for Synagogue.   In the traditional view, one is expected to reserve the finest garments and ornaments for wear on the Sabbath and holidays. A very good-looking tailored woman's pants suit or a quiet-colored sports jacket and slacks for a man might meet this standard, but, when in doubt, one does best to lean to the conservative choice—the dark business suit or fashionable afternoon dress.

Blue jeans, leisure suits, and a whole gamut of sports and play clothes have taken over the informal dress scene. In some communities such apparel is acceptable everywhere, at work and even in synagogue for both sexes. But the more conventional position is that obvious work clothes (the genesis of blue jeans) or clothes designed for a recreational pursuit are not appropriate for attendance at religious services. (See Chapter 4.)

Hat and **Tallit.**   For weekday morning, Sabbath, and holiday worship, the *tallit* (prayer shawl) and hat or skullcap are worn by all men in traditional congregations; in Reform temples they are generally not worn, although some men may use them if they wish.

Strictly speaking, a boy need not wear a *tallit* until he is bar mitzvah, and in some groups not until he is a married man, but in many congregations every male dons one upon entering. A visitor should follow the suggestion of the usher. Synagogues usually provide prayer shawls (in Yiddish, *taleysim*) for visitors and congregants on a rack in the lobby.

One does not carry the *tallit,* if he uses his own, on the Sabbath in Orthodox circles, but leaves it in the drawer under the seat on Friday evening. On holidays one may carry it. Some ultra-Orthodox men wear the *tallit* under their coats while walking to and from services to avoid actually carrying it. The practice of having a young child carry the *tallit* is open to question.

Upon arriving at the synagogue one puts the *tallit* on, with appropriate blessings, before entering the sanctuary. If it becomes necessary to step outside again for a few minutes, one leaves it at his seat. Although one may continue to wear the *tallit* while conversing with a friend in the lobby or on the steps or grounds, it is not proper to keep the *tallit* on when going into the lavatory.

At the end of the services, one folds the *tallit* and replaces it on the rack.

Traditional Basics.   An observant person always follows the basic Orthodox rules: segregated seating; modest dress; no smoking, carrying, or riding on the Sabbath or holidays; no bare heads within the synagogue building ever. The many variations of these practices from one modern congregation to another can cause problems for the less traditional or those with little experience in synagogue attendance.

One clue as to what to expect lies in the name: almost every congregation calling itself a temple observes Reform ritual or very liberal Conservative practices. When in doubt, it is best to follow traditional patterns.

Reform Variants. Sabbath services are more likely to be held on Friday evening than on Saturday morning, unless there is a bar mitzvah. Hats or yarmulkes are not necessary for men, although some do wear them. Most women wear hats or other stylish head coverings. One may carry a dress handbag and money, but not any object obviously workaday in nature, such as a briefcase. Riding and smoking are permitted.

TO DRIVE OR NOT TO DRIVE?

The nonobservant guest should be sensitive to the traditional prohibition of riding on the Sabbath and holidays. To avoid offending an Orthodox host, it is best to park one's car a block or two away and walk up to the synagogue. One should follow the same rule in a cab, and avoid driving up to the door. It is most tactful and considerate not to flaunt one's emancipation from traditional practices.

Like the Reform, most Conservative groups allow driving to services. In the suburbs, most of these synagogues have parking lots and it is expected that most of the congregants will drive because of the distances involved.

Ask! Having noted all this, one must next add that the observance of these customs varies from synagogue to synagogue, and sometimes from the administration of one rabbi to the next in the same congregation! It never hurts to ask when in doubt.

Weddings, Concerts, and Meetings. Since weddings are never held on the Sabbath or holidays, one may always drive to the synagogue to attend. This is also true of concerts, meetings, and any other secular functions that may be held in the public rooms of the synagogue.

Other "Unrestricted" Occasions. Other times when it is permissible to drive to any synagogue, carry money, handbags, and other objects, are Purim, Hanukkah, and other minor holidays, Selihot (midnight penitential prayers), and bar mitzvahs and other functions held on Rosh Hodesh (first of the Hebrew month) or nonholiday Mondays and Thursdays, when the Torah is read.

ATTENDING SERVICES

Entering.   Upon entering a traditional synagogue, a man puts on a *yarmulke* and *tallit*, either his own or one provided by the congregation. The skullcap or hat is kept on the entire time one is in the building, either at services, during any reception held afterward, or while socializing in the lobby or on the grounds.

If the books are on tables or shelves outside the sanctuary, one picks up a *siddur* (prayerbook) and Humash (Bible) on the way in. If they are not set out in the lobby, the books are usually at the seats. Ask an usher (or a neighbor who has extra books near him) for a prayerbook if they are not at the seat. It is rather disrespectful (and uninteresting) not to use a book and make some attempt to follow the service. All but the most old-fashioned of traditional congregations have prayerbooks with English translations alongside the Hebrew.

Where to Sit.   You may usually take any empty seat. Sometimes the seat may have a plaque showing a member's name on the back. You may sit there if the synagogue is crowded and it is late, on the assumption that the person named will not be attending. Otherwise, leave the named seats empty. There are always some seats up front; however, a visitor in a traditional synagogue should not take a seat at the eastern wall unless led there by an usher, as these are places of honor usually reserved for congregation dignitaries.

A couple in doubt as to whether they may sit together should wait to be directed by an usher to appropriate seats. If there are no ushers, it may be better for the man to enter the sanctuary first and scout the situation. The women's gallery is usually, but not always, upstairs. Sometimes it is at one side or in the back on the same floor.

Deportment.   The atmosphere at services may run the gamut from the very strict silence of the stylish Reform and Sephardic synagogues to the very easy family bonhomie of the small *shtibl* (Hasidic congregation).

As a visitor you should comport yourself formally and keep to the silence rule, even when you see others conversing during the service. A great deal of chatter is not in good taste for any congregants, but for the visitor it might be construed as taking a disrespectful liberty. You may offer a quiet, cordial greeting to the host or hostess at a bar mitzvah, but keep the small talk and family gossip for the reception.

Chatting during the Torah reading, which constitutes the study part of the service, is in very poor taste, although common in some congregations. Those who must converse should step out into the lobby.

Children. When you bring your children to regular services as guests at a bar mitzvah or to visit grandparents on holidays, drill them in what is expected of them, before the day. Be thoughtful enough to keep a watchful eye on them, and if the proceedings are lengthy and a child becomes restless, be ready to take the youngster outside to wait for the end of the service.

Children should never be sent outside to "play" without some supervision. There is too much temptation and opportunity to become unruly and mischievous while the adults are preoccupied within.

Arriving After the Service Has Begun. In Orthodox worship, it is normal for anyone entering after the service has begun to take up his prayerbook, start at the opening prayer, and read through the service rapidly and silently until he catches up to the rest of the congregation, standing for the prayers as the service indicates, even if the others are seated. This accounts for the slightly anarchic atmosphere in some old traditional and Hasidic synagogues.

Regardless of the nature of the congregation, certain conventions always apply when you arrive after the services have begun. It is customary not to permit entrance into the sanctuary during the sermon, the standing prayers, a cantorial solo, or announcements from the pulpit. Some congregations permit latecomers to enter and stand in the back so that they may hear the service while waiting for an appropriate break during which they may be seated. Sometimes the last few rows are reserved for late arrivals, who may sit there during a lengthy sermon or Amidah (standing prayer) and take seats down front later if they wish. Obey the directions of the ushers as to when you may enter the sanctuary and take seats. If there are no ushers, observe the same decorum, quietly slipping into a back seat if you can.

No matter what conventions are observed by the congregation, it is not correct, when taking your seat, to brush past a person who is still saying one of the standing prayers, especially the Kedushah (Sanctification), as the worshipper must not only not be distracted or interrupted, but may not move from the spot until he has finished this part of his devotions. Do not nod to or greet persons engaged in these prayers until they have finished.

Finding the Place. One may ask a neighbor on what page the ongoing prayer is to be found. It is most courteous, in replying, to hand the prayerbook you have been using to the newcomer, pointing to the place, and then to turn the place up for yourself in another book. This is usually handed over by the person inquiring, in exchange for the open one.

Leaving. One should not leave before the end of the service, except for pressing personal reasons. In traditional synagogues, women sometimes leave after the Kedushah (Sanctification) to ready the holiday meal, but to modern eyes this is demeaning. It is a holiday or Sabbath for all in the household, and one member should not reduce herself to servant status week after week. An exception may be made for a special festive occasion, such as a *kiddush* within the synagogue, where the hostess does not remove herself completely from the devotional scene and is preparing for a component of the service.

When the service is concluded, a man using the congregation's prayer shawl folds the *tallit* and returns it to the rack or shelf where he obtained it. Books are returned either to the seat racks or to the shelves where they were found originally.

It is customary to shake hands and exchange the appropriate Sabbath or holiday greetings with those seated nearby. In some congregations there is a receiving line set up after services so that the rabbi and other officiants may greet the worshippers as they leave.

A Stranger in the Synagogue. A refinement of the courtesy of greeting involves hospitality to the stranger one may notice at synagogue services. In small congregations, where most of the members know one another, the congregant has a duty at least to greet a nonmember at the end of the services. It is even more cordial, especially on the holidays, when the services are quite long, to introduce yourself at some break in the ritual and make the newcomer feel welcome.

A person new to the community may initiate this meeting by extending the greeting appropriate to the day and adding an introductory remark, such as, "I'm Marian Meyers and this is my husband Joseph. We've just moved to [or "are visiting"] Pittsfield."

A Note to the Non-Jewish Visitor. Visitors are always welcome in synagogues of any denomination. They should dress as for church attendance, including a hat for a man, and should avoid carrying anything or smoking on the Sabbath. Some synagogues require tickets of admission for High Holiday services, but never for the others.

USUAL TIMES OF SERVICES

Sabbaths and Holidays. Services are held in all synagogues every week on Friday evening, half an hour before sundown in the Orthodox, at various evening hours in others, and on Saturday morning. In addition, services are held on the eve of all holidays and the morning of the next day. There are special midnight services of music for Selihot (penitential prayers) before the High Holidays.

The exact times and dates are announced on the synagogue notice boards, in their bulletins, and in the religion columns of local newspapers.

Do not attempt to call a synagogue for information about services on the day (e.g., Friday evening or a holiday morning), as no business is transacted at that time and the offices of all synagogues are closed. (See Chapter 15.)

The Weekday Minyan. On weekdays, most traditional synagogues have services every morning and every afternoon from shortly before sundown into the early evening. They attempt to maintain a quorum (*minyan*) for the convenience of those who wish to say Kaddish (memorial prayers). One may phone the synagogue office to inquire as to exact times, a wise precaution, as they vary widely. Morning services are sometimes held at a very early hour, to accommodate those who go on to work from their devotions.

A man asked to make up a quorum should join in willingly. His participation will make it possible for others to perform a religious duty they could not otherwise carry out, such as reciting memorial prayers. Those who feel modest about their knowledge of the service should not hesitate on this account; it is their presence, if only to say "Amen," that makes the *minyan*. They may someday need the same courtesy when it is their turn to say memorial prayers.

In congregations where women are counted in the *minyan*, their presence is equally important and is also a *mitzvah* (a good deed).

PARTICIPATING IN THE RITUAL: "HONORS"

Jewish worship is regarded as a communal activity; indeed, one cannot perform an important part of the worship, Torah reading, or recite certain prayers, such as Kaddish, without a *minyan* (quorum of ten). A ritual of showing respect and love for the Torah has developed around the weekly readings. Since the Torah is considered the most holy object in the synagogue, participation in the Torah service is considered an honor.

The weekly portion of the Torah is read on Mondays, Thursdays, Sabbaths, and Rosh Hodesh. A table of the readings appears in the daily and Sabbath prayerbook.

Who Reads. The Torah is read from the hand-lettered scroll, which is written in an unpointed script rather different from the printed text. It is intoned or cantillated according to an ancient melody called the trope. Although all congregants are theoretically eligible to read, an expertise beyond the skill of the average synagogue member began to be looked for even in ancient times, and it became the custom to have an officially appointed reader, who performed the actual task, while those called up looked on silently, saying only the blessings before and after the reading.

Today, only bar/bat mitzvah boys and girls read the portions unassisted, although some congregations will permit readings by individuals who request the privilege and have the necessary skill. Great esteem is attached to clear, correct, and well-chanted reading.

The Ritual of Torah Reading.   The Ark is ceremoniously opened; the Torah scroll is taken out, carried in a formal procession through the sanctuary, and opened at the reading desk. The opened scroll is lifted on high and displayed to the congregation, either before the readings (among Sephardim) or when the readings are completed (among Ashkenazim). The process is then reversed as the Torah is ceremoniously rerolled, tied, "dressed" in its robes and ornaments, carried in procession through the synagogue once more, and put back into the Ark, which is then closed.

Each of these actions is performed by a different congregant, and being "called up" for them is an honor, with the assignment of an actual Torah portion (*aliyah*) ranking as the highest.

Names of the Honors.   The functions described above are usually referred to by their Hebrew names: opening the Ark, *petihah;* taking the Torah out, *hotza'ah;* untying and tying it up again, *gelilah;* lifting it up, *hagbah;* "reading" a portion, *aliyah;* closing the Ark, *hakhnasah.*

Assigning the Honors.   When there is no special occasion in the congregation, the synagogue officials (*gabbaim;* singular, *gabbai*) select the participants. However, when there is a bar/bat mitzvah, or an *oyfruf* (calling up of a bridegroom) or some other special celebration, it is customary to allow the family to name the recipients of the honors.

The Torah reading is broken up into segments; the number, depending on the day, may vary from three on a weekday to seven on a Sabbath. For special occasions, the number may be increased by subdividing these portions.

A host who desires to honor many family members and friends on a special occasion should consult with the *shammash* (sexton) or *gabbai,* and give him a list of the persons to be called, setting forth the Hebrew names of the persons receiving an *aliyah,* as they will be called up by this name. The first two portions are always assigned to a *kohen* and a *levi,* respectively.

When there are several functions on the same day, the other honors are divided among the hosts. A priority usually observed is that a bridegroom in the week just before or after his wedding comes first; next, a bar/bat mitz-vah; third, a new father; fourth, a person who is observing the *yahrzeit* (anniversary of death) of a parent; and fifth, a person rising from the week of mourning (*shivah*). After these, any congregant may be called.

Honors for Women.   Many Conservative synagogues now allow women to be called up for any of these functions, including Torah portions. Others, more traditional in nature, allow only bat mitzvahs to read a portion, and in addition, will regularly assign English passages and responsive readings to women members.

When women are called up, they follow the same procedure as that outlined below for men. In some synagogues they wear *tallit* and skullcap; in others, only a head covering.

Reform Practices.   Reform temples do not follow this ritual. They usually deemphasize congregational participation in the service, and there is no Torah procession, although this may vary from one congregation to another. Unless there is a bar/bat mitzvah, the reading of the Torah is done by the cantor.

Because many Reform temples do not have regular Sabbath morning services, the Torah reading may be done on Friday nights. Some also do not have regular weekday services. The schedule should be checked with the individual temple.

A woman may be given the honor of opening the Friday evening Reform service with the ceremonial candle lighting.

Procedure When Called Up.   For honors other than an *aliyah*, the *gabbai* will approach the person selected and ask him or her to take part. If you are reluctant to participate, you may politely decline the offer, but remember that the refusal may inadvertently slight the host of a festivity.

Do not decline out of a misguided fear of appearing awkward or ignorant. Many congregations pride themselves on doing things a bit differently and the *gabbai* is prepared, indeed eager, to help a visitor avoid embarrassing mistakes. The *gabbai* will give the signal when it is time to go up to the platform, to open the Ark, to draw the curtain, and so on.

A man who has not been wearing a *tallit* puts one on before going up to the Ark. Ascend the *bimah* from the right side. If there are doors as well as a curtain, the opening honor may be given to two persons.

Those who have opened the Ark remain on the platform while the Torah is taken out for the procession. They follow in the procession after the cantor, rabbi, and other officials until they have reached their seats.

Those who have been given an *aliyah* will be summoned with the traditional call *"Ya'amod* [Hebrew name] *ben* [Hebrew name], *hamishi"* ("Let him rise [name] son of [name] to the fifth portion," etc.). An honorific, such as *"morenu harav"* (for a rabbi) or *"ha bokher ha bar mitzvah"* (for a bar mitzvah boy) may be added before the name. A bar/bat mitzvah or a bridegroom is usually called up with a loud, festive chant. In some synagogues, only the number of the portion will be called, as *"Ya'amod hamishi."*

This call will come at the conclusion of the blessings for the previous portion. While the new reader is ascending, a blessing (*"Mi she Berakh. . . ."*—"May He who blessed our fathers . . . also bless. . . .") may be said for the previous reader.

The new reader stands at the reading desk to the right of the official Torah reader, who will point out the place in the scroll. You then take the end of the *tallit* in the right hand, touch it to the Torah, bring it to your lips, and kiss it. Then you recite the blessing.

When the portion and the concluding blessing are finished, you move over to the right side of the *bimah*. If a Misheberakh will be said, the official will ask your Hebrew name at this point.

You remain standing at the right until the next portion is concluded, to show reluctance to leave the Torah quickly. Then you shake hands with the reader, the *gabbaim*, the rabbi, president, and whoever else is on the platform, and, after descending from the left side of the *bimah*, with the people who offer greetings as you pass them on the way to your seat.

Congratulations are in order for having received such an honor. The usual greeting is *"Yasher koakh."* You shake hands and may add a thank you in response.

When the entire Torah reading is completed, the Torah is dressed in its covering and ornaments and returned to the Ark after another procession around the sanctuary. Those called up for the closing honors join in the return procession.

When the Procession Passes By. It is customary to turn toward the Torah as the procession moves slowly around the synagogue. As the scroll is carried by, one touches it with the *tallit* or the *siddur* (prayerbook), then kisses the *tallit* or *siddur*.

Youngsters at services may be brought close to the aisles and lifted up so they may participate in this ritual of honoring the Torah.

Donations. It is gracious to offer a donation to the synagogue if you have been honored, especially if a Misheberakh, with its pledge of charity, has been said.

Some bar/bat mitzvah hosts undertake to make one thank-offering on behalf of all their guests and the boy or girl being honored.

In modern practice these donations are not announced from the platform, although they may be listed in the synagogue bulletin.

THE JEWISH YEAR

And on your joyous occasions, your fixed festivals and new moon days, you shall sound the trumpets . . .

—NUMBERS 10:10

15. *The Hebrew Calendar*

WHY HEBREW DATES ARE "MOVABLE"

As anyone who has ever observed an anniversary, birthday, or *yahrzeit* (anniversary of death) according to the Hebrew calendar knows, the date corresponding to it in the conventional calendar changes from year to year, sometimes by as much as a month. The Hebrew calendar varies so widely from the Gregorian (civil) calendar because two differing systems govern the dates.

The Gregorian yearly cycle is based on the 365¼-day (actually 365 days, 5 hours, 48 minutes, and 46 seconds) revolution of the earth about the sun: the addition of an extra day every fourth year (Leap Year) causes the dates of holidays and the seasonal solstices to fall at almost exactly the same time each year.

The Hebrew calendar, on the other hand, is based on observation of the lunar cycle of 29½ days (actually 29 days, 12 hours, 44 minutes, and 3 seconds). Twelve lunar months account for only 354 days; if the calendar had no adjustments for the missing 11 days, the major festivals, which are agricultural in nature, would begin to occur at the wrong season of the year and all the other holidays would shift accordingly.

A complicated mathematical formula was arrived at in the fourth century by Hillel II (one of the last heads of the Sanhedrin), to stabilize the calendar. Briefly, the months have 30 and 29 days alternately, an extra day is added to adjust the date of Rosh Hashanah and Yom Kippur, and in leap years an extra month, Adar Sheni, is added before the month of Nisan, to regulate the date of Passover.

Names of the Months.   The names of the months are derived from the Babylonian. They are: Nisan° (corresponding approximately with April), Iyyar (May), Sivan° (June), Tammuz (July), Av° (August), Elul (September), Tishri° (October), Heshvan (November), Kislev (December), Tevet (January), Shevat° (February), and Adar (March). Months marked with an asterisk (°) have thirty days; Heshvan and Kislev are variable, and the others have twenty-nine days.

The Jewish year begins in the seventh month, Tishri, with Rosh Hashanah, also called the Solemn Day of Memorial (Yom Hazikkaron); however, Nisan is considered the first month, because of the verse in Exodus 12:2, naming this time of the great Exodus from Egypt as the first of months.

Because the yearly cycle was originally based on human observation of the moon, not on mathematics, all dates—holidays, anniversaries, the beginning of the months— are calculated from sundown to sundown.

Rosh Hodesh.   The first day of the month, coinciding with the new moon, is a minor festival in itself, Rosh Hodesh.

The date of the new moon, or the first of each Hebrew month (Rosh Hodesh), can be found by consulting the *luah* (Hebrew calendar) for the year. The date is announced in synagogue on the Sabbath preceding *(Shabbat Mevar'khim),* a reminder of the ancient custom of having the Sanhedrin proclaim the new moon with trumpets, signal fires across the land of Israel, and messengers to the settlements outside Israel.

Because the moon actually rises after twenty-nine and a half days, thirty-day months have a two-day Rosh Hodesh while the others have one day.

One Day or Two?   Rosh Hashanah, actually the Rosh Hodesh of a thirty-day month, has been celebrated for two days since a rabbinical ruling in ancient times ended the confusion over the proper date. At that time, Yom Kippur was limited to one day because of the rigorous nature of the fast, and the major holidays were kept as week-long festivals.

In the ancient Diaspora, the tradition was set of observing a full holiday for the first two days of each festival, just as for Rosh Hashanah, to be certain that the festivals were being celebrated at the same time as they would have been observed in Israel. Only Yom Kippur remained a single day of abstinence.

In modern Israel and among Reform groups, only the first day of the festivals is observed as a full holiday, except for Rosh Hashanah in Israel, where it is still two days. All Orthodox and Conservative groups keep to the two-day system outside of Israel, maintaining the link to ancient times despite the mathematical certainties of our era.

A SCHEMATIC CALENDAR
OF JEWISH HOLIDAYS

In Table 3, "Jewish Holidays," the major holidays are arranged in chronological order. The festivals and the High Holidays are indicated by an asterisk (°), evenings when candles should be lit by ♍, *Yizkor* (memorial prayer) days by (°°), and minor holidays by °.

Fast days, except for Yom Kippur and Tishah b'Av, are not shown.

Since Reform groups do not keep the second day of two-day holidays, they light candles only on the first evening.

DEALING WITH HEBREW DATES

Which Date to Observe. It is customary to use the Hebrew date when observing a *yahrzeit*. Some also use this date for tombstone inscriptions. However, most people use the civil date for birthdays and other anniversaries.

Those who observe the anniversary of their bar/bat mitzvah in synagogue generally keep to the Hebrew date, since this will coincide with the Torah portion they studied originally.

Finding a Corresponding Civil Date. A 100-year calendar from 1920 to 2020 can be found in the index to the *Encyclopedia Judaica*. A *luah*—the annual Hebrew calendar—can be obtained from one's synagogue in pocket or wall size. They are frequently distributed as a form of advertising by Jewish business concerns and are also published in diary format by most Jewish organizations.

A *luah* shows the corresponding civil date of each day and gives candle-lighting times, the Torah portion of the week, some prayer texts, often a five-year summary of major holiday dates, and other useful information. The dates run from September (Rosh Hashanah) to the following August. A *luah* is most easily acquired at the time of the High Holidays.

NUMBERING THE YEARS AND CITING DATES

The present Jewish calendar numbers the years from the date of Creation, as determined by biblical scholars. Thus 5741 (1980–81) represents five thousand seven hundred forty-one years since the beginning of the world, or, symbolically, since the beginning of consciously recorded time. The Christian world, on the other hand, began in the sixth century to date the years from the birth of Jesus, using the letters A.D. (Anno Domini), meaning

Table 3. Jewish Holidays

Approximate English date	Hebrew date		Holiday	Yizkor**
September	29 Elul (evening)	🕎	*Eve of Rosh Hashanah, (New Year)	
	1 Tishri	🕎	*First day, Rosh Hashanah	
	2 Tishri		*Second day, Rosh Hashanah	
September–	9 Tishri (evening)	🕎	*Kol Nidre, opening prayer of	
October	10 Tishri		*Yom Kippur (Day of Atonement)	**
October	14 Tishri	🕎	*Eve of Sukkot	
	15 Tishri	🕎	*First day, Sukkot (Tabernacles)	
	16 Tishri		*Second day, Sukkot	
	21 Tishri	🕎	*Eve of Hoshana Rabba	
	22 Tishri	🕎	*Shemini Atzeret (Feast of Conclusion, Eighth Day of Solemn Assembly)	**
	23 Tishri		*Simhat Torah (Rejoicing of the Law)	
December	24 Kislev (eve) to 1 Tevet		°First Hanukkah light (eight nights in all)	
January	15 Shevat		°Tu b'Shevat (New Year of the Trees)	
March	13 Adar		°Eve of Purim (Megillah reading)	
	14 Adar		°Purim	
March–April	14 Nisan	🕎	*Passover, first Seder (evening)	
	15 Nisan	🕎	*Second Seder	
	20 Nisan	🕎	*Eve of	
	21 Nisan	🕎	*Concluding days of Passover, seventh day	
	22 Nisan		*Eighth day	**
April–May	16 Nisan to 5 Sivan		Counting the Omer (49 days, no weddings)	
	27 Nisan		°Remembrance Day (Yom Hashoah, memorializing victims of the Holocaust)	

🕎 Candles lit   * Festivals, High Holidays   ° Minor holidays   ** Yizkor day

Table 3. Jewish Holidays *(cont'd)*

Approximate English date	Hebrew date		Holiday	Yizkor°°
April–May	5 Iyyar		°Israel Independence Day (Yom Ha'atzma'ut)	
	18 Iyyar		°Lag b'Omer (33d day of Counting Omer, weddings allowed)	
May–June	5 Sivan (eve)	♆	*Eve of Shavuot, Bikkurim	
	6 Sivan	♆	*First day, Shavuot (Feast of Weeks or First Fruits)	
	7 Sivan		*Second day, Shavuot	••
August	9 Av		°Tishah b'Av (Fast of the Ninth of Av, commemorating the destruction of the Temple)	
September	Elul		A holy month (Selihot—penitential prayers are said)	

♆ Candles lit   * Festivals, High Holidays   ° Minor holidays   •• Yizkor day

"In the year of our Lord," and referring to the time before that as B.C., "Before Christ." Thus A.D. 1981 means one thousand nine hundred eighty-one years after the birth of Jesus.

The A.D.–B.C. nomenclature is not acceptable to thoughtful Jews, sensitive to its meaning. The custom has developed, therefore, among Jewish teachers and scholars, when citing dates in the civil calendar, to use the abbreviation C.E., standing for "Common Era," instead of A.D., and B.C.E. ("Before the Common Era") instead of B.C. Thus the date of the rededication of the Temple by the Maccabees would be written as 165 B.C.E., and the date of its destruction by the Romans as 70 C.E.

Civil dates entered in Hebrew marriage certificates are generally cited as "June 22, 1980 C.E." There is no reason why a person desiring to assert his freedom from Christological references may not use such dating in all documents, or at least refrain from using the term A.D.

16. The Major Festivals

The first and last days of the festivals of Pesah and Sukkot, the first two days of the festival of Shavuot, and the High Holidays, Rosh Hashanah and Yom Kippur, are days of solemn worship, on which school attendance and work are not permitted in all branches of Judaism. They are celebrated by the observant with restrictions on daily workaday activities almost the same as those for the Sabbath.

HOLIDAY OBSERVANCE

The Orthodox do not drive, handle money or tools, or use the telephone on these days; however, cooking (for the holiday only) and smoking are permitted, except on Yom Kippur.

Among Orthodox, Conservative, and Reform groups alike, synagogue services and a home feast are basic to the observance of each holiday. Candles are lit in the home by the women on the eve of each holiday. The appropriate Kiddush is recited before the holiday meal.

The intermediate days of the week-long festivals are known as *hol hamo'ed*. Among the Orthodox, as little as possible ordinary work and business is done, although the usual daily activities are permitted if absolutely necessary.

YIZKOR

Yizkor (memorial) services are held during each festival and on Yom Kippur by synagogues of all denominations, although the day for Reform *Yizkor* may differ. Sephardim generally say *Yizkor* only on Yom Kippur. (See chapters on each holiday for details, and consult synagogue bulletins for exact times of services.)

HEBREW SCHOOL CALENDAR

Hebrew school vacations are usual during the week of Passover, and in the fall school generally does not start until after Sukkot. In Israel the school system follows this calendar.

17. Pesah/Passover and the Seder

Let every person in every generation think of himself as if he personally had gone forth from Egypt.

—HAGGADAH

Although Rosh Hashanah and Yom Kippur are the most solemn and spiritual of Jewish holidays, Pesah, recreating the catalytic event of Jewish history, ranks as the festival most closely associated with family, homecoming, and hospitality.

Pesah commemorates the deliverance of the Jewish people from Egyptian bondage. It is the festival of freedom, the keynote of Jewish identity. It is celebrated principally at home at the Seder, a ritual feast which should fulfill two important conditions: each person must experience the Exodus as though he or she personally had been freed from slavery, and the story must be told to the children from generation to generation in the language they best understand.

Rich in symbol and significance, family and child centered, and hedged about by important rituals and laws, Pesah is probably the festival that exerts the strongest emotional pull. Its political, ideological, nostalgic and gourmet elements make it the home holiday most widely observed even by those who no longer participate in the other aspects of Jewish worship.

FORBIDDEN FOODS (HAMETZ)

Fundamental to the holiday is the removal of all leaven and leavened food from the house and the substitution of matzo and matzo products for bread and ordinary cake. Scrupulous "spring cleaning" is undertaken by the observant to rid the house of any trace of *hametz* (leavened foods).

The strictness with which the law forbidding the eating of *hametz* is observed varies widely. Reform practice requires only the setting aside of all leavened bread and cake; at the other extreme are the ultra-Orthodox, who use no dairy products during Passover and change every food item and cooking and serving utensil in the house, sometimes even the very kitchen stove itself.

Practice also varies from one community to another. It is difficult to make a complete list of all permitted and forbidden foods without an addi-

tional list of exceptions. Such listing is further complicated by the prolifera-
tion of processed and synthetic foods.

Briefly, the observant do not partake of any food containing one of the
major grains: wheat, rye, barley, and oats. This includes biscuits, cakes, ce-
reals, crackers, hops, bread, rice, all liquids containing ingredients or flavors
made from grain alcohol (e.g., vanilla), and grain alcohols. Dried beans and
peas are also forbidden, as is any vegetable that may sprout.

During the holiday period, the observant use only wines and liquors certified kosher for Passover.

PERMITTED FOODS

All kinds of packaged and prepared foods are available for Passover; to be
acceptable, they should carry both the seal of a rabbinical group and the
Hebrew inscription כשר לפסח —*kosher l'Pesah*—"kosher for Passover."
This applies also to all products imported from Israel.

Most traditional synagogues issue a Passover bulletin with detailed instructions as to holiday preparations, permitted foods, and the rabbinical
supervision they accept as kosher.

Foods not *hametz* in and of themselves include meat, fish, fowl, all fruits,
vegetables except peas and beans, and, from freshly opened packages,
spices, coffee, tea, sugar, and salt.

THE SEDER

The word *Seder* literally means "order"—a ritual that is described in detail
in the Haggadah, the Passover text. It refers to both the Haggadah narration
and the special feast that is central to the story.

The Holiday Symbols.   The special preparations for the Seder table
should be started early, especially when many guests are expected. Children
should be involved in them as much as possible.

On a tablecloth kept for holiday use, one sets out the symbolic foods:
matzot (unleavened bread representing the haste of the departure from
Egypt; the Hebrew singular is *matzah*, the English, matzo or matzos); salt
water (for the tears of suffering and oppression); the roasted bone and
roasted egg (reminiscent of the sacrificial lamb and the Temple offerings);
maror, bitter herbs such as grated horseradish or bitter greens (for the bit-
terness of slavery); *haroset*, a mixture of chopped apples, nuts, cinnamon,
and wine (representing the bricks the Hebrews made for Pharaoh); *karpas*, a
green vegetable such as parsley or radish (symbolizing spring and hope for

the future); wine, the sign of joy and gladness, and a special goblet of wine for Elijah, symbolizing hope for the Messianic age.

Setting the Table. Three matzos are put into a specially sectioned case, or between napkins on a large plate set at the leader's place; on top of the covered matzos, or on the table alongside them, is placed the Passover plate (or a small tray) holding the symbolic foods, arranged according to the diagram in Figure 6.

Only a tablespoonful or so of *maror* and *haroset*, a single radish and a sprig of parsley, and a very small dish of salt water should be put on this plate. The rest should be set out in serving dishes to be passed around as called for in the narration.

Candles are lit by the women just before sundown. If there is room the candelabra may be placed on the table, but there is so much going on during the reading of the Haggadah and the meal that it is generally safer and more convenient to place the candles elsewhere, on the sideboard or mantel, where they can be seen but not be a hazard.

Other Seder Customs. The leader is usually seated in a cushion-filled chair against which he may recline while eating. It is a reminder of the ancient custom of reclining at banquets, and is considered the mark of a free man. Some set a cushion for each person. Children, in particular, delight in having their own pillows.

Setting the Individual Places. It adds to the festivity and importance of the occasion to use a special set of dishes and silver kept from year to year for this holiday.

Each individual place is set with a wine glass on a rimmed coaster or small saucer to hold the wine which will be dropped out of it during the ceremony, the silver that will be needed for the meal service later, and a small dish on the service place to hold *haroset*, greens, *maror*, and so on, as the service unfolds.

There should be a Haggadah for each person, preferably all the same edition, which makes it easier for all to follow the service. Children may be given a special illustrated text to keep up their interest.

A Kiddush cup is set for the leader (usually the father or grandfather), although there is no reason why a woman may not lead. If there will be more than one head of a household present, some set a Pesah plate and a Kiddush cup for each and have each one recite the holiday Kiddush that opens the Seder.

If there will be many guests at the table it may be easier not to set the dinner silver and service plates. Each place setting can be rolled in a napkin and the dinner plates stacked in readiness on a sideboard. Then at the end of

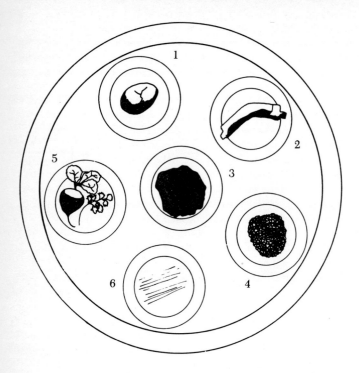

Figure 6. The Passover Plate. Set on top of or alongside three matzos. (1) roasted egg (2) roasted shankbone (*pesah*) (3) *maror* (bitter herbs) (4) *haroset* (chopped apples, nuts, spices and wine) (5) *karpas* (green vegetable) (6) salt water.

the first part of the narration the table can be quickly set for the meal service and the Haggadahs removed until it is time for Grace at the end of the meal.

How Much of the Symbolic Foods to Prepare.   There should be at least one portion (about a tablespoon) of each of the symbolic foods for each person at the table. In addition to the three matzos on the ceremonial plate, there should be at least half a matzo per person. Enough wine will be needed to fill the cup of Elijah once and the glasses of the others four times.

The wine glasses used should hold about three ounces. Only wine kosher for Passover may be used for the Seder.

Among traditionalists the service and the meal may not begin until after dark, since the Bible commands one to eat matzos "in the evening."

Those who follow the custom of Eastern Europe always begin the meal with a dish of hard-boiled eggs in salt water, regarded as a symbol of mourning for the Egyptians who were drowned at the Red Sea.

Afikoman.   After the blessing is said over the matzo, one half of the middle matzo is set aside, to be eaten later as the *afikoman,* the concluding bite of the repast. In families where each household head has made Kiddush it is also customary to have each prepare his own *afikoman* as well.

The Four Questions.   After the holiday Kiddush, which may be said either sitting or standing, the ritual washing, partaking of the *karpas,* and the preparation of the *afikoman,* the story of the Exodus from Egypt is recounted as the answer to "The Four Questions," often referred to as "Ma Nishtanah" from the opening Hebrew words "Why is this night different from all other nights?"

The questions are usually asked by the youngest child at the table. It is a center-stage moment and most children take it very seriously. They will want to be letter perfect in text and chant, and most youngsters do not mind rehearsing it thoroughly. If there are several young children present, the honor may be divided in several ways: each child may ask one of the questions in turn, or one child may ask the questions in Hebrew, another in English, and so on.

The Pesah ritual is a specifically child-oriented means of cultural transmission. The songs and games that have been interpolated into the ritual to retain the interest of children and impress the answer into their memory also make it fun for the whole family.

Hiding the Afikoman.   One playful custom is that of having the leader hide the *afikoman* at the beginning of the Seder. During the evening the children attempt to find and "steal" it, while the adults pretend not to notice. Since the service cannot be concluded without partaking of a bite of the *afikoman,* the leader must ransom this precious piece of matzo by offering a reward for it.

Opening the Door for Elijah.   In legend the prophet Elijah, disguised as a beggar, is supposed to visit every home on Passover. If he is received hospitably everywhere, the tale goes, the world is ready for the Messiah.

After the third cup of wine is drunk during the Grace, the cup of Elijah is filled to the brim and the children are sent to open the door for him. All rise to greet Elijah and sing a welcoming hymn. Occurring rather late at night, this is an occasion of innocent fun and mystification for youngsters, as the adults go about convincing them that the level of wine in Elijah's cup has really gone down while they were at the door to admit the invisible prophet.

WHAT LANGUAGE FOR THE HAGGADAH?

It has always been the custom to translate parts of the Haggadah into the vernacular, indeed, to use language so uncomplicated that even the youngest and most unsophisticated ("he who has not the capacity to inquire") may understand the narrative. In some modern households portions of the text that Zeyde (Grandpa) once used to explain in Yiddish are now read in English and all take turns reading. The selections should be chosen by the leader in advance, and, where possible, the reader should prepare the paragraph.

Some Conservative and Reform rabbis have added special passages to the Haggadah to reinforce solidarity with Russian Jewry and remembrance of the six million martyrs of the Holocaust. These make particularly appropriate English readings.

Even children too young to read the Haggadah text may be given a chance to tell part of the story in their own words. Older boys and girls may want to discuss their ideas of the meaning of freedom, slavery, and justice.

THE "BEGINNER'S" SEDER

A young family, facing the responsibility of preparing a Seder on their own if they have moved to a community distant from parents or relatives, should not hesitate to begin the tradition of having a Seder in this way, adding to the Hebrew ritual from year to year as their ability develops. The Haggadah text is complicated and the complete rendition in Hebrew can well take years to master. If they send their children to Hebrew school, the youngsters will add to the ritual each year with songs they have learned there.

THE TRADITION OF HOSPITALITY

Pesah is *the* family holiday of Judaism, the time when the clan gathers. It is traditional to invite those who are far from home, or have no family Seder to go to, particularly the poor, in fulfillment of the opening verse, "Let all who are hungry come and eat."

Not all families find it possible to have guests at their Seder table. Instead, many contribute to special Passover funds, *Maot Hittim*, through their synagogues. The money gathered is used directly for the poor of the community, to provide the makings of a Passover Seder. With the sharp rise in the cost of food, it has become a most necessary and worthwhile act of charity.

OBLIGATIONS OF A GUEST AT THE SEDER

When you are a guest, be careful to be prompt, since the ritual before dinner is long and all must necessarily wait for your arrival to begin.

It is obligatory to eat some matzo and partake of each of the four cups of wine at the Seder. You should also do your best to participate in the reading and singing. Questions and discussion are welcome; one is supposed to discuss the "wonders and signs" of the Exodus all through the night, as did the sages of old.

Dress as for an elegant informal dinner. A skullcap is worn during the entire service and the meal in traditional households. Smoking is permissible, as is carrying of holiday necessities, except when the holiday falls on the Sabbath.

If you wish to bring a gift or a delicacy for the Seder table, be careful, in selecting food items or liquors, to purchase only those that have the necessary *kashrut* labels. Standards of observance differ in various households, and it is best to observe tradition to avoid embarrassment.

Chocolates and other sweets, wines, cordials, preserves, and candied fruits, all popular choices, must all carry a rabbinical seal, not merely the words "kosher for Passover." Grain alcohols are not kosher. Properly certified plum brandy (*slivovitz*) and cherry liqueur (*wishniak*) are widely used instead.

For a nonfood gift you might select books and records on Passover subjects, an ornamental Haggadah, or one of the many beautiful ceremonial serving pieces to be found in Hebrew bookstores, sisterhood gift shops, or large specialty stores. A matzo cover, hand-embroidered, is a very personal gift that will be treasured for years.

PASSOVER CARDS

The practice of sending greeting cards for Passover is copied from Christian customs and is neither traditional nor necessary, although spreading. One should respond to such cards with a phoned or written thank you, but might avoid sending a card in return to stop the escalation of the exchange.

COMMUNITY SEDERS

Although people make great efforts to be with their families on this holiday, the sharp increase in the number of people, both young and old, who live alone has given rise to community Seders of many descriptions. They run the gamut from cooperatively organized student affairs to catered dinners in hotels and restaurants. Some synagogues sponsor group Seders on the second night or on both.

In general, it is probably better to spend the evening participating in some kind of Seder ritual than to be alone. A little energy and imagination put into organizing a Seder among a group of people who would otherwise be alone can return great dividends of fulfillment, whatever the level of ceremonial observance. In one Miami hospital, closed-circuit television is used to bring the Haggadah reading to the bed-ridden, so that they, too, may participate, with reported gains in morale.

PESAH DELICACIES

Traditional foods for Pesah include matzo-ball soup, *matzo brai* (fried matzo and egg), unleavened sponge, honey, and nut cakes, matzo meal pancakes, gefilte fish, and beet borscht. Strawberries and asparagus, both just coming into season, are also served as special treats.

YIZKOR

Memorial prayers are offered on the eighth day of Pesah in Orthodox and Conservative synagogues. Reform temple schedules should be checked individually.

18. Shavuot

. . . the season of the gift of our Torah.

—HOLIDAY KIDDUSH

Shavuot is a week-long festival called the Feast of Weeks, because it comes seven weeks after Pesah. It is also known as Hag Habikkurim, the Feast of First Fruits, because in ancient times it was a pilgrim festival, when one brought an offering of first fruits and new grain to the Temple, including a measure (*omer*) of new barley. It is sometimes called Pentecost (the fiftieth day).

This agricultural festival is also regarded as the birthday of Judaism, for it is the traditional date on which Moses descended from Mount Sinai bearing the Ten Commandments. Thus Shavuot commemorates the institution of an ethical and moral code fundamental to all mankind.

SPECIAL ASPECTS OF THE SHAVUOT SERVICE

The special reading for Shavuot is the Book of Ruth. The episodes take place during the spring grain harvest in ancient Israel. The emphasis on Ruth's acceptance of Judaism and the Torah makes the inclusion of women and girls in modern Conservative and Reform holiday services especially appropriate.

Many synagogues hold a group bat mitzvah for girls on this day. In some Reform congregations group confirmations of both boys and girls are held.

Since this is the traditional date for beginning the study of Torah, many synagogues hold special consecration ceremonies for young children about to enter Hebrew school. In some synagogues, part or all of the service is conducted by the graduating Hebrew school students and includes a welcome and consecration for the new students as the graduating class departs.

SHAVUOT THEMES

It is customary to decorate the synagogue and the home with fresh greens, plants, and spring flowers. Milk foods, especially cheese blintzes and cheesecake are served. Candles are lit by the women at home before sundown on the eve of the holiday.

Among the Orthodox there is a tradition of staying up all night to study Torah amid singing and rejoicing.

It is a pleasant family practice to read the Book of Ruth together in English.

YIZKOR

Memorial prayers are said on the second day of the festival in Orthodox and Conservative synagogues, on the first in Reform.

19. *Sukkot*

For in booths [huts] did I make the children of Israel dwell when I brought them out of the land of Egypt.

—LEVITICUS 23:42

Sukkot, the Feast of Tabernacles, a festival that begins five days after Yom Kippur, commemorates the forty years of wandering in the desert wilderness after the Exodus from Egypt, when the people lived in temporary huts. It also celebrates the ingathering of the fall harvest and is a holiday of thanksgiving both for the miracle of survival during the hazardous journey to the Promised Land and for the continuing bounty of the earth. The first Pilgrim Thanksgiving was based on this biblical festival.

SYMBOLS OF THE HOLIDAY

The symbols of Sukkot lend it an exceptionally joyful character. The *sukkah*, lovingly decorated, is the center of the home observances, and one takes as many meals as possible there during the week.

In the synagogue the men carry the *lulav* (a palm frond) with its companions, the *etrog* (a citron) and the branches of willow and myrtle, in jubilant processions.

THE SUKKAH

Every tradition-oriented family hopes to build a *sukkah*—a temporary structure in the yard, on the patio, or wherever else a convenient open space can be found on the home grounds. Apartment dwellers sometimes club together and get permission from their landlord to erect a *sukkah* on the roof or in the courtyard which all may share.

Basically, a *sukkah* must have three free-standing walls, which may be made of any materials from plywood panels to canvas stretched over a pipe frame. The roof must be made of loosely laid natural materials: any plant that grew out of the earth and was cut off from it, which includes everything from tall feathery foxtail weeds gathered from open lots to pine boughs, bamboo poles, or lath strips. The "roof" (*skhakh*, in Hebrew) should be spread thickly enough to shade the interior by day, but allow the stars to show through here and there at night.

It is traditional to decorate the interior in rich and fanciful manner, with rugs and tapestries for floors and walls, fine tablecloths, pictures, and garlands of flowers, fruits, and paper decorations hanging from the roof.

Building a *sukkah* is a truly high-key family experience in living Judaism. Everyone from the father to the youngest child can be involved in the building, decorating, and furnishing. Lanterns, folded birds, and chains of brightly colored paper, strings of popcorn or cranberries, and appropriate holiday drawings are projects especially popular with youngsters. It is traditional to hang apples, pears, clusters of grapes, red peppers, small eggplants and squashes, sheaves of corn and other harvest fruits, and vegetables amid the boughs or reeds of the roof thatch. The paper decorations, saved from year to year, become a family tradition.

THE FOUR SPECIES

Each congregant is supposed to purchase his own "Four Species," as the set of *lulav, etrog,* willow and myrtle is called. These can be obtained through the *shammash* of the synagogue (or in New York, on the Lower East Side or in Williamsburg from one of the many shops that specialize in these holiday items).

The branches of myrtle and willow are placed in a plaited holder that slips over the palm frond and makes them one with it. They should come with a plastic bag in which to keep them fresh during the holiday.

The *etrog* is carried in a special box lined with flax to prevent damage to the vital *pittam* (blossom end). Should this fall off, the *etrog* is no longer usable. An *etrog* is selected primarily for its beauty, color, perfect shape, and fragrance.

Blessings, referred to as *bentshn Esrog* in Yiddish, are said over the *lulav* and *etrog* by both men and women, according to a ritual described in the holiday prayerbook.

A congregant who does not have his own *lulav* and *etrog* may use one that is usually circulated through the synagogue so that all may perform the *mitzvah* of *bentshn Esrog.*

In Jewish neighborhoods one may be approached on the street by Hasidim bearing an *etrog* and *lulav* and invited to say the benediction. It is gracious to accept this courtesy and go through the ceremony, although you may refuse if you have already done it at home or in the synagogue.

THE FESTIVAL PERIOD

There is an extended period of rejoicing, actually covering eight or nine days, with three distinct observances. The first two days (only one day for the Reform and in Israel) are marked by the *lulav* processions and by feasting in the *sukkah*. Full holiday abstention from work, school, and business is observed on the opening and closing days of the festival.

The seventh day is Hoshana Rabba, the great Hosanna, a day of solemn prayer for salvation, the last day of synagogue processions with the *lulav* and *etrog* and the last day for meals in the *sukkah*. The eighth day (Shemini Atzeret) is a separate Festival of Conclusion and includes special prayers for rain (Geshem). The ninth day (once simply the second day of Shemini Atzeret) has become virtually a separate holiday—Simhat Torah, Rejoicing of the Law. On this day the weekly Torah reading cycle reaches a formal conclusion. The last two chapters of Deuteronomy are read and then the annual cycle is started once again with the first two chapters of Genesis.

In Israel and among Reform groups the observance of Simhat Torah is included in the Shemini Atzeret services.

CANDLE LIGHTING

Candles are lit in the *sukkah* on the opening and closing nights of the holiday. They should be handled with great care to avoid fire. Short candles should be used, with the holders placed on a metal tray, and they should not be left unwatched.

Candles are also lit in the house on the eve of Simhat Torah in Orthodox and Conservative groups.

SUKKAH *HOSPITALITY*

Hospitality is very much in the spirit of the holiday. It is customary to invite those friends and neighbors who could not build one for themselves to recite the Kiddush in your *sukkah*.

Some families give a party for their children's friends in the *sukkah* and receive their adult friends at a holiday *kiddush* on the festival days or the Sabbath of the festival week.

Most synagogues build an elaborate *sukkah*, have the holiday kiddush said there, and host a Hebrew school *sukkah* party. In some congregations a box lunch in the *sukkah* for adults (or families) is a feature of *hol hamo'ed* (midweek of the festival), giving all who desire to participate an opportunity to eat in the *sukkah* at least once during the holiday week.

In some communities it is customary for families to send gifts to ornament the *sukkah*, or contributions toward the cost of the *kiddush* and the fruit decorations. Many people are needed to cut greens, decorate the interior, and help set up and serve the *sukkah* repasts. It is a pleasurable *mitzvah* to serve your community in this way.

The blessings to be said in the *sukkah* will be found in the festival prayerbook. A hat or yarmulke is worn during blessings and the repast, except among Reform Jews.

APPROPRIATE GIFTS FOR SUKKOT

Wines, liquors, cakes (especially honey pastries), chocolates, fruit baskets, and other delicacies are all appropriate gifts for a guest to bring to a *sukkah* party. If the host is Orthodox, care should be taken to select kosher products, especially wines and candies. A small serving dish or decorative object for the *sukkah* would also be suitable.

TRADITIONAL SUKKOT FOODS

It is customary to partake of apples dipped in honey, saying the appropriate blessings, after the holiday Kiddush and before the meal is served. Dishes made with honey, such as *tsimmes* (prunes and other fruit, carrots, and honey) and *tayglakh* (a honey pastry) are also served in many traditional homes, to symbolize the hope for a "sweet" year.

SIMHAT TORAH

Simhat Torah is a highly colorful synagogue day, for all the scrolls are taken from the Ark and carried in processions around the sanctuary at least seven times, or as many times more as will give all the congregants a chance to participate. There is much singing, dancing, and rejoicing over drinks and sweets.

Children join in the procession carrying holiday flags; the older ones may be allowed to carry the small Torah scrolls. Rejoicing with children is so central that one often sees fathers in traditional synagogues carrying their very young children about on their shoulders as they join the dancing round.

SIMHAT TORAH HONORS

The persons called up for the concluding portion of the scroll (Hatan Torah) and the opening portion (Hatan Bereshit) are especially honored. In many congregations it is customary for them to host a *kiddush* after the services. It is usual also to make a donation to the congregation as thanks for the distinction conferred.

VISITING OTHER SYNAGOGUES

In neighborhoods where there are many traditional synagogues, it is a happy custom to visit from one to the other during the evening and morning of Simhat Torah and take part in as many services as possible.

A nonobservant visitor should remember to wear a hat or yarmulke and avoid carrying anything.

YIZKOR

Memorial prayers are said on Shemini Atzeret in all congregations.

20. The High Holidays

It shall be a solemn rest unto you . . . a holy convocation . . . a memorial declared with a blast of horns.

—LEVITICUS 23:23–25

Known also as the Days of Awe (Yamin Nora'im) the High Holidays—Rosh Hashanah and Yom Kippur—are the most solemn and sacred days of the Jewish year, so universally observed by Jews that in New York City they have become official school holidays. In other areas, with much smaller Jewish communities, the closing of Jewish-owned businesses on these days has impressed their significance on the non-Jewish world.

DECORUM FOR THE "NON-PRACTICING" JEW

Self-respect, ethnic pride, and an appreciation of the freedom to be openly Jewish would all indicate that even the non-observant person, who perhaps never goes to synagogue, should accord some dignity to these days. Precisely because the civil calendar does not accord legal holiday status to these days, as it does to the Christian holy days (such as Christmas and Easter), a Jew, no matter what his religious convictions are, should not work on Rosh Hashanah or Yom Kippur, nor keep his place of business open.

Trading time off with co-workers of other faiths makes this possible even in emergency or vital occupations, such as medicine, the armed forces, the police and fire departments, and so on. Those who may hesitate to assert their right to "equal time" might reflect on the fact that the Christian world is well aware that these are holy days for Jews.

It is not hypocritical to demand respect for the traditions of one's people, if one accords them proper respect and value himself. It is demeaning to flaunt one's disregard for one's cultural and ethical heritage by working and otherwise ignoring and downgrading the day.

For the nonobservant, respect for the day not only means not working, but also keeping children home from school, dressing appropriately when faring forth within the Jewish community, and refraining from such public desecration of the day as washing the car or mowing the lawn during this time off from work.

Those who wish to use the time for recreation should do so discreetly. It is unseemly to parade about with golf or tennis gear on these days; even the Jewish resorts which feature special holiday "packages" close the sports facilities while services are in progress.

Activities suitable to these days, apart from synagogue attendance, are visiting friends and family in the afternoon or evening, walking in parks and other places of natural beauty (but not dressed for hiking!), serious reading and meditation on the introspective themes of the day, and other quiet, reflective pursuits.

The evenings when the holidays end are occasions for much rejoicing, and are appropriate hours for going out for entertainment.

THE THEME OF THE HIGH HOLIDAYS

Because Rosh Hashanah (literally, "the head of the year") falls on the first of Tishri, by tradition the date of the Creation of the world, it has become the Jewish chronological New Year. In prayerbooks and in the Bible, it is referred to as Yom Hazikkaron, the Day of Remembrance (of Creation), Yom

Teruah, the Day of the Blowing of the Trumpet, and most important, as Yom Hadin, the Day of Judgment.

Yom Kippur, coming ten days later, is known as the Day of Atonement. These two holidays and the time between take on an introspective and awesome quality because of their underlying themes of judgment, contrition, and atonement. These are days for self-examination, new resolutions, earnest efforts at correcting one's faults, and at righting wrongs and settling quarrels between friends and relatives. The New Year motif lends a social, happy overtone to the underlying solemnity of this period.

OBSERVANCE

The holidays are observed with equal solemnity by all branches of Judaism, except that Reform and Conservative congregations permit driving to and from services if it is too far to walk.

Rosh Hashanah is observed for two days by all but the Reform group, who keep only one day. In Israel also, Rosh Hashanah is a two-day holiday.

Smoking and cooking for the holiday repast are permitted on Rosh Hashanah, but not on Yom Kippur.

It is customary not to schedule weddings or banquets during these ten solemn days.

Some people visit the graves of departed family members before Rosh Hashanah, during the month of Elul. (See Chapter 85, "Visiting the Cemetery.")

THE ETIQUETTE OF FORGIVENESS

During these ten days of introspection one is supposed to ask the forgiveness of any person one may have wronged or slighted during the year. It is a time for patching up family disputes, business or professional misunderstandings, and the like. Tradition, recognizing that there is wrong as well as right on both sides of any controversy, requires that the younger person ask the pardon of the older one. The tradition also recognizes how difficult it is to forgive, in requiring that one *must* forgive anyone who is sincerely contrite.

THE MAHZOR (HOLIDAY PRAYERBOOK)

On the High Holidays, many new readings and prayers are added to the usual Sabbath liturgy, so that a special prayerbook is used for Rosh Hashanah and Yom Kippur services, called the *Mahzor* in Hebrew. These are usually provided by the synagogue and nowadays all have parallel Hebrew and English texts.

If you plan to visit an old traditional synagogue or will be worshipping abroad, it is best to have your own *Mahzor* along. It is permissible to carry the *Mahzor* (and *tallit*) to and from synagogue on Rosh Hashanah, but on Yom Kippur it should be brought to synagogue on the eve of the holiday and left there for the next day's service, to be carried home after the concluding service the next day.

21. *Rosh Hashanah*

THE SHOFAR

The *shofar* is the traditional ram's-horn trumpet used since the days of Moses to announce the new moon, the Sabbath and holidays, to summon the people of Israel to solemn meetings, to battle, and to judgment.

Hearing the blowing of the *shofar* is a central obligation of the Rosh Hashanah worship. The service provides for 100 repetitions of the trumpet calls, placed in groups at the conclusion of the main sections of the liturgy.

It is customary to bring small children to synagogue toward the end of the service so that they may hear the *shofar*. The time is usually announced and one should check, so that youngsters will not become restless during long preliminaries.

The *shofar* blast is a stirring link to the historic beginnings of the Jewish people. Wherever services are broadcast for the homebound the *shofar* ceremony is included, and it is a common decorative symbol on holiday cards.

HOLIDAY SYMBOLS

On Rosh Hashanah eve candles are lit by the women at home, with special holiday benedictions to be found in the prayerbook.

The holiday table is set with two loaves of hallah, wine, and, in addition, apples and honey. The hallah is baked in a special holiday shape: either round, suggesting God's crown, as a "braided ladder," symbolizing the ascent of prayers to heaven, or as two wings, suggesting men's similarity to the angels. Some top the round loaf with a birdlike shape, to symbolize an angel.

After the appropriate holiday Kiddush, Sheheheyanu, and the blessing over bread have been recited, a special blessing is said over the apple, expressing the wish for a sweet and fruitful year. A slice of the apple and the first bite of hallah are dipped in the honey. (The text can be found in the prayerbook.)

On the second night of Rosh Hashanah, it is customary to serve a new fruit of the season, such as a melon or persimmon, so that the Sheheheyanu benediction may be said this night as well.

All kinds of honey pastries, candied fruits, and other sweets are served as holiday refreshments.

JEWISH NEW YEAR GREETINGS

Verbal Greetings.   From the eve of Rosh Hashanah until the end of the second day one says *L'shanah tovah tikkatevu,* "May you be inscribed for a good year." The response is *Gam atem,* "The same to you." One may also use the English expression "Happy New Year." Other variants will be found in the section on traditional greetings in Chapter 3.

In the week or two before Rosh Hashanah one may also offer this greeting when meeting Jewish friends or colleagues whom one does not see often, and include the greeting in correspondence.

New Year Cards.   Greeting cards expressing many variations of the New Year wish are customarily sent to all one's relatives, Jewish friends, and colleagues. A text or design that includes the traditional *l'shanah tovah* is preferable. Reproducing a favorite photo or a child's drawing makes a most personal and interesting card. On special-order cards you may want to leave the date out of the text, so that you can use the cards from year to year.

This once-a-year correspondence can be changed from a mere mechanical stimulus-response routine by the addition of a personal touch. Even an imprinted card should be signed; better yet, a sentence or two of family news or a few cordial words of inquiry and regret at not meeting more often may be written on the flyleaf. A harmonizing colored ink may be used for signature and addressing if desired.

If you are not certain whether an acquaintance is married, the card should be addressed to him or her alone and sent to the office, not the home. (See Chapter 60 for other variations of addressing.)

Cards may be signed either with given names, such as "Helen and Paul

Weinstein," or, more formally, "Mr. and Mrs. Paul Weinstein." These are matters of individual taste, governed to a large extent by the degree of relationship with the persons to whom the card is sent. With close relatives, you do not need the family name at all, unless there are many cousins with the same first names.

A card may be signed for the entire family as "The Weinstein Family" or "Helen and Paul Weinstein and Family" or, enumerating all the family members, as "Helen, Paul, Jonathan, and Miriam Weinstein."

Card sending should not be allowed to escalate into an overwhelming clerical task. It is both pleasant and important to send greeting cards to close friends and relatives whom you do not see often or who live at a great distance, not so essential when you will encounter them at services, at work, or in the neighborhood, and be able to extend timely good wishes personally.

Cards from Non-Jewish Friends. Non-Jews may properly send greeting cards of the season to Jewish friends. The response obviously should not be a return holiday card. Instead, you thank the sender personally, by phone or on seeing him next, or may write a brief note. If the sender is a business acquaintance whom you do not really know well, no response is necessary at the time, although you might want to add the name to a list for Christmas or secular New Year greeting cards. (See Chapter 31.)

When to Send Cards. Cards should be sent out about two weeks before Rosh Hashanah, so that they arrive before the holiday and allow time for a response if the person has not already sent you a card. If you receive a card from a person who is not on the family mailing list, the name should be added for the next year.

Sometimes unexpected cards arrive after Rosh Hashanah. It is correct to use New Year's greeting cards to reply to them until the end of the festival season (Simhat Torah), although purists look for cards with the Hebrew legend *G'mar hatimah tovah,* "May you be sealed for a good year," the appropriate greeting for Yom Kippur and after.

You may also return the greeting personally with a phone call, or when you see the sender next.

SYNAGOGUE GREETINGS

At the conclusion of services it is customary to shake hands with seated neighbors and friends, offering the appropriate holiday greetings. Family members often kiss instead of shaking hands.

When the rabbi, cantor, and synagogue officials form a receiving line in the lobby, one offers them the holiday greeting and a handshake in passing through the line. One may offer a brief comment on the services.

VISITING

Visiting friends and relatives to exchange good wishes is a feature of the day. In synagogue, little children are brought to greet grandparents; older children seek out their parents and grandparents in the same way, when all live in the same community.

Afternoon at-homes of an informal nature are also popular; since all have dined handsomely at midday, no refreshments other than beverages, cake, and fruit are necessary.

TASHLIKH

Among the very pious it is customary on the afternoon of the first day (or, if it is a Sabbath, the second) to walk to a body of free-flowing water to perform the *tashlikh* ritual, a symbolic casting-off of one's sins. This custom persists among the less observant in the form of a dressed-up family walk in a park or along a pleasant boulevard in the late afternoon, before evening services begin.

APPROPRIATE GIFTS

A holiday guest might seek out a book, a hallah cloth, or other ceremonial object from Israel; the usual flowers, honeycake, fruits, sweets, or wines are also appropriate. Some avoid giving nuts, because the Hebrew letters of the word can also form an acrostic spelling "sin" (!).

22. *Yom Kippur*

Yom Kippur, the solemn Day of Atonement, is regarded as the Sabbath of Sabbaths, the most sacred day of the year, for on this day the heavenly judgment, first entered on Rosh Hashanah, is sealed and made final. It is also known as the "white fast," because, unlike the "black fast," Tishah b'Av, it is not a day of mourning but a day spent divorced from all earthly and physical concerns, concentrated instead on self-examination and prayer.

In keeping with this theme, the synagogue is usually decorated with white flowers and white curtains for the Ark. The cantor and rabbi wear white robes, the male congregants white yarmulkes, and the women, either all white when that is fashionable, or some white accessories.

YOM KIPPUR ABSTINENCE

Among the observant, the abstinence of Yom Kippur includes total fasting for all over the age of thirteen (except the sick or weak), abstaining from sexual relations, refraining from major ablutions (although washing while dressing for the day is permitted), not using leather shoes (out of compassion for animals), or cosmetics. All the usual Sabbath restrictions also apply.

These rules are followed with only minor modifications by all groups—Orthodox, Conservative, and Reform—except that the more liberal groups will condone driving to services if one must.

THE MEAL BEFORE THE FAST

A festive meal is served in the late afternoon, before the fast begins. Honey is served as part of the meal. Highly seasoned foods should not be served, to lessen the problem of thirst during the fast. Many serve a fish dish as a symbol of plenty in the coming year.

CANDLES

It is customary to light a *yahrzeit* candle as a memorial to the deceased members of the family, just before leaving for services. Holiday candles are also lit either at home or at the synagogue upon arrival there. It is safer not to leave ordinary candles burning unattended at home.

BLESSING THE CHILDREN

Just before leaving for synagogue on the eve of Yom Kippur, many families follow the custom of having the children gather together so that the father may bless them. The Sabbath and the Priestly Blessing are used, and also a special blessing for Yom Kippur. A mother raising her children alone may bless them in this way also.

KOL NIDRE

The ancient chant of Kol Nidre, intoned all over the world as the sun goes down on Yom Kippur eve, has an almost hypnotic fascination for anyone with even minimal Jewish identification. It embodies centuries of persecution, redemption, and renewal, and is one of the most dramatic moments in the services.

It is recited just before sundown. All the Torahs are taken from the Ark and ranged on the *bimah* in recognition of the solemnity of the thrice-repeated abrogation of all vows made under duress or emotional strain, all oaths unfulfilled because of some negligence or inability.

One should try to arrive well before sundown, an hour when one may still drive to services and carry *tallit*, prayerbook, and slippers or shoes to be left in the synagogue for the next day's use.

A NOTE TO VISITORS

Although practically all synagogues require membership and/or the purchase of tickets for reserved seats for the High Holidays, most will admit visitors to some area of the synagogue so that they may hear Kol Nidre or Yizkor.

A nonobservant visitor who has come to hear Kol Nidre should be aware that it is not proper to leave until the evening service is completed. Only in the few synagogues that still conduct a lengthy Kol Nidre appeal for charity may one leave as the hour grows late.

A pledge to give charity is an inherent part of the penitential ritual; it serves to validate one's prayers. One should be meticulous about this donation in synagogues where no extended appeal is made. The actual contribution is generally made by mail just before or directly after Yom Kippur.

Visitors who intend to drive home after the evening service should be sensitive to the Orthodox prohibition of riding and park their cars away from an Orthodox synagogue, so that they may drive off without offending the observant community.

alty and courage over anti-Semitism, of intelligence over sottishness and brutality. No battles, no martyrs, and a story that celebrates the triumph of a "mere woman," Esther, over the classic villain Haman and his foolish tool King Ahasuerus. The name is derived from the word *pur*—a lottery—the method by which Haman chose the date for his planned massacre of the Jews.

The classic story itself is the center of Purim observance, for tradition required that one hear the reading of the Megillah (scroll) in synagogue. The day is a minor holiday, and work, school, and other activities may continue as usual, although there are so many celebratory events in observant communities that it becomes a truly festive day.

***Purim*-shpil.** The Purim story, or Purim-*shpil*, is often acted out in Grand Guignol style in Hebrew school, or honored in masquerade parties for youngsters. One can see dozens of little Mordecais and Queen Esthers in the group, but only a dedicated clown wants to dress up as Haman or Vashti!

Reading the Megillah. Revelry, satire, and noisemaking characterize the reading of the Megillah. One attempts to "blot out" the name of Haman whenever it is read aloud. This is done with *groggers* (rattles or noisemakers similar to those used on New Year's Eve) or hearty stamping of the feet. The reading is often done in comical style as well.

Most synagogues take up a collection, usually "half a shekel" or fifty cents, reminiscent of the half-shekel tax of ancient Temple days. The money is given to charity.

Visitors should come prepared with change, and contribute graciously to this collection and to any merrymakers who approach them. Simple, direct charity is one of the keynotes of the holiday.

Holiday Foods. A Purim feast or *seudah* in the afternoon is customary. Many serve roast duckling, but the main symbol is the *hamantash*, a triangular pastry filled with prunes or poppyseeds. Kreplach, triangular meat-filled pastries, are also eaten. The triangular shape represents the hat said to have been worn by Haman; however, Sephardim call these *oreas de Haman*—Haman's ears.

This is the one holiday on which tradition allows indulgence in drink, enough to make it difficult to distinguish Mordecai from Haman when reading!

Shalakhmanot. The sending of gifts to friends and to the needy (*shalakhmanot*) is an ancient tradition of Purim, set forth in the Book of Esther.

Reform, Conservative, and Orthodox alike still observe it, but in varying ways.

Traditionally, you send a gift of at least two kinds of fruit, cookies, or sweets to at least one friend within your community, usually hand-delivered by a costumed youngster. The gift should be modest (no florist's baskets!) but should be prettily wrapped. Avoid breakable containers, since the gift will be carried by a child filled with the spirit of fun.

The messenger is rewarded either with a few coins or a return gift for his family, or (better!) both. You may also give the messenger his little gift and send your own child with the return gift for the family.

In this tradition, charity is also given to at least two needy individuals. Even the poor are expected to give to others.

The more people you give to, the better. In very large Orthodox communities some men don an appropriate costume and rollick from door to door soliciting alms. Passersby may also be approached.

Prepare for a day of visiting services and friends by having a pocketful of change. No "beggar" should be refused, and dispensing a coin or two to each will enable both sides to fulfill the *mitzvah* of Purim giving since all the money collected goes directly to the poor.

The Unexpected Gift. In some communities an attempt is being made to revive *shalakhmanot* and you may receive an unexpected gift. You may not refuse the gift, and must send something in return to the family sending the present, and to one other. With a little forethought, you can be prepared with some goodies in the pantry and small change in hand. The custom leads to a good deal of neighborly fun for the children, with a benevolent overtone much different from the objectionable spirit of Halloween "trick or treat."

The Less Traditional Purim. In less traditional communities the Purim ritual is much more sedate, the Megillah reading more decorous, and the charity dispensed more impersonally. There is often a costume party for children. The date is a popular one for a synagogue dance, masquerade, or other festivity.

HANUKKAH

. . . a great miracle happened here.
—NEW ISRAELI THEME FOR HANUKKAH

Hanukkah, the Festival of Lights, commemorates the historic victory of the Maccabees over the Syrian-Greek tyrant Antiochus more than 2140 years ago. The Hebrew name of the holiday is derived from the word for dedication, a remembrance of the cleansing and rededication of the ancient Temple to Jewish worship after it had been defiled by the Syrians.

This joyous holiday, replete with festive lights, feasting, and merrymaking, goes on for eight days. It is, however, a minor holiday and school and business activities may be carried on as usual. It is observed by Reform, Conservative, and Orthodox.

Hanukkah has universal significance as the triumph of religious freedom, of idealism over corruption.

Symbols of the Holiday. A special menorah (candelabrum), called the *hanukiah,* is lit each of the eight nights of the holiday. It has nine candle-holders, one for each night and one for the *shammash* or servant candle, which is used to kindle the others. The menorah may be made of any suitable material: glass, ceramic, or metal. A well-designed menorah can be a decorative object in the home all year; many old silver and brass ones are antiques of considerable value. Some old menorahs are oil-burning.

Some households use electric menorahs. These are not permitted by some traditional groups unless a candle or oil-lamp menorah is also lit. Others object to the electric menorahs on purely symbolic grounds, because they so much resemble Christmas lights.

The text for the festival is the expression *nes gadol haya sham,* "a great miracle happened there." The initial letters of this sentence are the four characters engraved on the four sides of the Hanukkah *dreydel,* the spinning top used for the traditional holiday game.

How to Light the Menorah. Whether one uses brightly colored small candles (available from Hebrew bookstores, groceries, or the synagogue) or oil and wicks, the procedure for lighting the menorah is the same. In either menorah, one light is kindled the first night, two the second, and so on. Each night the *shammash* is lit as well, making a total of forty-four candles or wicks that will be needed.

The candles or wicks are placed in the menorah starting at the right side as you face it. First light the *shammash,* then use it to kindle the newly added light first, then the others from left to right. When all are lit, the appropriate blessings and hymns are chanted. The whole family should be present if possible. A yarmulke (or scarf for women) is worn during the ceremony.

The menorah should be placed at a street-facing window, so that passersby may see and enjoy the light. The *mitzvah* is to gaze upon the light and be reminded of the miracles of Hanukkah.

A metal tray or a sheet of aluminum foil may be used to catch drips and avoid accidents.

The candles are lit after dark, except on Friday evening, when they are lit just before sundown, before the Sabbath candles.

Who May Light Candles.　Although the duty is the father's, it is especially festive to let each child who is old enough light his or her own menorah alongside the father's. The additional *hanukiahs* might well be those made by the children as crafts projects.

A woman may light the candles for her family. She, too, may have her own menorah if the individual lighting ritual is followed. There is an old tradition that the women of the household rest from their work while the Hanukkah candles are burning, in honor of Yehudit, the heroic daughter of the High Priest Johanon.

Hanukkah Gifts.　It is customary to give children small gifts, either on each night of the holiday or on the eighth night. By tradition this is usually "Hanukkah *gelt*"—money in the form of shiny new coins. Some use chocolate coins wrapped in gold foil stamped with symbols found on Israeli coins. One may also use a plastic *dreydel* filled with candies and some chocolate coins. These are especially appropriate as party favors.

Children should be encouraged to make small gifts to give each other and their parents, but sensitive parents will make an effort to avoid parallels with Christmas and an orgy of present exchanging. Although the holiday often falls around the twenty-fifth of December, Hanukkah is *not* the "Jewish Christmas."

Hanukkah Parties.　Many parties are given at this time, for family and friends and especially for children. A traditional food is the pancake, especially the East European potato latke. The fun includes playing *dreydel* or other games such as cards, checkers, chess, or dominoes.

Decorations, invitations, and favors for a children's party are easily and most charmingly made by the youngsters, who also enjoy acting out the story of the Maccabees. A dress-up box helps in the impromptu fun.

Appropriate Party Gifts.　Since there are no restrictions on riding and handling money or carrying, Hanukkah has become a popular time for hospitality among the observant. A guest may bring any of the usual "hostess" or "dinner" gifts, but an item of Jewish interest is particularly appropriate. In this category one may choose pictures, ceremonial objects, books, or records, for example.

Other Observances.　As part of the general rejoicing the home should be decorated for the season. Children may make many of the symbols—menorahs, *dreydels*, the *nes gadol* letters, and the like—out of construction paper, clay, or other craft materials. Many posters and banners are also available through Hebrew bookstores or sisterhood gift shops.

In its recollection of the victory of another small band of Jewish warriors, Hanukkah has become an especially meaningful holiday in Israel. Expressing this historic connection, the traditional phrase has been changed to *nes gadol haya po,* "A great miracle happened *here.*"

Hanukkah Cards. Although it is possible to buy greeting cards for Hanukkah, the custom of sending them far and wide is a mimicking of Christmas customs and has no real basis in Jewish tradition. It is a pleasant idea to send holiday greetings to close friends or family members whom you do not see often, but you should beware of letting this friendly gesture escalate into a meaningless, tiresome exchange of commercial sentiment. If you receive a Hanukkah card from a Jewish acquaintance, an informal thank you in person or mention in correspondence is appropriate. You need not return an equivalent card.

In making up their Christmas lists, non-Jews sometimes send Hanukkah cards to their Jewish acquaintances. This gesture, while courteous, is not a conventional Jewish observance; it is, however, certainly more suitable than their sending a Christmas card to a Jewish friend. On receiving a Hanukkah card from a non-Jewish friend you may, if you wish to, send a Christmas card in return. In this situation each person would be giving fitting recognition to the holiday of the other.

The greeting cards made by children in Hebrew school activities are quite another matter. They should be sent out to doting relatives or hung up as holiday decorations in the home, to give the youngsters a meaningful part in a celebration that is uniquely theirs as Jews.

Store and Office Decoration. In some offices and stores, Hanukkah greetings are posted and decorations put up. As an addition to the holiday festivity that is an appreciation of cultural diversity, the action is praiseworthy, although some may decry the impulse to "assimilate" Hanukkah into Christmas and rob it of its historic distinction.

TISHAH B'AV

The "black fast" of Tishah b'Av, a day of mourning for the destruction of the Second Temple in 70 C.E. (and also of the First in 586 B.C.E.), is observed by Orthodox and Conservative, but not by Reform congregations, who have dropped the formal service since the establishment of the State of Israel.

In those communities where it is still observed, Tishah b'Av is the culmination of a period of mourning for the many disasters that have befallen the Jewish people. Although work and school go on as usual, it is a fast day.

The Three Weeks and the Nine Days. Three weeks before Tishah b'Av is the beginning of a subdued solemn time for the traditionally observant. The day is said to be the one on which the first breach was made in the walls of the Temple. During this period no weddings or public festivities are held. Among the very observant, no meat or wine is served during the last nine days of the three weeks, and no new clothing worn, except on the Sabbath. Some also refrain from shaving or cutting the hair.

No weddings are held on the day of Tishah b'Av itself, even in Reform circles where the fast is no longer kept.

Those who do not observe this historical mourning period should take more traditional practice into account when planning dates for large parties, such as engagement or anniversary celebrations, and also in the dinner menus served to more observant guests at the quieter gatherings they might attend during this time.

Observances. On Tishah b'Av the traditional synagogue is draped in black and lit only by candles. In some, the worshippers sit on low benches or on the floor, removing their shoes, as mourners do.

Dirges (*kinot*) and readings from Lamentations (*Eikhah*) are chanted to special holiday melodies. It is an occasion for a rather awe-inspiring synagogue visit.

The visitor should wear a hat and come prepared for the low seating. For an evening visit it is a good idea to slip a small flashlight into one's pocket or handbag. Some congregations use flashlights instead of candles to read by, and invariably there are never enough to go around. Also, stairs, hallways, and so on will be dark.

During the morning services the *tallit* and *tefillin* are not worn.

Some children's camps hold very impressive services and pageants on this day, which generally falls in early August.

LAG B'OMER

Lag b'Omer is a numerical acronym derived from the letters forming the date, the thirty-third day of the Omer period between Pesah and Shavuot. It commemorates the cessation of a dreadful plague that ravaged Palestine, and in particular the students of the famed Rabbi Akiva, during the Roman siege in the second century C.E.

Sefirah. The seven weeks of the Omer period are referred to as *sefirah* (counted) days. In memory of the plague in which tens of thousands of people died, the days have come to be regarded as a time of semimourning, during which no weddings or public festivities are permitted by Orthodox and Conservative groups. On Lag b'Omer, however, since it marks a happy event, there are no restrictions and all kinds of rejoicing are permitted.

Lag b'Omer Picnics. It has become customary to hold a picnic or campfire for youngsters on this day, usually sponsored by the Hebrew school, although it could be a family outing. It is a pleasant day for a children's party. Since it generally falls early in the spring, it is prudent to have alternate plans in mind in case of rain.

One tradition of the day is to engage in archery in the park or out in the country to commemorate the heroic students of Simeon bar Yochai, a great teacher. The outings and field days of Lag b'Omer are unique in the honor they accord to scholars and teachers.

YOM HA'ATZMA'UT: ISRAEL INDEPENDENCE DAY

The Fifth of Iyyar is celebrated in Israel with great revelry and patriotic display such as military parades, floats, children's parades, and rallies. A still-emerging holiday, its keynote is rejoicing. Some efforts are being made to develop a *haggadah* (legend) for a kind of Seder honoring the miracle of the new state and the preservation of the Jewish people. It is a good occasion for fundraising parties and public celebrations.

YOM HASHO'AH: HOLOCAUST DAY

Yom Hasho'ah (the twenty-seventh of Nisan) commemorates the martyrs of the Holocaust. It is generally observed by special services in synagogues and will ultimately develop a ritual and symbols of its own, as teaching and understanding of the Holocaust continue.

THE SABBATH

Remember the Sabbath day, to keep it holy.

—THE FIFTH COMMANDMENT, EXODUS 20:8

24. *The Sabbath as a Concept*

The concept of a Sabbath, a regularly recurring, universal day of rest, is counted one of Israel's most precious gifts to the world. Lovingly described as a "queen" or "bride" in hymns of welcome, the Sabbath eve ushers in a day set aside from mundane cares and occupations, free from the domination of worldly masters, a memorial to the Creation and the Exodus from Egypt.

The civilizing influence of a day of rest extended to all—slaves, servants, animals, and strangers, as well as the Israelites—cannot be overestimated. The ancient Greeks, for all their philosophy, lived on the labor of slaves and scoffed at the Jews as lazy and barbaric because of their insistence on not working one day out of seven. Since that era, attitudes have reversed so completely that it is the person who takes no time off who is regarded as somewhat unbalanced, a "workaholic."

A DAY OF REST

Before the advent of the five-day week, keeping the Sabbath presented a difficult employment problem to the Orthodox, especially since Sunday, the Christian Sabbath, was a legal day of rest. Now that Saturday is also a free day for most, it has become a secularized "day off," during which many who are not observant shop, indulge in sports, or take their children or themselves to all kinds of lessons and service appointments, regardless of religious obligations.

Orthodox, Conservative, and Reform alike ascribe paramount importance to the Sabbath, ranking the day ahead of all the holidays but Yom Kippur, which is regarded as the "Sabbath of Sabbaths." In all groups, the Sabbath is observed as a day of rest, worship, and family observance. One is expected to abstain from all work or school activities, attend synagogue services, and enjoy the home rituals of the Sabbath. Both the intellectual and the physical delights of the day should be savored to the utmost: study, sleep, rest, fine food, drink, and clothes, and love and companionship.

It is only in the degree to which they restrict "work" activities that the Reform, Orthodox, and Conservative positions differ.

"WORK"

What constitutes "work"? This question has generated rabbinical discussion through the ages to this day, as life continues to change technologically. Electricity, automobiles, elevators, radio, and television are some of the innovations that the Orthodox are concerned with today.

The Mishneh Torah sets forth thirty-nine categories of "forbidden tasks," all of which are avoided by the Orthodox. Many other common activities are forbidden by rabbinic law. Basically they are all pursuits concerned with daily, mundane life (handling money, for example), or activities that result in a physical change in the environment (such as gardening).

Some of the workaday activities proscribed by the Orthodox include cooking and baking, housework, kindling or extinguishing a fire (which includes using the automobile, all electrical appliances and lights, the telephone, and the doorbell), cutting or tearing, writing, carrying, sewing and craftwork, buying or selling, playing a musical instrument, or handling any item whose actual use is forbidden on the Sabbath.

Orthodox services are held at sundown on Friday evening and during the morning hour on Saturday.

Reform Practice. The Reform practice modifies the Sabbath restrictions to an absolute prohibition only of work at one's job or profession, and school attendance. Positive activities related to the Sabbath are encouraged, such as study of the Bible portion and other Jewish writings, and family activities, such as Sabbath meals and attendance at services together. Activities discouraged are those which are not consonant with the spirit of the Sabbath as a day of rest from worldly concerns. One may drive to services, use electricity, and carry Sabbath necessities.

The traditional home rituals—candle lighting, Kiddush, and blessing of the children—are observed without changes. Services are generally held after dinner, at about 8:00 P.M., on Friday, instead of at sundown. Some temples have Saturday morning services only when there is a bar/bat mitzvah.

Conservative Practice. Conservative practice follows a middle course between these two. The time of Friday evening services may alternate between sundown and after dinner, but Saturday services are held regularly during the morning hours.

The home rituals are followed without change. As in Reform groups, one may drive to services, use electricity, and carry objects needed for the Sabbath. However, some of the congregants may lean toward Orthodoxy in observance; the degree of liberalism practiced by others may vary widely.

25. *Guidelines to Sabbath Observance*

For the traditionally observant, there are, in a sense, no Sabbath problems. They follow the rules carefully and do not accept invitations that would cause them to violate tradition.

For those whose personal practice is free of most restrictions, or who do not observe the Sabbath, there are often social occasions when they are not certain what is permitted and what is not. The non-Jewish guest also faces questions in this area. A Sabbath visitor who is not Orthodox should follow a few simple guidelines when in doubt.

Between sunset on Friday evening and sundown on Saturday, *do not* drive up to the door, carry anything while outdoors, smoke, or use the telephone. Do not ring the doorbell, unless, as in an apartment house, there is no other way to get in. Otherwise, knock at the door, instead of ringing the bell and wait to be admitted, even if the door has been left unlocked for the Sabbath (more and more rare).

On the positive side, come prepared with a yarmulke, hat, or scarf for a head covering, greet people with the traditional expressions—"*Shabbat shalom*" (Hebrew) or "*Gut Shabbos*" (Yiddish)—and above all, eat, drink, and enjoy! You are supposed to make an affirmative contribution to the good cheer of the day.

When you are a house guest, ask permission before turning lights on and off. By interfering with the setting of an automatic timer or a nightlight, you may inadvertently cause an embarrassing situation, since an Orthodox host may not ask the visitor to turn the lights on once more.

26. Home Ceremonies

The Sabbath is ceremoniously ushered in and out with joyous home rituals, many of which devolve upon women. These observances are the same in all branches of Judaism.

CANDLE LIGHTING

Candles are lit in the home by the women, with the appropriate benedictions, about twenty to thirty minutes before sundown on Friday evening. At least two candles are lit, although some add one more for each member of the family.

Plain white candles, the kind usually sold in boxes labeled "Sabbath candles," are used. The tapers used for dinner parties are not practical because they are designed to burn for a long time.

Once the candles are lit, the candlestick may not be moved, and the candles must be allowed to burn to the end. Placing a few drops of water in the candlestick cups before inserting the candles assures that the flame will go out when the wax melts down to the water level, instead of guttering in the accumulated melted wax. Bobeches or aluminum foil may be used to catch any drip. Some also place the candlesticks on a metal tray for added safety.

The table should be set and all meal preparations completed before candle lighting. The candlesticks should be set on the table, or, if this is not practical, nearby, where their light can be seen and enjoyed through the meal.

Young girls may light their own candles together with their mothers to learn the ritual and have an active part in the celebratory aspects of the Sabbath, although usually it is the female head of the house who lights them herself. (It is customary for a woman to cover her head with a lace scarf or white kerchief while lighting the candles and saying the benediction.)

Lighting the candles ushers in the Sabbath for the household. The greeting after candle lighting is *"Shabbat shalom"* or *"Gut Shabbos."*

A weekend guest may be invited to light her own candles or she may simply say the benediction over the candles lit by the hostess.

MEALS ON THE SABBATH

Tradition requires that three festive Sabbath meals be eaten—dinner on Friday evening and on Saturday at midday after services, and a lighter supper just before sundown. In this hurried, socially fragmented age, these repasts provide a special time for the family to be together.

It was customary in European villages to save the finest produce of the week for the Sabbath meals. With the endless variety available in modern markets, many families make an effort to reserve certain seasonal delicacies, such as asparagus, melons, or strawberries, for these meals, and to serve certain family specialties only on the Sabbath.

The traditional menu should include wine, two unsliced loaves of hallah, a meat or fish dish, and the best of fruits and vegetables. A sweet, preferably sponge or honeycake, is also usual.

The customary Sabbath main courses are those that can be prepared ahead on Friday and kept warm or easily reheated to serve the next day. There are many different community traditions, and new ones are being created as lifestyles change. A guideline for considering new entrees would be the simple rule that no cooked dish may be prepared from scratch during the Sabbath; this would rule out all broiled, grilled, and fried foods.

The table should be set with the best china, silver, and glassware on a fine white tablecloth. Plastic placemats could be used at children's places to protect the cloth from spills. (See Table Setting in Chapter 6.)

GUESTS

It is an agreeable and ancient tradition to have guests at the Sabbath table, especially those who would otherwise be alone, or who are new or temporary residents. In many college communities, tradition-oriented families try to provide a homelike experience for Jewish college students by inviting them to a Sabbath meal.

OBLIGATIONS OF THE SABBATH GUEST

The nonobservant or non-Jewish guest visiting an observant household should remember that the rules of the Sabbath apply to the late-afternoon period.

One should express thanks for the hospitality with a post-Sabbath phone call or note. If the occasion seems to call for a gift (a birthday or anniversary, for example), it should be sent to the home before the Sabbath.

In Conservative and Reform households, although the rules may not be so strictly observed, a guest should follow the more traditional customs, avoiding any activity that is clearly workaday in nature.

THE RETURN FROM SYNAGOGUE

A pleasant ritual is followed in some homes, where the family members returning from sundown services at the synagogue on Friday evening gather about the table to sing the Sabbath hymn, *"Shalom Aleykhem,"* welcoming the Sabbath angels to the house.

The father (or the mother) may then bless the children with the traditional benedictions found in the Sabbath prayerbook. Some men also chant *"Eshet Hayil"*—"A Woman of Valor"—from Proverbs, in honor of their wives.

RITUALS OF THE FESTIVE MEALS

Kiddush. The Sabbath meal begins with the sanctification of the wine (*Kiddush*) by the male head of the house. Only kosher wine may be used for Kiddush. Most households have a special Kiddush cup, usually silver, used only on the Sabbath.

In some families it is the custom for all to stand; in others, all but the person saying Kiddush may sit. Either custom is correct.

The males all wear skullcaps for this benediction and the Hamotzi, in all branches of Judaism. Among the Orthodox, the skullcap is worn throughout the meal and the evening. A host should have extra skullcaps on hand to offer to guests who may not have their own. It is a tactful way to indicate the need to cover the head.

Hallah and Hamotzi. Two uncut loaves are used for the benediction over bread (Hamotzi) at each meal, as a reminder of the double Sabbath portion of manna received by the Israelites in the desert during the years of the Exodus.

The hallah may be any shape—braided, round, or oblong—are all traditional. If large loaves are impractical for a small family, one may buy small hallah-shaped rolls at Jewish bakeries, and use either one large and one small loaf, or two small ones for the hallah at each meal.

The hallahs are covered with a cloth or a white dinner napkin before the candles are lit. After reciting the Kiddush, the head of the family removes the covering, holds up the loaves, and recites the blessing over bread. The others respond, "Amen." He then cuts the bread, distributes slices around the table, and the meal may begin. Some sprinkle the hallah with salt before tasting it.

In some households the Hamotzi is said while all remain standing after the Kiddush. (See Chapter 11.)

Zemirot. Many beautiful hymns and table songs (*zemirot*) have been created to enhance the joy of the Sabbath. In traditional homes they are sung between courses and before the final Grace, which is also sung to a special Sabbath melody. This custom is followed by Conservative and Reform groups as well, many of whom have added songs in English.

Singing *zemirot* adds to the unhurried, leisurely atmosphere of the Sabbath meal. Children should be encouraged to teach the family the songs they have learned in Hebrew school, and to participate in *zemirot* and Grace so that they become proficient. It is a mark of refinement, as well as a religious obligation, to take part in these convivial observances when dining out in traditional company.

Grace After Meals. The full Sabbath Grace is chanted after each meal (except breakfast) when there are at least three males present, using a special Sabbath melody.

Seudah Shelishit (Shalosh Seudot). The third meal of the Sabbath, *seudah shelishit* (sometimes called *shalosh seudot*), is taken in the late afternoon. When the days are short it usually consists of fruits and other light refreshment. When the days grow longer, a more elaborate light supper is served. It is often the occasion for hospitality and informal visiting.

The *seudah shelishit* is sometimes served in the synagogue social rooms between the conclusion of an afternoon study session or lecture and the beginning of the evening services.

HAVDALAH

The Sabbath is ushered out with *Havdalah*, during which a special braided candle is lit, the scent of spices enjoyed, and a blessing said for the new week to come.

The ceremony begins when three stars can be seen in the sky.

It is customary to have children hold the candle and the spice box.

The greeting after Havdalah is *"Shavua tov"* or *"Gut vokh,"* "A good week."

As soon as Havdalah has been said, one may turn on lights, use the phone, and in general return to weekday pursuits.

MELAVEH MALKAH

Tradition regards the extension of the Sabbath mood as desirable, and so some families eat yet a fourth meal, after Havdalah, as a farewell to the

Sabbath Queen (Melaveh Malkah). This is also a suitable occasion for an informal "at-home," since guests living at some distance may ride, and instrumental music and other non-Sabbath pursuits are now allowed. The usual party refreshments are served.

At this hour one may carry gifts to the home. All other weekday activities are permitted, as the Sabbath is over.

27. Entertaining on the Sabbath

With its traditions of hospitality, rejoicing, and savoring the delights of leisure, good food, and wine, the Sabbath has become a favored time for family and communal entertaining. Any of the three Sabbath meals may be the occasion for a dinner party; the *kiddush, oneg Shabbat, seudah shelishit* or Melaveh Malkah, times for buffet receptions as elaborate or informal as one wishes.

THE FESTIVE KIDDUSH

Occasions when one may wish to tender a *kiddush* buffet at home or at the synagogue include bar/bat mitzvah, the *oyfruf* of a bridegroom, announcement of an engagement, birth of a child (particularly a girl), graduations, birthdays and anniversaries, and celebration of other important family events.

Congregations often host a communal *kiddush* on the Sabbaths of the festivals or in celebration of major synagogue events, such as the welcome of a visiting lecturer, honors to the rabbi or cantor, women's or children's Sabbaths, and the like.

Refreshments may range from simple cakes, nuts, sweets, and wine to a grand catered buffet luncheon. Traditional foods include herring and smoked fish, gefilte fish, potato and noodle kugel, chopped liver, strüdel, honey and sponge cakes, and every delicacy of the season.

Before planning the refreshments to be served in the synagogue, one should check the regulations carefully. Some congregations allow only food prepared by approved caterers; some, including Reform congregations, have definite rules as to the kinds of food that may be brought in. Others will permit only food that has been prepared in their kitchens, under supervision.

Paper and plastic dishes and cutlery, especially when serving a large group, are correct, in fact, desirable, as avoiding "work" for the hostess.

OTHER PARTIES

Seudah shelishit and Melaveh Malkah parties are generally held to celebrate a homecoming, welcome a distinguished guest, introduce a newly married couple whose wedding was held elsewhere, bid farewell to departing travelers, or extend holiday hospitality to a large group of friends and relatives.

Refreshments may be of the "high tea" kind—little sandwiches, cold salads, fruits, nuts, pastries, punch, wine, and other beverages. Hallah is generally not served, to eliminate the need for ritual washing or formal Grace. The menu is usually light and limited to foods that can be prepared ahead of time and served without heating.

WHEN A COMMITTEE SERVES

Many congregational festivities are prepared and served by volunteer committees, men as well as women. Such groups function very well when all of the duties are clearly spelled out and assigned. If it is a very large reception, each subcommittee (cooking, serving, and cleanup, for example) should have its own head, responsible to a chairperson for the entire event.

When the food is to be prepared by a committee, the various dishes on the menu may be assigned to individuals to prepare, or a uniform recipe, for noodle kugel, for instance, given to several cooks, each of whom makes one batch at home. When the synagogue kitchen is large enough, a group may work together there to prepare and store food on the spot.

In any case, the timetable should provide for all the preparations to be completed and all food delivered early on Friday; if there is adequate freezer and refrigerator space, Thursday afternoon is even better.

Table setting, serving, and cleanup are duties which could be assigned to teenagers. The teamwork makes the communal activity fun, and its obvious importance to the success of the day is a great builder of enthusiasm.

MENUS THAT AVOID DIETARY PROBLEMS

Not only are some holidays considered *milchig* (dairy), but *parve* (neutral) or dairy menus in general avoid problems of *kashrut* for both host and guests. Fish, a traditional Sabbath food, may appear in many guises from gefilte fish to salmon mousse. Cheeses, noodle and potato puddings made with *parve* shortenings, salads, and fruit dishes are all attractive on a nonmeat menu. Avoiding meats and shellfish still allows for a wide and sumptuous choice of foods. (Orthodox synagogues may require the use of kosher cheese.)

ONEG SHABBAT

The expression *oneg Shabbat* means the "delight of the Sabbath" and is a term applied to an informal gathering after services on Friday evening or on Saturday afternoon; it may be held either at home or in the synagogue. Light refreshments are served, Sabbath songs sung. Sometimes there are informal discussions as well.

Many congregations hold a regular *oneg Shabbat* afternoons, at which young people's activities are sponsored, such as folk dancing, singing, discussion groups, and appropriate games and outdoor pursuits.

The Friday evening *oneg* in some congregations has become the time to celebrate a bat mitzvah, with more elaborate refreshments appropriate to the occasion. (See Chapter 48.) Receptions honoring synagogue officials are often the occasion for a festive *oneg*.

AN ONEG BIRTHDAY PARTY

A Saturday afternoon might be a good time for an *oneg* birthday party, when the date is a Sabbath. In an Orthodox home the birthday candles would not be lit till after dark. One could use little flags or icing rosettes to decorate a cake instead of candles. Tiny paper pennants attached to toothpicks, each one bearing the name of a guest, might also be used instead of candles. Birthday presents for Orthodox youngsters should be sent ahead or after the Sabbath.

28. The Single-Parent Household

When children are being raised by a single parent, observance of the Sabbath and the holidays seems to present problems, especially when the family lives far away from grandparents or other married family members.

In Jewish law, any of the home ritual obligations of the absent parent can be performed by the other, regardless of sex. A man may light candles on the Sabbath, a woman recite Kiddush or Havdalah. A woman should not only prepare a Passover Seder for her children, but may also conduct it. She may preside over any of the holiday home rituals as well.

There is no legalistic reason why young children should be deprived of Jewish family observances because one of the parents no longer lives in the household. Continuing to keep the Sabbath and holidays during the children's early years will prepare them to assist the mother or father when they reach the age of thirteen, at which time a girl may light candles, a boy recite Kiddush or Havdalah. The family religious life will approximate more closely that of the two-parent home, and be enhanced by the warmth and richness of an enduring tradition.

HOSPITALITY: *HAKHNASAT OREHIM*

Great is hospitality . . .
—TALMUD, SABBATH 127A

Hospitality for the wayfarer is one of the most ancient and highly regarded of virtues in Judaic philosophy. In fact, the sin of Sodom was sometimes characterized as a lack of hospitality. Extending oneself for a guest was expected. By the Middle Ages, this hospitality had become a communal responsibility, so that a Jewish traveler could always be sure of finding a kosher meal and a place to sleep in any Jewish community. The laws of hospitality applied even to non-Jews.

In modern times, this concept has been extended to generous reception of the student, persons in the armed forces, and all travelers in need of assistance. Sabbath guests are especially welcome.

29. *Some Thoughts for Host and Guest*

Rabbinical writings from the earliest times are filled with precepts concerning the *mitzvah* of hospitality, principles which apply strikingly well to our day. For example, "A guest who unduly troubles his host is considered unworthy" (Derekh Eretz Zuta, 8).

In today's servantless households, being a worthy guest translates into making one's own bed, cleaning up the bathroom facilities after using them, helping with serving meals and clearing up afterward, avoiding trivial requests for special foods or comforts, following the household customs in ritual observances, and participating in a positive way in the activities of the day or event.

A guest has an obligation to add to the happy atmosphere of a social occasion and to express his sincere appreciation of the host's efforts on his behalf. When they can, guests should contribute to the meals or the entertainment by bringing or sending gifts of food or drink, paying for some of the meals eaten out, theater tickets, or other admission fees. Treating the children to some little pleasure they would especially enjoy is another gracious way to return hospitality. Thank-you notes after a visit are important.

The host shows true graciousness when he allows a guest to reciprocate. It is gauche to be the kind of host who never allows a guest to pick up a check or bring a gift, especially when this refusal is vociferous, or as one sometimes sees in restaurants, almost quarrelsome.

LIVING IN
A PLURALISTIC WORLD

Im ayn ani li, mi li?—If I am not for myself, who will be?
—PIRKE AVOT 1:14

30. *Jewish Holidays and the Civil Calendar*

Most people are so accustomed to the order of days in the civil calendar that they are unaware that, in effect, it legislates the *Christian* Sabbath—Sunday—and the *Christian* holidays—such as Easter Monday, Good Friday, and Christmas Day—as official days of rest. Adherents of other religions have had to petition for the right to keep differing holidays. This assertion of minority rights is a fundamental act of self-respect.

The High Holidays are recognized everywhere as the most solemn days of the year for Jews. In cities with large Jewish communities these dates are taken into account when planning school calendars, subscription series, and large-scale public meetings. In New York, for instance, the City Opera Company routinely notes the eve of each Jewish holiday in its calendar, and the city's schools and universities are closed on Rosh Hashanah and Yom Kippur. In smaller communities there is sometimes an information gap. One must assume that it is a combination of insensitivity and ignorance that causes the scheduling of college or voter registration or a school trip on a major Jewish holiday.

The intelligent self-aware Jewish community, imbued with contemporary ethnic pride, need no longer silently withdraw from such events or participate with a smothered sense of guilt or inferiority. A courteous visit or letter to the persons in charge of such events can serve to transmit the information they need to avoid such scheduling embarrassments, provided it is done well ahead of time.

Some publishers of calendars now include notations as to the holidays of other faiths. In consulting these, it is important to remember that Jewish holidays always begin on the eve of the day given as the date in commercial calendars.

Apart from religious considerations, feelings of Jewish dignity and pride should lead the Jewish community to insist on the recognition of their holidays as important dates to be taken into account in the town's business, civic, social, and educational life.

The rabbi usually works with the town boards to establish these principles. It then behooves the Jewish townspeople to follow through by keeping their children out of school and in planning their business and social calendars.

JEWISH HOLIDAYS
AND THE CONDUCT OF BUSINESS

From an ideal point of view, all places of business should be closed on the High Holidays at least; from a more observant stance, on the Sabbath and all other holidays as well. When it is not possible to do this, those Jewish employees who seek time off for religious observance should have it freely granted to them, if not as actual days off, then as time exchanged with employees of other faiths.

When a place of business is closed in observance of a holiday, the reason should be given, otherwise there is not much group solidarity to be gained from the practice. Many a small-city newspaper carries advertisements announcing the closing of stores and offices in observance of the day, while the stores themselves often post signs listing closing hours and days.

The telephone-answering machine may also be used advantageously during such closings. A recorded message can extend holiday greetings to the caller, and information as to when the office or store will again be open. The message might say: *"Hag same'ah!* [or *"L'shanah tovah!"*] Faber Distributors is closed in observance of Rosh Hashanah. We will reopen for business on Wednesday, September 24 at 9:00 A.M. Meanwhile you may leave a message with your name and phone number and we will return your call on Wednesday. Please wait for the signal before you begin to speak."

Many people use the answering machine at home in the same way, to avoid the interruption of holidays or Sabbaths with phone calls. The message states that they will not be answering the phone until a certain time because of holiday or Sabbath observance.

The Jewish professional or business person who chooses to ignore his holidays in planning his meetings and appointments should realize that the Christian world is usually well aware of them and regards this willingness to be compromised as one more instance of Jewish materialism. A helpful objective guideline is the question, "Would a Christian schedule this activity for Christmas Eve or Good Friday or Easter Sunday?"

Usually a simple explanation is sufficient to adjust the dates at the time the plans are made.

JEWISH HOLIDAYS AND THE PUBLIC SCHOOLS

Unlike Catholic Holy Days of Obligation, when Catholics are required to attend Mass, but may afterward carry on their usual daily activities, the major Jewish holidays require complete cessation of all workaday pursuits. This is true of Orthodox, Conservative, and Reform practice, although the Reform calendar differs slightly because they observe only one day of each two-day festival.

In most communities, the rabbi or the Jewish Community Council notifies the school board of all Jewish holidays, with the request that no important examinations or other vital school matters take place on those days. The student's absence is excused, but, of course, the day's work must be made up.

Problems sometimes arise on the senior high school and college level with Saturday scheduling of important examinations or classes. Sunday or weekday testing dates are available for College Entrance Board examinations and for some college orientation sessions. It is usually possible to substitute other days or other courses for the ones offered on Saturdays. The issue should always be raised well in advance, and a letter from the rabbi may sometimes be needed.

"THE JEWISH EASTER": HOLIDAY TERMS

Whether out of some friendly "ecumenical" impulse or out of genuine ignorance as to the difference between Christian and Jewish practice and belief, people sometimes refer to Pesah as the "Jewish Easter" and Hanukkah as the "Jewish Christmas." Neither reference is correct and both are offensive, implying that Jewish observance has no validity unless equated with a Christian practice.

Sensitivity can best be heightened by asking whether Christians would accept a reference to the Christian Passover. Such a comparison, while perhaps historically correct, is completely askew in terms of doctrine and the rituals that have evolved over the centuries.

Although they occur at approximately the same time in midwinter, Christmas and Hanukkah have nothing whatever to do with each other.

Even the custom of giving little gifts to children on Hanukkah has only a superficial resemblance to the spate of presents called forth by Christmas celebrations.

To those aware of Jewish history, both Christmas and Easter are alive with painful memories of persecution and cruelty. Keeping the holidays properly sorted out may help to preserve a peaceful neighborly relationship in our own time. Each faith has its own richness of tradition and to refer to their festivals in careless parallels belittles and distorts both. Mutual respect mandates the use of proper terms for the holidays without false comparisons and confusion.

31. Coping with Christmas

Christmas is so embedded in American life that one would have to live at a place far removed from TV, radio, and print media to escape its pervasive presence. The Jewish family can be almost overwhelmed by the surge of sentiment, opulence, and color that sweeps over the world at Christmastime. It heightens for some the feeling of being a minority people, which indeed we are, whether or not we participate in Yuletide activities. Somehow, each family must come to terms with the significance of Christmas and decide on the place it will have in their lives.

Christmas, in the religious sense, is obviously not a Jewish holiday, even though it honors the birth of one who was a Jew. Since one can hardly deny the existence of this glamorous holiday, one must decide on an individual basis whether to take the children to see the community or a neighbor's tree, whether to perpetuate the department store Santa Claus myth, and so forth.

Christmas trees, wreaths, glittering decorations, and Santa Claus seem inappropriate in the Jewish home; calling a tree or a wreath a "Hanukkah bush" gives it no Jewish validity, and to some ears is a desecration. Moreover, some Christian sects decry Christmas trees as pagan or idolatrous practices, while others have begun a campaign against the excessive commercializing of Christmas.

The season of bright good cheer can best be enjoyed as a festival of goodwill sponsored by another community, without adopting its symbols and entering into the religious aspects of the celebration.

CHRISTMAS MUSIC

There is a wealth of beautiful, albeit religious, music for Christmas, a good deal of it performed in churches. Jews who go to a church to hear a Christmas Mass or an oratorio should be aware that it is a religious service and should not make the mistake of proceeding to the altar rail to take communion. They should sit or stand when others do, but should not kneel in prayer or genuflect before the altar. (See Chapter 88, "Visiting Churches.")

GREETINGS AND CARDS

On a personal basis, it is proper and pleasant to extend holiday greetings to Christian friends, neighbors, and colleagues on the occasion of their major festival. The custom of sending cards in the name of a business firm or professional is also widespread, although certainly open to scrutiny. Is the clientele largely Christian? If not, why Christmas greetings?

Cards selected by a Jewish sender are never appropriate if they have a religious motif. There are many designs stressing the peace and goodwill themes of the holiday and expressing the wish for a happy new year that are more suitable. Such holiday greetings would not be offensive to the Jewish people on a business list and would express the cordiality of the sender without any religious involvement.

Jews should not send Christmas cards to each other, but many, caught up in the "goodwill, good cheer" spirit, do. The response to such an unexpected card may be a personal note or nonreligious greeting card, or a phone call, expressing cordial wishes for the new year, without reference to Christmas.

GIFTS AND TIPS

Since the Christmas season is traditionally a time for thanking people, it is also a time for giving tips or gifts to employees, service personnel, and other persons important to one's life.

The tipping rituals in apartment buildings and large offices are well established. These are usually handled individually in apartment houses and in the form of tip pools in offices. If the service people in your office have been unusually helpful or pleasant, it is a nice touch to give some small gift personally, such as a carton of cigarettes, a fruitcake, or a box of candy, as well as contributing to the tip pool.

Mail and newspaper carriers, babysitters, hairdressers, telephone-answering personnel, and other regular service employees should also be tipped or given a gift.

Presents for a child's teacher can be a problem. It is best to check local regulations. In many public school systems it is illegal to give gifts to teachers, yet the custom continues. An elaborate present is not called for, but if all the children in the class are bringing something to a class party, it is not really fair to make your child the exception by not sending some gracious little gift. If you feel genuinely grateful for a teacher's work with a child, write a cordial letter of thanks at the year's end. Teachers often appreciate these notes far more than the perfunctory bottle of toilet water or box of soap.

A Jewish teacher in a largely Christian school, knowing that students may bring gifts, should accept them graciously. Usually the teachers respond by providing refreshments for a class Christmas party. Teachers new to a school system should consult their colleagues. In some schools, especially on the high school level, teachers who wish to play down the Christmas idea do so by limiting the Christmas party and stressing the legal restrictions on gifts.

The whole issue of Christmas trees, Christmas decorations, and carol singing in classrooms and assemblies is deeply involved in questions of religion in the schools and the separation of church and state. In must be dealt with in each community on a local basis, and in these matters Jewish residents are entitled to and should voice their opinions.

HAPPY OCCASIONS

BIRTH

Be fruitful and multiply. . . .

—GENESIS 1:28

The birth of a child is not only a great personal joy to its family, but also the fulfillment of the positive commandment to increase and multiply. This is both a *berakhah* (blessing) and a *mitzvah* (duty).

32.   *It's a Boy!*

THE BRIT MILAH

Every male child becomes a member of the Jewish community at birth through the ceremony of circumcision—*brit milah* (in Yiddish, *bris*)—which is one of the signs of God's covenant with the Jewish people, and with him in particular.

The circumcision is performed on the eighth day following the birth of the child, even if it is a Sabbath or a holy day. If the child is born at twilight, or at night, a rabbi should be consulted about when the eighth day falls, as the days are counted from sundown.

If the health of the child does not permit, the *brit* may be postponed until he is strong enough, but all branches of Judaism forbid the circumcision of an infant younger than eight days, and demand that it be conducted as a religious rite that includes the prescribed prayers and benedictions.

Since most new mothers now have very short hospital stays, the *brit* will take place either at home or in the outpatient facility provided by some hospitals, where the baby may be brought on the eighth day. In most cases the *brit* at home is the best choice for the comfort of both baby and mother.

Jewish parents should resist any pressure of the hospital or pediatrician to have the circumcision "routinely" done during the three days (or less) that the mother is in the hospital, or conversely, to have it postponed to some later date. Some doctors may set this as much as three months later. As noted above, circumcision at any time other than the eighth day after birth is against all Jewish law; it also greatly increases the risk of the procedure for the infant.

Before the excitement and confusion of the delivery, parents should make it clear to the hospital and doctor that they intend to have a ritual *brit*, should the baby be a boy.

In traditional practice the circumcision is done by a *mohel*, a religious functionary especially trained to perform this rite. Reform groups permit the circumcision to be done by a physician, but require that a rabbi be present to recite the benedictions, unless the physician himself or some member of the family is able and willing to do so. A *minyan* (quorum of ten men) is not necessary, but is desirable.

The *brit* may be held at any time of the day, although the morning is generally preferred. On Fridays, it is usually held as early in the morning as possible, to avoid interfering with the Sabbath.

It is customary to serve a *seudah*, a feast in celebration of the event.

The Mohel. Most doctors will admit, when consulted, that a good *mohel*, with his specialized experience in performing this operation, is more expert at circumcision than a physician who may do only a few procedures a month. It is interesting to note that when England's Crown Prince Charles was circumcised, Queen Elizabeth, with all of Britain's most distinguished surgeons to choose from, selected Dr. Jacob Snowman, the official *mohel* of the London Jewish community, to perform the operation.

A good *mohel* is one who is clean, trained in hospital asepsis, and concerned for the parents, for whom this may be more trying than it is for the baby! He should be ready to visit the baby before the *brit* and check out his health, explain the aftercare needed to both mother and father, and see the child once more after the circumcision to check on the healing. He should also be available to answer questions that may come up during this time.

The fee for the circumcision should be discussed when the *mohel* is retained for the *brit*. If it is done in a hospital, inquire about any additional fees when the arrangements are made.

As with a physician, one follows the *mohel's* directions in the ritual and provides whatever assistance and equipment he requests.

A *mohel* may be found through the recommendations of your rabbi, a Jewish-oriented hospital, your relatives or friends, or through the classified pages of Anglo-Jewish weeklies, where many of them advertise. They will travel to suburban communities; the fee will then, of course, include the *mohel's* travel expenses.

Invitations. A *brit* is a family affair, but close friends of the parents and grandparents may also be invited. Invitations are usually telephoned because of the short time between the birth of the baby and the *brit*.

Among Orthodox people, attendance at a *brit* is a *mitzvah,* and an invitation to one should not be refused. Therefore, to avoid embarrassing those who might be unable to drop their daily affairs at short notice, one does not directly invite Orthodox guests by asking, "Will you come?. . ." One merely informs them that the *brit* for the new baby will be at a certain time and place.

The child is not referred to by his name until after the *brit.* (See "The *Brit* Ritual" below.)

Honors for Guests.   It is customary to give special honored roles in the ceremony to various members of the family or to close friends, so that they may share in the *mitzvah.*

Essential to the ceremony, and therefore the highest honor, is the role of the *sandak*—"the holder," or godfather—who holds the baby during the actual circumcision. This is usually the grandfather, but it may be a friend or another relative.

In addition, one may have a *kvatterin* (a Yiddish word for a kind of godmother), who takes the baby from the mother and gives it to the *kvatter* (also Yiddish, for a kind of godfather), who takes the baby to "Elijah's chair." Two additional honors may be given to men, one who will place the baby in the chair, and another who will then take him to the *sandak.* One may honor still another man (instead of the father) who will hold the baby during the blessing over the wine, and finally another woman who will bring the baby back to the mother.

At an Orthodox or Hasidic *brit* one sometimes sees the baby, on his pillow, being handed ceremoniously to each man present, and then, in the room for the women, to each woman present, so that all may have a part in the *mitzvah.*

THE BRIT *RITUAL*

***The* Brit Service.**   At a traditional *brit* the mother is not present, although when it is done at home she may be in the next room. In Reform practice, the mother may be present and may recite with her husband the blessings usually said by the father alone.

It is customary to light many candles in the room as a symbol of rejoicing, and to set aside a chair for the prophet Elijah, who is called the angel of the Covenant, and is regarded as the guardian of small children, particularly at circumcision.

The baby, carried on a pillow, is placed in the lap of the *sandak,* or on a table against which the knees of the *sandak* touch. The father stands by, hands the knife to the *mohel,* thus making him his agent, and the circumcision is performed by the *mohel,* or at a Reform *brit,* by a physician.

Blessings are recited by the rabbi or *mohel,* the father (and sometimes the mother, if she is present), and the guests.

The blessing over wine is said, and a few drops given to the baby. During this blessing the child's name is announced. Part of the text of this blessing reads:

> Our God and God of our fathers, preserve this child to his father and to his mother, and let his name be called in Israel [baby's name] son of [father's name]. Let the father rejoice in his offspring and let the mother be glad with her children. . . . May the little child, [baby's name], become great. As he has been entered into the covenant, so may he be introduced to the study of the Law [*l'Torah*], to the nuptial canopy [*l'huppah*], and to good deeds [*u'l'ma'asim tovim*].

The phrase *l'Torah, l'huppah, u'l'ma'asim tovim* is often incorporated in a congratulatory remark, to which one responds "Amen."

A special prayer is also offered for the well-being and perfect healing of the circumcised infant. The full text of the *brit milah* service may be found in any complete book of daily and Sabbath prayers.

After the ceremony the baby is brought back to the mother, if she has not been present, by another female relative. The wine cup is also brought to the mother so that she may drink from it and recite the blessings herself.

***The* Brit Repast.** The circumcision ceremony is followed by a joyful repast, with a menu similar to that for a brunch. The refreshments served should include hallah, so that the special Grace for the *brit* may be said, wine and liquors for *kiddush* and *lehayim,* and, traditionally, herrings and other breakfast delicacies. Cookies, honey and sponge cakes, egg *kichel,* nuts, and dried fruits are also traditional.

The responsibility for preparing this feast usually devolves upon one or both grandmothers. Some women bake and prepare frozen foods beforehand, in the last few weeks before the child is born. But the atmosphere of the meal should be informal. Paper dishes, plastic tableware, and glasses are sensible, and quite correct.

When the *brit* is performed in a hospital, refreshments may or may not be permitted, and the number of guests will be strictly limited. In general, it is better to have the ceremony at home.

A Brit in the Synagogue. Occasionally, some families have the baby circumcised in the synagogue, and hold the *brit* repast there as well. When the synagogue permits, the circumcision is performed at the reader's desk toward the end of the morning service. All present are invited to the festive *kiddush* and breakfast afterward. This practice not only assures a *minyan* for the ceremony, but also makes it possible to accommodate many more guests than at home.

Announcing the Baby's Name. A child is not referred to by its name until it is formally named at the *brit* (or in synagogue, for girls). In Orthodox circles one does not ask directly what the baby's name is until after the *brit* or naming; one may ask indirectly, "What name will you give him (or her)?" (See Chapter 34.)

His First Hat. The baby will need a hat for the ceremony. A little cotton or corduroy cap that ties under the chin is best. If the smallest size baby cap is too big, a tuck may be taken in the crown all around the hat. No attempt should be made to dress the baby in anything but a little shirt and a diaper. A decorative baby shawl or receiving blanket may be used as a wrap for the child.

SHALOM ZAKHOR/SHALOM N'KEYVAH

A pleasant old tradition worth more general observance is the custom of having a *shalom zakhor* (welcome to the male) on the Friday evening before the *brit*. This is a simple collation of chickpeas (traditional), fruits, sweets, and beverages, held in the home, for close friends and family. The guest of honor is the father, in celebration of his preparing to perform the important *mitzvah* of *brit milah*.

This gathering should be kept most informal and simple. Only family and very close friends should be invited, by telephone or in conversation.

In keeping with the modern attempt to enhance the status of women in Jewish ritual, such pre-*mitzvah* parties (*shalom n'keyvah*, or welcome to the female) are sometimes held prior to the formal naming of a girl in synagogue.

THE PIDYON HABEN *RITUAL*

The father of a first-born male child traditionally has not only a special joy, but also a special obligation—to perform the ritual of *pidyon haben*, redemption of the first-born.

According to tradition, when the first-born Jewish males were spared during the plague visited upon Egypt, God consecrated them to His service in the Temple, and it was necessary to redeem them from this service with a payment of five shekels of silver. The custom is still practiced among traditional Jews. Reform congregations have done away with it, and instead expect both parents to participate in the synagogue naming of all their children.

In a traditional *pidyon haben*, a celebratory feast is given on the thirty-first day after the child's birth (unless it is a Sabbath or a holiday). The father presents his child to a *kohen* (a member of the priestly clan) and offers the money for his redemption. Some carry the child in on a specially decorated cushion. The *kohen* accepts the money and returns the child to the father, pronouncing the Priestly Blessing and prayers for the child's well-being. The money may later be returned by the *kohen* or it may be used for *tsedakah* (charity). (The child of a *kohen* or a *levi*, either mother or father, is exempt from this ceremony.)

The full text of the ritual is in the daily and Sabbath prayerbook.

33. *It's a Girl!*

NAMING A GIRL

In traditional practice, the birth of a girl is noted by giving the father an *aliyah* (call) to the Torah on the Sabbath that falls closest to thirty days after the birth. The child's name is announced after the reading. Passages from the Song of Songs are recited, then the blessing for girls:

> May He who blessed our mothers Sarah, Rebecca, Rachel, and Leah, Miriam the prophetess, Abigail and Esther the queen, bless also this pleasing little girl and may her name be called [girl's name], daughter of [mother's name]. . . . May He give to her parents the joy of seeing her happily married, a radiant mother of children, rich in honor and joy to a ripe old age.

If all has gone well, mother and child can be present. The mother may then say the Hagomel (thanksgiving) service in thanks for deliverance from peril (also said after the birth of a boy). After services the congregation is generally invited to share the family's joy at a festive *kiddush*.

SIMHAT HABAT

Some families have a home party when the baby is a month old, a kind of parallel to the *pidyon haben*. It is often referred to as a *simhat habat*, rejoicing for a daughter.

More and more, however, a girl is named in the synagogue on the first Sabbath after her birth. The child, of course, is not present. The father is called to the Torah and the blessing is pronounced, but the main festivities usually take place at home, where the mother and baby are, and the celebration is very similar to a *brit* feast.

Among Sephardim, the naming of a baby girl is first done at home, before guests invited for a celebratory meal. Later, at a time when both parents and the child can attend synagogue, the baby may be brought to services to be blessed and to have her name publicly announced.

There have been some attempts in recent years to create meaningful *brit* or covenant ceremonies for girls. Parents interested in exploring this new ritual should give it thought before the child is born, so that the readings they use are not put together hastily. Havurot, youth movements, Hillel rabbis, and the magazines of modern progressive Jewish organizations are good sources of ideas.

34. *Birth Announcements*

While birth announcements may be as whimsical and creative as one wishes, the most tasteful choice is the conventional double visiting card edged in pink or blue, or a simple folder that spreads the happy news with the least cute treatment.

One may decide to write only a few brief notes to those close friends or relatives who cannot be reached by phone and let word of mouth spread the news further.

SAMPLE TEXTS

For a printed announcement, the vital statistics would be the names of the parents, name of the baby and its sex, date of birth, and if desired, the home address. An informal announcement might read:

16 Carter Road
Becket, Massachusetts

We joyfully announce the birth of our daughter, Abigail, on Friday, April eleventh, 1979.

Bob and Judy Newman

If there are older children, their names may be added to the text, which could read:

We joyfully announce the birth of Jonathan's sister, Abigail, on Friday, April eleventh, 1979.

Bob and Judy Newman

More formally, a card could read:

Bob and Judy Newman
take great pleasure in announcing
the birth of their daughter
Abigail
Friday, April eleventh, 1979
[Address]
[optional]

Birth announcements should not be sent indiscriminately to all your casual acquaintances. (It does seem to be asking for gifts.) You may, however, post a card in a large office or other place of employment, assuming that your colleagues would be genuinely interested in the good news.

Announcements may be sent out at any time after the child is formally named in synagogue or at the *brit*, generally within the first month after birth.

WHEN A WOMAN KEEPS HER MAIDEN NAME

If a woman has decided to use her maiden name after marriage, when the birth of a baby is announced in the newspapers the notice would read: "A son was born to Alice Brown and Joseph Siegal on [date] at Central Hospital [city]. The child's mother, who has retained her maiden name, is the daughter of [etc.]." An announcement card would carry the two parents' names instead of the usual "Mr. and Mrs.":

Alice Brown and Joseph Siegal
take great pleasure in announcing, [etc.]

35. Names for a Jewish Child

WHY IT IS IMPORTANT TO HAVE A HEBREW NAME

Every Jew, male or female, needs a Hebrew name. The name will be used whenever you are called up to the Torah, on your marriage contract (*ketubbah*), at a bar or bat mitzvah, on the occasion of a special blessing, and finally, on your tombstone and in memorial prayers.

Hebrew names go both forward and backward in the family line, since an individual's name is linked to the name of the father, or in Reform practice to the name of the father and mother. For some special blessings, in traditional practice, the name of the mother is used. Thus it is also important to know the Hebrew names of your parents and to carry your own Hebrew name forward in the full names of your children.

A boy's name is expressed as "Moshe ben [son of] Barukh." When the mother's name is used also, it would be "Moshe ben Barukh v'Rivka [and Rebecca]." A girl would be called "Sarah bat [daughter of] Barukh," or "Sarah bat Barukh v'Rivka."

NAMING CUSTOMS

Among Ashkenazim, it is customary to name children for a deceased relative whom one wishes to commemorate, usually a parent or grandparent. Sephardim use the names of living relatives. Among Reform Jews, either custom may be followed.

Actually, there are no laws directly concerning the choice of names. Some more traditional Ashkenazim are extremely sensitive to using the name of any living relative, especially in the mother's or father's direct line of descent, considering it an evil omen for the older person. Others are offended if a deceased ancestor's name is not used, no matter how much the young parents may dislike it.

If a name that is traditional in your family does not please you, one possible way to change it without offending your own parents or grandparents is to go back to its roots. Hebrew names were often passed on in the form of diminutives; thus one may discover, for example, that Sender, too shtetl-sounding for some, is derived from Alexander, Sadie from Sarah, Bessie from Elisabeth. The original name may be more acceptable to all. There are so many variants and combinations of names that some agreeable compromise is always possible.

The choice of a name for your long-awaited child is a highly personal matter and the decision should not become a source of family controversy. From biblical times on the actual naming of the baby has been done by the mother, and she should have the last word.

CHOOSING A NAME

Although the baby has no voice in choosing a name, he or she must carry it all through life. Names are considered by many to have mystical and magical qualities; certainly a child's name has a psychological effect on its personality. It follows that the selection of a name should not be made lightly.

Certain principles of good sense should guide. The first and last names should make a euphonious combination; the name should be distinctive, without being outlandishly original. Names to be avoided are those that give rise to embarrassing nicknames or puns, that do not combine well with the family name, that have initial letters that spell an unseemly word, or that have clearly non-Jewish connotations. Generally avoided are those Bible names with unfavorable associations such as Esau, Ishmael, Jezebel, Job, Cain, Caleb (meaning dog), Lot, etc.

WHY A JEWISH NAME?

A Jewish child should have a Jewish name; if not for family or religious reasons, then for reasons of ethnic pride alone. Such names include names from the Bible, names from modern Hebrew literature, the original Hebrew names of the forebears being commemorated, and Hebrew names that express an idea, embodying a grace, a virtue, the qualities or aspects of a pleasing natural object, animal, season, or event. Many such interesting new names are current in Israel, including Ariella (lioness), Herut (independence), Aviva (spring), Ari (lion), Orah (light), Roni (song), Illanah (tree). Using new names, your grandmother, the *bubbe* Hinda, could be commemorated by the name Ayalah (doe), or your grandfather, *zeyde* Simha, as Gil (joy).

ANGLICIZING YIDDISH AND HEBREW NAMES

After the twelfth century the custom developed of giving a child two sets of names, one civil, required by law to be in the vernacular (the equivalent of an English name today), and the other Jewish (or religious), in Hebrew or

Yiddish. Many strange combinations resulted, sometimes yielding totally new names that at first glance seem to have no relation to the originals. An example is the derivation of Tillie and Yenta, two names that today are rather disliked. Both come from the fashion of adding to the name Sarah, which means "princess," the Latin or Italian civil name Gentilia. In time, only the nicknames remained as popular names. Thus were born the names Molly, from Malke (queen), which was often added to the name Esther, and Shprintze from Esperanza, a direct translation of the name Tikveh (hope).

Frequently a second name was added when a person was dangerously ill, to thwart the powers of darkness. In searching through a family tree for a traditional name, one often finds three- or four-part given names that are the result of this old superstition.

A modern trend is to simplify these names and to go back to the original Hebrew. To some, the most pleasing and refined names in English are the exact translations of the Bible names from which most of these Yiddish diminutives or multinames derive. Thus Shmulik is properly rendered in English as Samuel, Rashke as Rebecca, Dubeh or Dvashe as Deborah. Choosing this form has the practical advantage of giving the child the same name in Hebrew and English and thus assuring that he or she will not forget the Hebrew name over the years.

Should a more "English-sounding" name be sought, the direct translation of the idea expressed by the name is also a good choice; thus Hannah, which means charm or grace, could be rendered in English as either Anne or Grace, Nehama may be Comfort or Consolation, and Barukh may be Benedict (blessed).

THE INITIAL-LETTER SYNDROME

Some people arbitrarily take only the initial letter or sound of the Hebrew or Yiddish name and use that as a basis for selecting an exotic or stylish English name. There is usually little to recommend this practice except personal whim. Often, the result is that a strongly original name, rich in family and biblical nuances, gives way to a rather common name of little distinction, as a Zipporah (Hebrew "bird," the wife of Moses) who is called Florence (from the Yiddish for bird, Faygele). Even worse, a Hayyim or Chaim ("life") may be transformed into a Christopher (Christ-carrier). To some purists all these transformed names, many with Christological or pagan associations, are inappropriate for a Jewish child and are, in a sense, a denial of his heritage.

If the parents, despite family tradition, wish to use a non-Jewish name as the primary given name for the child, the Hebrew name should be added as a middle name and used in Hebrew school and in synagogue services.

BOYS' NAMES FOR GIRLS

It may not be wise to take the name of a male forebear and turn it into a girl's name (as Morris to Marcia or Shaul to Charlotte), for then, should the parents later have a boy, the name they would have liked to give him will be unavailable to them. Of course, the same holds true with regard to girls' names for boys.

In general, the name should clearly indicate the sex of the child; names that do not are often embarrassing, especially during the early school years.

RESOURCES

Questions about names can sometimes be resolved by consulting the community service departments of YIVO, the Jewish Theological Seminary, or referring to some good name books. A most recent publication is *A Dictionary of Jewish Names and Their History* by B. C. Kaganoff (New York: Schocken Books, 1977), which also contains much data about family names.

36. *Some Special Cases*

THE ADOPTED CHILD

A male child adopted into a Jewish family must be circumcised according to ritual either on the eighth day (if adopted as a newborn), or as soon as possible after adoption. If the child was routinely circumcised at birth, the ritual of the *brit* is completed after adoption by drawing a ceremonial single drop of blood.

If the child is a girl, she should be formally named in synagogue as soon as possible after adoption.

The usual celebrations are held after these ceremonies.

If the child's natural mother was not Jewish, or her religion is unknown, the child will also be inducted into the Jewish faith at the time it is named. A rabbi should be consulted as to the proper procedure.

ANNOUNCING AN ADOPTION

The couple who have finally achieved a legal adoption are as joyful, and blessed as much, if not more so, than natural parents. They may send out formal announcements of the happy event if they wish, but the wording will be somewhat different, and the cards should not be sent out until the adoption is final.

The actual birth date of an adopted child should not be included in the announcement; it may lead to active speculation as to who the natural parents are, and even to embarrassing or annoying calls and letters from persons who think they may be the natural parents. It is better to give the age of the child instead.

A formal announcement would read:

> Mr. and Mrs. David Gold
> are happy to announce the adoption of
> Jonathan
> aged seven months
> > 25 Maple Lane
> > Ridgewood, New Jersey 07452

Some parents prefer to use the word "arrival" instead of "adoption." An informal announcement might then read:

> David and Eleanor Gold take pleasure in announcing the arrival of Jonathan, aged seven months.
> > 25 Maple Lane
> > Ridgewood, New Jersey 07452

An adopted child generally celebrates his real birthday.

THE HALF-JEWISH CHILD

If the mother is Jewish, then according to all religious law the child is Jewish. Consequently, the *mitzvah* of the *brit* and of naming apply to such a child as they do to one who is of full Jewish parentage, except that the father does not present a boy child for his circumcision or a girl for her naming. This is done by a male relative of the mother, or by the rabbi. Practice differs in various communities.

If the mother is not Jewish, but signifies her intention to bring the child up as Jewish, the rabbi should be consulted as to the proper procedure for inducting the child into the Jewish faith.

CHILDREN WHOSE PARENTS
ARE NOT MARRIED

A child born to a Jewish couple who are living together without being married may go through the ritual of the *brit* and of naming. Whether the father himself may present the child for the ceremonies is a matter to be discussed with a rabbi. If the parents could legally be married, Jewish law does not consider the child illegitimate.

If the mother is raising the child by herself, the rabbi or a male relative may carry out the father's function. The naming is then usually done privately, without mention of the father's name.

37. *Other Pleasant Customs*

GIFTS

Baby showers may be given for the expected arrival, but not by members of the family. Gifts of money for the baby may be in the form of cash, or checks made out in the mother's name; bonds are drawn payable to either the child or the mother. Because of the strong feeling against preparing too much in advance, most gifts are given after the child is born and its name announced.

It is a thoughtful touch, when there is an older child, to bring or send a small present for the big brother or sister, together with the gift for the new baby. A little story book, some crayons and a coloring book, or a small toy go a long way to alleviate that "left-out" feeling that assails an older sibling when the new baby comes home and becomes the center of so much attention.

A TREE FOR THE NEW BABY

In some communities it is customary to plant a tree to commemorate the birth of a child: a cedar for a boy, a pine or a cypress for a girl. In the old tradition the hope was that the trees, growing with the children, would furnish the wood for the *huppah* poles when they were married.

Parents who are not fortunate enough to have a garden in which to plant the tree might choose an indoor tree, such as a Norfolk pine in a pot, or plant some trees in Israel.

It is a pleasant way to mark the advent of a new life and watch its progress through the years.

THAT FIRST HAIRCUT

Now that so many young men wear their hair long, it is not so startling to observe that Hasidim and other very Orthodox Jews do not cut a little boy's hair until he is three years old. A very festive party is held on the birthday, at which the oldest person present is honored by being allowed to cut the first curl; if he is a *kohen* (a member of the priestly clan) it is a great honor to the family to have him do it. The other guests may also be allowed to cut a tiny snip each.

It is always agreeable to have a party, and a first-haircut celebration would be fun for the family, no matter what the age or sex of the child.

38. Yihus: *The Family Tree*

Merit and distinction derive from intellectual family connections, a Jewish concept that values alliance to and descent from a scholarly family. In rabbinical writings such ancestry is said to convey more honor than riches and is the desideratum when arranging a marriage. Thus the *yihus-brif* (family tree) became an important document.

Apart from honor, there is a sense of communication over the generations, past and future, that makes the creation and maintenance of a family tree a particularly warm and enriching family project. Tracing the family line back from the present is an activity that joins the generations together; tracing today's cousins can be rewarding. Including Hebrew names, marriage and birth dates, and the *yahrzeit* dates of deceased relatives makes it a useful document as well. Some add a note as to the occupation of each person.

A family record page is the simplest way to begin. A useful form might be set up across two facing pages of a photo album, preserved under the plastic sheets, but accessible for new entries as needed. The extra width gives enough room to list the children of marriages in the family. The pages following could be used to mount pictures not only of family members but of homes the family has lived in, graduation programs, newspaper clippings, and other biographical mementoes.

Data about family branches and ancestors (aunts, uncles, grandparents, and the "greats") can be set up on similar pages headed "Father's Family" and "Mother's Family."

It is also interesting to collect reminiscences of the past from older members of the family and transcribe them for mounting in the album.

A suggested form might look like that shown here.

PARENTS

FATHER _____ _____
English name   Hebrew name

Son of _____

and _____

Born _____

In _____

MOTHER _____ _____
English name   Hebrew name

Daughter of _____

and _____

Born _____

In _____

Married _____

In _____

CHILDREN †

NAME _____ _____
English   Hebrew

Born •_____

Bar/Bat Mitzvah _____
date

Son (daughter) of _____

and _____

of (place) _____

Born _____ †

married on • _____

NAME _____ _____
English   Hebrew

Born •_____

Bar/Bat Mitzvah _____
date

Son (daughter) of _____

and _____

of (place) _____

Born _____ †

married on • _____

YAHRZEITS

Name _____ (English/Hebrew)

Date _____ (Hebrew/English)

* Place may be added on another line
† Page may be extended to allow listing the children of each marriage

BAR/BAT MITZVAH

And all thy children shall be taught of the Lord.

—ISAIAH 54:15

39. *Bar Mitzvah Basics*

WHAT IT MEANS TO BE
A "SON OF THE COMMANDMENTS"

The bar mitzvah is a Jewish ceremonial occasion so well-known that a definition of the term appears in Webster's dictionary, which effectively makes an English term of the Hebrew expression. The phrase bar or bat mitzvah, literally "son or daughter of the commandments," connotes the attainment of religious and legal majority by a boy or girl who is now under personal obligation to carry out the commandments (*mitzvoth*), and who assumes full responsibility for his or her own conduct. Technically speaking, one becomes a bar mitzvah by attaining the age of thirteen, and no special ceremony is necessary to bring this majority into effect. Since many of the rights once granted a bar mitzvah are now governed by secular law, only religious duties remain: to observe the commandments, to don *tefillin* (phylacteries) and *tallit* (prayer shawl) in daily prayer, to make one of a *minyan*, and the right to be called up for the reading of the Torah, an *aliyah*.

Being called up to the Torah for the first time, as the culmination of a period of formal training, and the congratulatory celebration attaching to this *aliyah*, form the core of bar mitzvah ceremonies in traditional practice.

The minimum participation usually expected in Orthodox and Conservative congregations is the reading of the *maftir*, the *haftarah*, and the blessings attached to these Torah portions. The boy is also expected to make a speech (*derashah*) of some scholarly nature. (See Chapter 44.) In some traditional synagogues the young man may also conduct as much of the Sabbath service as he has mastered.

In Reform congregations that permit individual bar mitzvahs, the Torah portion may be read in English or Hebrew, or the boy may merely recite the blessing before and after the reading by an official of the congregation. Generally, he will also deliver a speech.

In recent years, more and more Conservative synagogues have ended the differentiation between bar and bat mitzvah and now allow girls who are qualified by their religious training to have an individual bat mitzvah at Sabbath morning services, with the same degree of participation as a boy. Everything that follows in this chapter about the boy's bar mitzvah should be read as applying equally to a girl who is preparing for such a bat mitzvah.

Whatever the ceremony, it marks an important passage in life for the youth, a peak moment of joy for the parents and relatives, and hence an occasion for festive rejoicing, feasting, and giftgiving.

PLANNING AHEAD

Preparing for a bar mitzvah involves much more thinking ahead than merely selecting a date and calling in a caterer to serve the feast. In planning the event together, families will find themselves examining their religious values and their identification with Judaism. The decisions should be made in family conclave; above all, the young person who will be the center of the celebrations must be given a meaningful part in the deliberations. Both the family budget and the child's wishes and abilities should be taken into account. His bar mitzvah should be an event that he creates, not something that merely happens to him at the behest of adults.

FORMAL TRAINING REQUIREMENTS

Thoughtful parents should make a synagogue affiliation early on, and begin to send the child to religious school in good time, so that he may complete the educational requirements of the institution without strain. Most synagogues require from two to four years of religious instruction, during which the youngster is expected to master the language skills, the prayers, and the understanding of his people's faith, history, and culture that will enable him to assume his responsibilities as an adult in Judaism, and carry out the traditional part of the service with sincerity, accomplishment, and grace.

The degree to which he will participate in the service should be decided on by the child and his teacher as the time draws near. Parents, especially fathers, should be supportive, but not so demanding of performance that they create trauma for the boy. The father should be content to star in his own part of the service and not aim for a vicarious glory in seeking a role for his son that is beyond reasonable expectations. The child should feel the satisfaction of an adult accomplishment and not the terrors of a disgraceful failure before all his friends and family assembled.

The Handicapped Child.   If a child suffers from some learning disability or physical handicap, it is most important to consult the rabbi early, so that a plan of study may be prepared that will enable the boy to take his place in the community of adults and achieve all that his abilities permit. With proper guidance, no child need be deprived of a bar mitzvah because of physical, emotional, or learning problems.

Moving into a New Community.   Difficulties often arise because of the mobility of modern life. Where a family has just moved into the community with a child approaching bar mitzvah age, it is essential that they consult a rabbi as soon as they can, so that a proper program can be planned in the short time left. Some of the study time requirements may be waived. Even if a private tutor is engaged, it is important that the boy attend religious school, so that he can make some friends in the community among his contemporaries.

The Parents' Responsibility.   It is manifestly unfair of parents, especially those with no synagogue affiliation, to make little or no provision for a child's Jewish training and then suddenly decide, when the boy or girl is twelve, that it is expedient, for fashionable reasons, to have a big, splashy bar mitzvah, forcing an ill-prepared child through a difficult, often meaningless ordeal so that the parent's social impulses can be gratified. To offer as an incentive to the child the many gifts he will receive is reprehensible, and an introduction to the world of adult hypocrisy. Fortunately, the boy's involvement in Jewish training often brings the whole family into the fold of Judaism once more.

PREPARING FOR A PUBLIC APPEARANCE

Thirteen is not only bar mitzvah age, but also an awkward hobbledehoy time for most boys. Bearing in mind that their son (and also their other children) will be on dress parade on this day, families should begin formal social training well in advance of the occasion, practicing company table manners, developing skill in passing foods, cutting up meats, helping oneself gracefully from platters, using the correct silver and glassware at a formal setting.

It is also wise to practice introductions, shaking hands, introducing guests to each other, accepting congratulations and gifts graciously. While fond relatives kiss him and comment on how much he has grown and how well he read his Torah portion, the young man must smile and smile, and be every inch the gentleman.

If a formal evening dinner dance is planned, some dancing lessons may be in order. Even though most young people do today's disco steps at a very early age, boys sometimes need coaching in dancing with Grandma and Mama, and some training in their obligation as the young host to partner their young lady guests at least once during the evening.

THE QUESTION OF KASHRUT

Those who are observant of *kashrut* (the Jewish dietary laws), or who intend to use a kosher caterer, need no instruction in this matter. But when the family does not follow the kosher tradition in its daily life, their decision on the food to be served at the reception raises questions of propriety and even of Jewish self-respect.

The day of a boy's bar mitzvah, which is a ritual affirmation of Judaism, is not the time to serve a banquet of *terefah* (forbidden) foods. Many Reform congregations, despite the fact that their members are free of the obligation to observe all dietary laws, stipulate that no *terefah* foods may be brought into the temple when the reception is held there. Even if one is not using a kosher caterer, it is possible, and desirable, to order a menu that avoids pork, shellfish, and the mixing of meat and milk. The very people who do not ordinarily observe the dietary laws when they eat in restaurants will be the most critical if they find shrimp salad and baked ham on the reception table. And most important, the observant among the guests will not be able to partake of a *terefah* repast at all; so-called neutral foods, such as fish, cheese, or vegetables, become unclean when served on the same table as *terefah* foods.

THE GRAMMAR OF "BAR MITZVAH"

One hears very frequently the vulgar and incorrect use of the phrase bar mitzvah as past participle, as in "He was bar mitzvahed last year." There is no such usage possible. The expression "bar mitzvah" is a noun, meaning either the young man or the celebration involved. Thus, a boy *becomes*, or *is*, a bar mitzvah; his parents celebrate his bar mitzvah. One should make every effort to use this phrase correctly.

40. Choosing a Date

Traditionally, a bar mitzvah should be held on the Sabbath immediately following the child's thirteenth birthday (according to the Hebrew calendar). However, there are factors that may operate to modify this. One is the intense competition in some synagogues for the available dates. Others may be vacation schedules in summer months, conflicts with heavy school schedules, and other festivities within the family circle.

At the time one first consults the rabbi about educational requirements, a tentative date should be set. This can be made final at whatever time ahead the synagogue calendar necessitates. If need be, two boys may share the same date. Once the Sabbath is set, the boy will begin to study the Torah portion for that week and changes become very difficult.

PROVIDING FOR SABBATH OBSERVANCE

Since the vast majority of bar mitzvahs occur at Saturday morning services, and families and friends may gather from great distances to attend, Sabbath observance for the Orthodox requires special advance preparations. Provision must be made to accommodate Sabbath-observing relatives and friends from Friday afternoon to Saturday night or Sunday morning at a hotel, motel, or a friend's home somewhere within walking distance of the synagogue and to arrange for kosher meals for them during this time. Smaller than the bar mitzvah reception, the other Sabbath meals can be pleasant, intimate family occasions.

Should such arrangements not be possible, a part of the bar mitzvah celebration, usually a formal dinner or buffet reception, may be held after sundown on Saturday, or on the Sunday, to allow Orthodox relatives and friends to travel to the party.

DATES THAT ARE NOT SABBATHS

A better choice, when Sabbath observance poses a problem is to seek a date that does not fall on the Sabbath. The basic requirement is that the day chosen be one on which the Torah is read as part of the service, that is Monday, Thursday, or Rosh Hodesh (one of the first two days of the new Hebrew month, which often falls on a Sunday). Such a choice makes it possible to have a very festive gathering on a Monday or Thursday legal holiday or on a Sunday morning, thus avoiding problems of housing, travel, and many meals away from home for one's guests.

Such days lend themselves very well to less formal entertaining, such as festive brunch or luncheon, and to observance of the thirteenth-century decree that only those who participated in the service should be invited to the feast.

It may be necessary to ask the rabbi specifically about such days, as most people tend to think only of the Sabbath in connection with a bar mitzvah.

THE MINHAH BAR MITZVAH

A bar mitzvah may be held at the afternoon service (Minhah) on the days the Torah is read. Choosing such a time on Sabbaths when the days are short makes it possible to go on to a reception and dinner immediately after the evening service (Ma'ariv) and Havdalah (end of the Sabbath). The evening celebration then does not become separated from the religious occasion, and those guests who do not travel on the Sabbath can still attend the reception after dark.

41. Bar Mitzvah Celebrations

A PLEA FOR SIMPLICITY

Once the day and date are set, it is time to decide on the kind of celebration to be arranged. And here we must enter a plea for simplicity. What was initially a minor ceremonial recognition by the community of the individual's informed acceptance of his religious duties has, in our day, mushroomed into a series of formal social occasions whose festive aspects rival elaborate weddings; indeed, the weddings are often anticlimactic to some bar/bat mitzvah celebrations.

In some communities a social competition develops, egged on by caterers, that can only be compared to the Pacific Northwest Indian potlatch—an orgy of destructive spending. There is no limit to the ideas that caterers, and sometimes one's well-meaning relatives and friends, can dream up to magnify the ostentatious display of wealth at such an occasion.

Even in the seventeenth century, Lithuanian rabbis were inveighing against those who spent too much money on festive meals, so that those modern rabbis who preach sermons criticizing functions that involve "too much *bar* and not enough *mitzvah*" have historical precedent for their remarks.

Good taste and good sense should come together at this time. Parents should recognize that the bar mitzvah, while a peak happy occasion, is only a promise of the future. The young person has, after all, merely achieved a certain chronological age and finished a preparatory training course. He has made an emotion-filled affirmation, and taken the first step toward adulthood. But there are many more happy events to come in the life of the family, perhaps college training and a start in a profession to be paid for. There may also be other children to provide for. It makes little sense to go into debt to provide an opulent affair far above the family's normal lifestyle, especially when true refinement would indicate a celebration in proportion to the place of the event in the life of the individual, no matter what the family's finances.

The guiding principles should be, first, that the boy and his religious affirmation must not be swallowed up in an adult extravaganza designed to pay off social obligations, make business contacts, and generally impress others; and second, that the festivities should appropriately express the beauty and primacy of the religious occasion and the sincerity of the family's rejoicing.

RECEIVING AFTER SERVICES

In keeping with the underlying religious nature of a bar mitzvah, the most appropriate celebration is one that follows immediately after the services. At that time one may sponsor a *kiddush* in the synagogue reception rooms for the entire congregation, to be followed by a luncheon or buffet for invited guests, to be held there also, or at home.

Kiddush in the Synagogue. Essential to the *kiddush* are wine and hallah (the Sabbath bread) or cake. If the congregation is very large, one may arrange for a simple table set with wine already poured into glasses and with platters of cookies and sliced cakes (especially honeycake and sponge cake, symbolizing a sweet life). Nuts, sweets, and fruits are also appropriate. Hors d'oeuvres are not necessary unless the *kiddush* is meant to substitute for a luncheon. One should check with the sexton as to the number of congregants, other than invited guests, who might be expected to partake of a congregational *kiddush*.

In Orthodox gatherings, hallah is not served, since one must wash the hands before partaking of bread, and say Grace afterward, even though a full meal was not eaten.

After the group gathers in the room, the rabbi or some honored member of the family, usually the grandfather, recites the blessings over the wine and hallah (if served). The hallah is cut into small portions and passed to the guests. If bread is not served, the guests may recite the appropriate blessings over cakes and sweets as they help themselves.

If a more elaborate buffet or luncheon is planned after the *kiddush* for one's invited guests, the hallah and the *Hamotzi* (blessing over the bread) may be reserved for that part of the celebration. The blessing procedure is the same.

Receptions in the Synagogue or Community Center.   Faced with large guest lists and small, servantless homes, most families decide to use community facilities, either the reception rooms of the synagogue or temple, or those of a nearby community center. Some large apartment complexes have community rooms that are available to their residents, but these must be carefully checked for privacy and suitability. There is frequently a resident caterer connected with such rooms.

In dealing with the caterer, it is necessary to keep a firm hand on the arrangements to maintain simple elegance. Many extras, such as monogrammed cocktail glasses and swizzlesticks, "Torah scroll" menus (sometimes adorned with the boy's picture), extravagant floral decorations, wine waiters, ice sculptures, and gargantuan arrays of food, are not only not necessary, but in dubious taste.

Music.   In most traditional synagogue settings, instrumental music and ballroom dancing are not permitted on the Sabbath. Singing and spontaneous folk dancing are.

The Bar.   Although a *lehayim* (toast to life), a toast to the parents, grandparents, and the bar mitzvah himself, are very much in order, care should be taken to keep the bar service within the bounds of moderation characteristic of Judaism. It is altogether appropriate to serve only sacramental wine for *kiddush*, a champagne punch or champagne and suitable red and white wines, if one wishes to avoid hard liquors. The ubiquitous wine waiter and bar cart circulating among the tables and pressing alcoholic drinks on the guests is, to some, offensive at a youthful celebration.

For the many children who will be present, it would be best to have a separate soft-drink bar, serving sodas, fruit juices, and nonalcoholic punch. Bartenders should be specifically instructed not to serve liquor to underage guests.

RECEIVING AT HOME

The ideal place for a bar mitzvah party is in one's home. The intimate family air of the day is best maintained here, and of necessity a more informal, personal atmosphere and a more limited guest list will result. Acquaintances and business associates will not expect to be invited to such an occasion, and it is thus possible to keep the gathering smaller without offending anyone.

Receptions at home may range in scope from a formally served seated luncheon for a small group to a seated buffet or an elaborate stand-up reception, or indeed, take in all three.

It is possible to receive a large number of guests in a smaller home by staggering the "at-home" hours on the invitations, inviting the closest family group for lunch immediately after the services, another group of friends for a *shalosh seudah* (the third Sabbath meal) in the late afternoon, four to six or seven o'clock, and yet a third group for an evening collation which will begin about an hour after sundown.

Such an extended party can be taxing, especially if one does not have a regular household staff. A wise hostess will hire outside help for serving, bartending, and clearing for the day, so that she can enjoy it with her guests. It is really not right to allow (or expect!) guests to help, yet they often feel pressed to do so when the hostess is obviously swamped.

Glassware, dishes, tables, chairs, and linens may be rented for the day. Paper napkins and plates, and plastic glasses, knives, and forks, may be used at an informal buffet. The use of disposable dishes, glasses, and cutlery avoids problems of *kashrut* if one's home is not strictly kosher. Many charming matched sets of disposables are available for party use; the very best, heaviest quality should be selected.

Garden Parties. In the warmer months, a large group may be very pleasantly entertained at a garden party, if the grounds at home are extensive enough. The same staggered-hour plan may be followed. Children will be less troublesome outdoors, but one is, of course, at the mercy of the weather, and should be prepared to move the party indoors if the day is inclement.

A tent may be rented for the day to eliminate worries about the weather, but it is usually rather expensive, and in very hot weather one may sometimes find the garden deserted and the guests revelling inside the air-conditioned house. Despite all these reservations, a green lawn and flowering garden make a most delightful informal setting for a bar mitzvah celebration.

"At-Home" Menus. Menus for "at-home" entertaining may be as simple or elaborate as one wishes. Homemade delicacies give the chefs of the family a chance to star. With a large freezer at one's disposal, it is possible to start cooking and baking well in advance. In many communities close friends and relatives undertake to prepare their *spécialités de maison* for the hostess. Such dishes should be delivered early on the Friday, to avoid unseemly carrying on the Sabbath, and to give the hostess time to plan for their serving.

Many kinds of food can be ordered from delicatessens and kosher take-out places, ranging from cold cuts and salads to hot dishes. Delivery should be arranged on the Friday, as noted above.

Caterers and Party Cooks.   There are some caterers who will transport a wide range of facilities and their staff to one's home and take over the complete responsibility for the party. Every detail is taken care of, and it is almost magical to see the entire festivity appear and disappear without much work on the part of the hostess, but it is often more costly than the very same party held at the caterer's establishment. The date often must be reserved well in advance.

In many communities there are party cooks who will come to one's house, prepare the menu agreed upon, and clean up the kitchen afterward. The hostess must discipline herself to stay out of the kitchen completely, and may have to arrange separately for additional help to serve. She may also have to oversee the necessary marketing, equipment rental, set-up of the bar, tables, and serving area, and the like. Apportioning the responsibility for these details should be done at the time the date is reserved.

Special Provisions for Young Guests.   By its very nature, a bar mitzvah celebration will include many preteen youngsters, and their even younger brothers and sisters. They should certainly be invited to services and any daytime receptions, and are often the most delightful and spontaneous part of the company.

After services, however, where they have had to sit still for a long time, and are often quite hungry, they can descend upon a beautifully arranged sweet table or buffet and make a wreck of it in a few minutes. Every effort should be made to provide a separate area for youngsters, where they can enjoy themselves without constraint. A special menu might even be served to them, of such favorites as hamburgers, hot dogs, or spaghetti.

If one's home has a recreation room, it could be turned over to them. The young host will take great pleasure in planning a soda fountain, disco dancing (if the family's Sabbath observance permits), and other teenage amusements.

A thoughtful hostess will also make provision for the babies in the family by arranging for babysitters during the morning services (check with the synagogue), and a changing and nap area at home, away from the social tumult. The babies will bring pleasure to all their doting relatives, and this is, after all, a family party.

To the Parents of Young Guests. A long day of formal festivities is hard for young people to take. Young boys and girls who are to be guests at such functions should be drilled by their own families in acceptable reception, dinner, and dance behavior.

Even when some special area has been set aside in which the young people can enjoy their own kind of fun while the adults are partying, the parents of young guests cannot abdicate their responsibility for the actions of their children.

FORMAL SATURDAY EVENING AND SUNDAY RECEPTIONS

When the principal bar mitzvah celebration is to be held after the Sabbath is over, it is customary to fete those guests who attend services with a small *kiddush* reception, and sometimes a small family luncheon immediately afterward, reserving any elaborate hospitality for either Saturday night or Sunday. In spring and summer months, when the Sabbath days are very long and a reception could not traditionally begin until about nine o'clock, Sundays are usually the preferred days.

Such bar mitzvahs escalate rapidly in cost and complexity, involving, as they must, two large parties, an additional set of formal clothes for the family, floral decorations in two or three different reception areas, and two liquor bills.

It is in poor taste to hold a formal dinner dance on a Saturday night, at which youngsters are dressed up in tuxedos or junior formal gowns, and kept up till very late hours in a hotel ballroom, while their parents and their friends drink and cavort.

A practical and appropriate choice for a post-Sabbath festivity would be either an elegant Sunday luncheon or a midday reception and dinner. Out-of-town guests will be able to arrive and depart the same day, and the party will end early enough so that the youngsters may calm down and get to sleep at a reasonable hour.

Very young children are not invited to evening parties, or to formal functions on Sundays.

Entertainment. Music always makes a social gathering more festive. Records may be used at home to provide sound ranging from light classical background to disco music for dancing. A strolling guitarist, accordionist, or violinist is a very pleasant touch if one does not wish to engage a dance band.

If entertainment is offered at large dinners, it should be borne in mind that the young adults present are very young indeed. Masters of ceremonies, comedians, dancers should be reminded that this is a "family affair." Even magicians have been known to enliven their acts with off-color jokes!

The Dais. The old-style dais table, at which parents and honored adult guests are seated with the bar mitzvah boy, is seen less and less. Nowadays there is often no dais at all; instead, the youngsters are all seated together in one section of the room with their own soft-drink bar.

Parents and grandparents may then be seated at other tables (not together at one) so that each group has its own host or hostess, as it were. In such a set-up, leaving one's table to circulate among the guests avoids the awkwardness of a tableful of empty places.

The Birthday Cake. Since a bar mitzvah revolves around achieving a certain age, a birthday cake is generally included in the menu even though the celebration may not fall on a boy's calendar birthday. It is used as a centerpiece on a buffet table, or as the focus of an elaborate dessert ritual at a seated meal.

The cake may be shaped like an open book, a Torah scroll, or a *Magen David,* but one in the form of the Tablets of the Ten Commandments is not considered correct. By cutting into such a cake, one is symbolically breaking the Tablets once again.

At catered dinners, the master of ceremonies generally makes an entertainment of lighting the candles. There will be fourteen (one for good luck), and the honor of lighting them, one by one, is distributed among grandparents, aunts, uncles, siblings, cousins, and finally the proud parents. In a small family, some of these honors may go to a boy's best friends. If the family is very large, a whole group of relations (aunt, uncle, and their children) may be called up together to light one candle.

On the Sabbath, fire may not be kindled; hence in traditional circles little flags are often used, to be inserted in the cake instead of candles.

If you choose to have such a ceremony, it would be best to be prepared for it before the day by making up a list with the names correctly set out for the master of ceremonies ("Uncle Joe and Aunt Dorothy," not "Mr. and Mrs. Epstein"), and perhaps a few words about their special relationship to the bar mitzvah. Some families prepare a little verse about each candle-lighter, which may be read by the master of ceremonies or someone in the family who enjoys public appearances.

The honorees deserve the courtesy of being told ahead of time, so they may prepare a congratulatory remark. If there are great-grandparents or other aged relatives to be honored, an escort to the center of the stage is a thoughtful gesture.

It is customary to save the last candle, symbolizing a good future, for the mother and father to light.

FLOWERS

The use of flowers makes any party more festive. The family may contribute to the flower fund for the decoration of the *bimah* (synagogue platform), and will, of course, want some floral centerpieces for synagogue buffet and dinner tables. Floral decoration of the synagogue interior is not usual.

At home, flowers may be used as freely as one wishes. Any blossoms of the season are appropriate, with the exception of Christmas poinsettias and Easter lilies.

Since flowers wither rather quickly (sometimes in direct relationship to their costliness!) some families choose to forego these decorations and instead give flowers or plants to a hospital ward or home for the aged. Others make the gracious gesture of sending the decorations to such an institution when the party is over.

42. *The Guest List*

WHOM TO INVITE

Among the people who must be included in any guest list are:

1. The family
2. The bar mitzvah's close friends, but *not necessarily* their parents, if they are not acquaintances of the host and hostess
3. The boy's bar mitzvah teacher (if he had a special tutor) and family, and perhaps a favorite teacher or two and their spouses
4. The rabbi and his family

The list may be widened to include friends of the parents and grandparents who have some interest in the boy. You may also wish to return the hospitality of friends who have invited the family to their bar mitzvah celebrations.

Try not to invite anyone who does not know the bar mitzvah, or have some interest in his education and future. By keeping to this rule you can avoid having the celebration escalate into an *omnium gatherum* at which you repay all sorts of social obligations or entertain business associates who have no real connection with the guest of honor—your son or daughter.

THE BAR MITZVAH BOOK

Once the matter of who is to be invited is settled, a master guest list should be set up. Properly arranged in a notebook, this list has many uses: addressing invitations, checking responses, noting seating plans, arranging overnight accommodations, recording gifts and their acknowledgment. It is a valuable aid to both the parents and the young man in keeping details under control during a hectic time.

It is helpful to divide the list into separate groupings for the mother's family, the father's family, and friends and business associates. Even the closest relations, such as grandparents, should be listed, to avoid embarrassing omissions when doing addressing, place cards, and the like.

Within each group, the list should be alphabetical, and separated once more into local and out-of-town guests. It should include not only full names, as they will be used for addressing envelopes, but also the familiar name by which the bar mitzvah is to address each person. He will be meeting many relatives he hasn't seen since he was a baby (as they will all remind him), and will need this help in maintaining poise and ease in greeting them, and later in writing thank-you notes.

A suggested set-up is shown here. It works out best when laid out across two facing pages of a notebook.

Such a list may also be set up on index cards in a file box, but the notebook seems more practical, especially since it is to be handled by a youngster.

It is helpful to include in the bar mitzvah book the names, addresses, and telephone numbers of stationers, caterers, florists, rental services, and motels used, together with notes on the quality of performance and prices charged. The menus of the various meals served can be noted, with comments. Samples of all cards used can be kept here, too. If friends and relatives have prepared some special dishes, you may want to note this, and perhaps the recipes as well.

You will find the book very useful later for many other family social functions.

Bar Mitzvah Book

Local Mother's Family Name, Address, Phone	Called	Reply[1]	No. of persons	Table no.[2]
Bernstein, Mr. and Mrs. Harold Marianne and Allan	Uncle Hal, Aunt Mae	A	4	
1005 Parkway West, 10458 (413) 874-2096				
Out-of-Town **Mother's Family**				
Cohen, Mrs. Maurice	Tante Edith	A	1	
50 Circle Boulevard Philadelphia, PA 19103 (215) 486-7089				
Davis, Mr. and Mrs. Albert Elizabeth and Joseph	Uncle Al, Aunt Barbara	A	4	
83 Memorial Drive Chicago, IL 60605 (312) 632-1005				
Finkel, Dr. and Mrs. Harry 97 Longwood Drive Philadelphia, PA 19103 (215) 486-7900	Uncle Hershy, Tante Ita	R	0	

Totals
  No. guests expected (±)————
  No. rooms needed————

[1] If more than one meal is involved, break this down (and add columns for each function),
e.g., for *kiddush*————
            luncheon————
            Sunday buffet————
[2] For a seated meal.

OBLIGATIONS OF THE WEEKEND HOST

When guests come from a distance for the weekend, although they pay for their hotel rooms themselves, the host family has obligations of hospitality to them in addition to the reception plans for the bar mitzvah itself. The

Gift	Thank-you Note	Overnight at	Special needs
Webster's 3d Ed. unabridged dictionary	5/27	—	—
check—$50	5/27	the Goldsteins 72 Lakeview	rent folding wheelchair
Israel Bond—$100	5/27	Pineview Motel[3] 2 doubles	send phone number of limo service; have limo meet at airport
brown sealskin wallet	5/20	—	—

[3] Guests pay for their own rooms; host makes reservations for them.

family should expect to make hotel reservations and to arrange to have planes and buses met (a car service may be used, for which guests pay themselves). They should also expect to provide for dinner Friday evening and Saturday evening, and a Sunday brunch, if necessary.

43. Invitations

WHAT IS CORRECT?

The bar mitzvah is unique in being a major social event centered around the education of a child. Although one may follow formal protocol for invitations, there is a felt need for "something different." This is readily apparent when one examines the sample books of social stationers. A bewildering array of colors, typefaces, styles of folding, and variation of texts is shown. Most of these unconventional invitations are ostentatiously ornate.

Socially correct invitations may be as informal as handwritten notes to a small group of relatives and friends, or as severely elegant as the formal invitation to a wedding. The choice should be dictated by the nature of the party planned. Whichever of the forms given below one decides on, certain basic principles of good taste in correspondence always govern.

The paper chosen must be of the very best quality one can afford, and off-white or pale pastel in color. Gray, ivory, buff, or pale blue are all correct. Black ink is always correct, but other conservative dark colors may be used, such as brown, very dark blue, deep green, or violet. Bear in mind that the addresses should be written in matching ink, and be certain it is available before ordering unusual color combinations. Deckle edges go in and out of fashion; they are correct for informal use.

Forms to Be Avoided. An incorrect combination is the folder which carries the bar mitzvah's name or monogram on the first page and the invitation on the third page. The hosts are the boy's parents; it is they who are issuing the invitations (and paying the bills!) and the boy's name or monogram should not appear, nor should the invitation be signed by him, although such samples can be seen.

In addition to improper monograms, all kinds of questionable ornaments are shown. It is best to avoid the embossed *Magen David*, gold Torah scrolls, badly drawn Lions of Judah and Tablets of the Commandments, and so on. Any ornamentation chosen must be truly artistic to be really effective. In this, as in fashion and art, less is more.

English and Hebrew Texts. If you are using only an English text, it should appear on the first side of a folded sheet. When a Hebrew text is used as well, the most appropriate choice is to have the Hebrew and English face each other on the inside pages (English on the left, Hebrew on the right). You may alternatively choose to have one text on the first page and one on

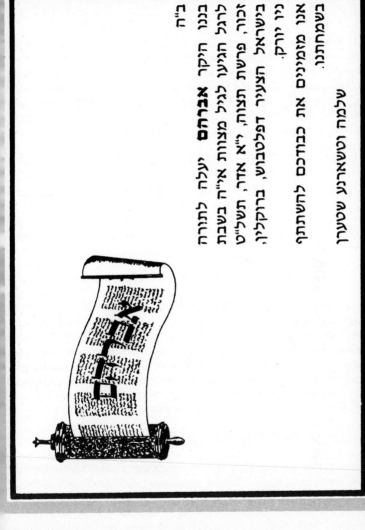

Figure 7. A hand-lettered Hebrew text. Used as a cover, it is decorated with the boy's name (*Abraham*) superimposed on a Purim *megillah*, appropriate to the date of the bar mitzvah, Purim.

the third page, in which case it is a problem which text is to come first. The family's values will decide this matter.

The Hebrew script should be hand-lettered for the most pleasing effect. In English texts the Roman Gothic or Italic families are handsome, legible, and in the best taste.

Use of Bible Verses. A pleasing adaptation of Hebrew styles is to use as an ornament a Bible verse on the first page of an informal folder, with the invitation on the third page. If you select a large-size formal invitation that will be folded in half again, the text may appear just under the fold on the last page, which will become the cover. In this size or the smaller folder, the text should be placed in the upper left portion of the page, enclosed in quotation marks, and the source given, e.g.,

> "And the child grew and the Lord blessed him."
>
> Judges 13:74
>
> "And all thy children shall be taught of the Lord."
>
> Isaiah 54:15

The choice of a fitting verse should be made by the boy and his teacher.

WHEN TO SEND OUT INVITATIONS

Invitations should be sent out at least four weeks ahead of time. Around holiday and vacation periods, and in June, when there are many weddings, six weeks' advance notice to guests is advisable.

Since engraving or printing may take several weeks, it is best to order the invitations at least seven or eight weeks before they are to be sent out. You can usually pick up the envelopes from the stationer at the time you place the order and start addressing them beforehand if your list is very long.

THE FORMAL INVITATION

Religious services are formal occasions; hence the phrase "the honour of your presence" is used in a formal invitation (with the British spelling "honour"), not "the pleasure of your company." The form most closely paralleling a wedding invitation follows. This text calls for the most formal type-face and the best off-white paper. If all the guests are to be invited to a celebration after services, only one card is necessary.

Two envelopes, inside and outside, are used, and addressed in the same manner as wedding invitations. (See Chapter 60.)

> Mr. and Mrs. Harold Levine
> request the honour of your presence
> at the Bar Mitzvah of their son
> Alan
> Saturday, the twenty-sixth of May
> at ten o'clock
> Temple Petach Tikvah
> Ringwood Drive
> Great Neck, New York
> and afterward at luncheon

or

> and afterward at luncheon at home

R.s.v.p.
40 Colt Road
Great Neck, New York 11204

A more appropriate text follows. It places more emphasis on the essential part of the bar mitzvah ceremony—the calling up to the Torah. Two envelopes should be used with this text, as with the above. Note that here one card also is used, for a reception to which all guests are invited.

> Mr. and Mrs. Harold Levine
> request the honour of your presence
> at Sabbath services
> when their son Alan
> will be called to the Torah
> as a Bar Mitzvah
> Saturday, the twenty-sixth of May
> at nine o'clock
> Temple Petach Tikvah
> Ringwood Drive
> Great Neck, New York

Reception
following services
R.s.v.p.

THE INFORMAL INVITATION

You may send handwritten notes to the guests if the list is not so long that the writing becomes an impossible chore. The penmanship should be as neat and clear as possible. The round "social secretary" style is favored. Black ink on very good off-white or pale pastel paper is the best choice.

This handwritten note may be reproduced by the offset printing process on a carefully chosen art folder, or a specially designed verse, illustration, and text may be hand-lettered and printed by the same process. You may combine Hebrew and English texts by this method.

Failing such original talents, you may choose to have the text set up in a cursive typeface and engraved or printed.

Although almost any color of paper and ink and any kind of display type may be selected in keeping with the informal style, it is best to avoid "trendy" styles and ostentatious decorations.

Some suggested texts follow:

Our son, Alan, will be called to the Torah as a Bar Mitzvah on Saturday, the twenty-sixth of May, at Temple Petach Tikvah, Ringwood Drive, Longmeadow, New Jersey, at nine o'clock. We would be honoured to have you join us at services on this happy day and afterward at luncheon.

Belle and Harold Levine

Please reply
40 Colt Road
Great Neck, New York 11024

When all the guests are invited to the services and then later to an evening reception at home, the last sentence of the invitation might read:

Please share our simha by joining us at services and in the evening from seven-thirty till eleven o'clock for a reception at our home.

Another variant of the informal text might read:

Please share our simha on the occasion of the Bar Mitzvah of our son, Edward Marc, by joining us at Sabbath services on the twenty-sixth of May at nine o'clock at the Paloverde Jewish Center, 300 Mountain Drive, Los Angeles, California, and afterward at Kiddush.

Evelyn and Philip Berman

R.s.v.p.
75 Woodhill Boulevard
Los Angeles, California 90010

Only one envelope is necessary with an informal invitation.

SOLVING NAME PROBLEMS

When the Parents Are Divorced. Even though his parents are divorced, the bar mitzvah is still the child of both, and wherever possible the invitation should be issued in their joint names, thus indicating that, despite their unhappy marriage, they love their child and are proud of his progress toward adulthood.

When the divorced parents are hosting the bar mitzvah together, a formal invitation might read:

Mrs. Ann Stone
and
Mr. Daniel Stone
request the honour of your presence
[etc.]

If the divorced parents do not wish their names to appear together as above, the invitation may read simply:

The honour of your presence is requested
at the Bar Mitzvah of
Alan Levine
Saturday, the twenty-sixth of May
[etc.]

When the Parent Is Remarried. If the parent of the bar mitzvah has remarried, the formal invitation should read:

Mr. and Mrs. David Golden
request the honour of your presence
at the Bar Mitzvah of her son
Marvin Levine
[etc.]

Note that "son" may be replaced by "Mrs. Golden's son," or "his son, Marvin" (no surname, as it is the same as his father's).

Such name problems may also be solved by an informal text reading:

Joan's son, Marvin Levine, will be called to the Torah as a Bar Mitzvah Shabbat morning, May the twenty-sixth, at nine o'clock, at Temple Shalom, 5700 Lakeshore Drive, Chicago, Illinois. Please join us for services and afterward at Kiddush.

Joan and David Golden

Note that the boy uses the surname of his father, but his mother has re-married. One might also write only "Marvin Levine will be called," etc.

Where there are name problems, it is important to have a reply address that indicates to whom a response is to be sent.

When the Mother Is Widowed. A widow properly continues to use her deceased husband's name. A formal invitation would read:

Mrs. Harold Levine
requests the honour of your presence
at the Bar Mitzvah of her son
Alan
[etc.]

However, if she decides to use the informal wording she may sign the note "Belle Levine."

ENCLOSURES

Reception and Dinner Cards. If it is not possible to use one invitation because some guests will be invited to services and a Sabbath *kiddush*, but not to other later parties, enclosure cards will be necessary. These are done on matching smaller cards in the same typeface and may be enclosed in matching envelopes.

When the whole family has been invited to the synagogue service and *kiddush*, but only the adults are asked to a formal evening reception, the envelope of the reception card would be inscribed only with the adults' names.

For a reception at home:

At Home
four to seven o'clock
40 Colt Road
Great Neck, New York

R.s.v.p.

Note that cards with varying hours may be used to invite people at different times during the day. The master guest list must then be divided into categories to keep track of the number of people expected at each function.

For a Sunday celebration:

Dinner
Sunday, the twenty-seventh of May
at five o'clock
Ringwood Country Club
Great Neck, New York

R.s.v.p.
40 Colt Road
Great Neck, New York 11024

If travel directions will be needed, a separate printed card, without envelope, may be enclosed.

Response Cards. Although most conventional etiquette books inveigh against the enclosure of response cards, they are nonetheless widely used, and hence are shown by most stationers, although some still resist making them up. The matter should be considered on practical rather than conventional grounds.

When the guest list is large (over one hundred), the return of response cards provides a very efficient file of acceptances and regrets, and a handy set of cards with which to work out the seating arrangements. For the guest, in these hurried and less formal times, it is also a convenience to have the card and the addressed envelope ready at hand to return.

On the other hand, the cards are expensive to print, and postage rates continue to climb. Such cards are really unnecessary with informal invitations, or when the invitation list is small, and their omission is certainly the most conventionally correct procedure.

The decision as to the inclusion of a response card should be made on these practical grounds. One need not be intimidated by outworn conventions, or the preferences of the stationer (whether for or against the cards).

If they are used, they are made up on matching cards, like the enclosure invitations, with a printed envelope addressed to the host, and with stamps affixed for return.

TELEPHONED INVITATIONS AND RESPONSES

No bar mitzvah can be so informal as to permit a casual, telephoned invitation. A specific time and place are involved and it should be recorded in writing. Moreover, when each person wishes to chat for a few moments, the time spent in telephoning can be inordinate.

By the same token, a telephoned response is burdensome to the hosts. It is a simple courtesy to write a reply. (See Chapter 62 for the form used for a formal acceptance or regret.)

Those invited should respond promptly. It is inexcusable not to reply if one does not intend to attend the function. The courtesy of an invitation demands the courtesy of a response, even if that must be a "regret."

The only exception to the "no telephone" rule is a sudden last-minute change in plans caused by illness or some other unforeseen event. Even in such circumstances, if time permits at all, it is better to write so that some record of the change exists.

44. Synagogue Procedures

THE BAR MITZVAH'S PART

Aliyah: *Torah Reading.* The ritual part of a bar mitzvah occurs during the Torah reading (described in Chapter 14) at the Sabbath, Monday, Thursday, or Rosh Hodesh services. The bar mitzvah is expected to read parts of the week's portion. Usually these are the *maftir* from the last portion in the Torah scrolls, and the *haftarah* or additional portion from Prophets. He also chants the blessings before and after each portion. A boy who is well-versed in Hebrew may undertake to chant the entire Musaf (additional) service.

In traditional services these passages are chanted in the ancient *trop* (cantillation or reading melody). In Reform services the reading is sometimes in English and much abbreviated.

The Speech (Derashah). It is also traditional for the boy to make a speech, in Hebrew at Orthodox bar mitzvahs, in English at others. The content may range from a learned discourse (*derashah*) on the Torah portion read to a simple speech in which the bar mitzvah expresses his gratitude to his parents for their love and care, thanks his teachers for their help and the guests for sharing in his *simha,* and discusses the meaning of his bar mitzvah to him. Most rabbis require the youth to write the speech himself, although there are some congregations which have a set speech, sometimes in the form of a prayer, that all bar mitzvahs deliver without variation.

The speech is made at the conclusion of the Torah reading, before the sermon by the rabbi. The rabbi or the president of the congregation calls the boy up for the presentation of a gift from the congregation. The rabbi sometimes speaks directly to the bar mitzvah and then invokes the Priestly Blessing.

Developing Poise. During this service the young man will be expected to walk from his seat in the congregation to the *bimah* (raised platform), to walk in the Torah procession, to shake hands with the synagogue officials, to be seated on the *bimah* during the remainder of the services, and in some congregations to take part in a formal recessional and receiving line. For shy or retiring individuals this is an ordeal, and practice in meeting people, shaking hands, walking slowly in front of a group, standing, and sitting still are helpful in overcoming awkwardness.

In the last few months preceding the bar mitzvah, the family should make it a practice to attend Sabbath services, if they do not do so regularly, so that they all, and in particular the boy himself, may become familiar with the ritual and become known to the congregants. Being at ease in the synagogue itself does a great deal to lessen the tensions of the day. Regular attendance at junior services, where young people officiate, also helps a boy develop poise.

For a "Sweet Future." In some Orthodox or Hasidic services little bags of sweets (nuts, raisins, and small candies) are distributed among the guests. When the boy finishes his chanting, he is showered with the sweets (taken out of the bags, of course) as an expression of the wish for a sweet and fruitful life. Care should be taken to supervise small children during this pleasant moment, and the actual number of goodies in each bag should be very small, so that there are no problems.

THE PARENTS' PARTICIPATION

The Father. The father of the bar mitzvah is also given an *aliyah,* the third portion (unless he is a *kohen* or *levi;* see Chapter 14). The father is expected only to recite the blessings before and after the Torah reading, which is usually done by an official of the synagogue. In most traditional and Conservative synagogues, he also recites a special blessing as the parent of a bar mitzvah.

Barukh shepetarani (meonsho shelazeh).
Blessed be He who has relieved me (from the responsibility for my son's conduct).

In Reform congregations the Sheheheyanu blessing is substituted, since Reform Judaism rejects the idea that parents are responsible for the transgressions of their children. The full text of this blessing will be found in Chapter 12.

Sephardic congregations do not use the Barukh Shepetarani blessing.

Fathers who have not had an *aliyah* in some years should practice the blessings beforehand. A bar mitzvah often creates a vicarious tension for the father that can lead to an embarrassing blankness of mind at the critical moment.

The Mother. In some synagogues women may be called up, either for the traditional *aliyah* or to read some part of the service in English. This is optional for women. The mother, who is under a great deal of social tension on the day, may prefer not to appear on the platform. On the other hand, she may derive a great deal of satisfaction from the honor. The choice is hers in synagogues that permit women to participate in the Torah service.

HONORS FOR GUESTS

Participation in any part of the Torah reading is an honor. The principal honors are the seven Torah portions themselves (*aliyahs*). These may be divided up to number more than seven if need be; the minimum number of verses for each person is three. The most "honored" *aliyahs* are the third, always reserved for the boy's father, the sixth, and the seventh, *maftir*, always the bar mitzvah's portion. The other honors are described in Chapter 14.

Traditionally, most of these honors go to the bar mitzvah party, although some may be allotted to other congregants who have an occasion meriting any *aliyah*. The division of the passages and the allocation of the honors should be arranged in consultation with the sexton (*shammash*), who is in charge of the order of the services. The list should be written out, containing the Hebrew names of the honorees, and given to the sexton, in traditional synagogues before sundown on Friday.

Those guests who are to receive honors should be told in advance, especially if they are to be given an *aliyah* which requires the recitation of blessings.

A person who is to be honored with a Torah portion is called up to the *bimah* by his Hebrew name and that of his father. The call is "*Ya'amod* [name of person] *ben* [name of his father]" ("Let him rise, [name] son of [name]"). The host should ascertain these names ahead of time; they are sometimes disconcertingly different from the English. It may be hard to recognize in "Aharon ben Nachman" good old Uncle Artie!

The bar mitzvah is called up with a louder and more festive chant, and is granted a special honorific preceding his Hebrew name. His call is

"Ya'amod ha bakhur ha bar mitzvah [name] ben [father's name]." Thus he is given his title for the day: "The young man who is a bar mitzvah."

In Reform congregations the mode of reading is much modified, with considerable variety in practice from community to community. The section read is generally much shorter and members are not called up to recite the blessings. The procession and the elevation of the Torah may be omitted. In some temples the reading is in English.

THE RECESSIONAL AND THE RECEIVING LINE

In most synagogues the rabbi will announce a procedure for leaving the platform, requesting the congregation to remain in their places until he, the cantor, and the bar mitzvah celebrants have reached the rear of the synagogue. They will form a receiving line there, usually in this order: president, rabbi, cantor, bar mitzvah, hostess, host. The members of the congregation will then all have the opportunity to extend congratulations and good wishes.

Conversations should be kept to a minimum to avoid holding up the line. The bar mitzvah should be instructed to pass along correctly the names of those to whom he has been introduced.

A receiving line at other functions planned for the celebration is a most unnecessary formality. More agreeable and less stilted is the practice of having host, hostess, and grandparents circulate among their guests for conversation and felicitations.

45. Appropriate Attire

DRESS FOR SYNAGOGUE SERVICES

Men of the Family. Synagogue dress for the family should approximate that worn for holiday services. The young man, his father, brothers, and grandfathers, should all wear conservative suits, white shirts, and ties. Sports jackets, leisure suits, and blazers are too casual for such a solemn day. Shoes should be conservative in style, well-polished, and should "walk quietly." If the weather is very cold or rainy, a dress topcoat will be needed.

A hat and/or yarmulke will be necessary in traditional congregations. Most young men prefer ornate skullcaps to hats these days.

It is a nice touch to provide festive, colored satin skullcaps for all the male guests at a reception. These may be ordered imprinted inside with the boy's name and the date. A color that complements the floral decorations is usually chosen. White is generally not used, being reserved for High Holiday services, and sometimes for weddings.

Women of the Family. The mother of the bar mitzvah naturally has a desire to dress up for the occasion. She is usually still quite young and glamorous herself. However, she must remember that she is really not on center stage on this day, and is dressing for attendance at religious services.

Good taste decrees a becoming costume, restrained in color and cut, that will permit wearing a hat gracefully, as the head covering is *de rigueur* in traditional synagogues. Gloves are essential too. Although some women wear bits of lace or a bow and flower arrangement in place of a hat, these rarely look as smart as a well-chosen hat.

The best choice is either an ensemble of dress and coat or jacket, or a soft suit. A dress to be worn without a coat or jacket should not be too décolleté and should not be sleeveless. Indeed, long sleeves are usually more graceful and formal than short. There are no specific rules about colors, but many women try to avoid wearing black at joyous occasions. The best choice is a soft, subtle shade of the color one finds most becoming.

Although women have begun to appear at services in pants, these are really too casual for such an important occasion, or else so ornate and "at home" (in lace or flowing jersey, for example) as to be slightly ridiculous.

Makeup and hair styles should be as flattering as possible, but never extreme. Glittering eyeshadow, bizarre nail polish and lipstick colors, and heavy perfumes are out of place, no matter how momentarily chic for other occasions. Mascara should be waterproof—the most stoic mother will shed a few tears on this day.

She should wear her best jewels, but not all at once! As for shoes, comfort is as important as style, for a hostess will find herself standing most of the day. Unless the sanctuary is frigidly air-conditioned, furs should not be worn indoors during the service.

The same principles would govern the attire of the grandmothers.

The sisters of the bár mitzvah should be dressed prettily, but avoid the really outré in style and makeup. Long country-style dresses are charming for young girls. Even for teenagers, pants are really not in the best taste in any synagogue. Unmarried girls need not wear head coverings.

Little children should be dressed in outfits that are comfortable as well as attractive.

In traditional congregations handbags will not be used.

Guests. Guests would follow the same general rules of attire for synagogue attendance, except that they need not dress up quite as much.

In traditional synagogues a head covering will be needed—a hat or yarmulke for all men and boys (even very little ones), and a hat, lace square, or scarf for married women. If in doubt as to the nature of the congregation, it is best to plan for a hat of some kind, as it is always in good taste at services, while arriving bareheaded may sometimes prove to be an embarrassment.

In Orthodox practice, it is forbidden to carry anything on the Sabbath, hence handbags, umbrellas, and briefcases are not permitted in traditional synagogues.

DRESS FOR EVENING
AND SUNDAY FUNCTIONS

Dress for parties given in the evening or on Sundays would follow the general custom for the hour and formality of the occasion and the season of the year. The mother of the bar mitzvah should, even in evening dress, avoid extreme décolletage.

For any reception held after 4:00 P.M. and running into the evening hours one may dress as for a cocktail party. A male guest's choice (if he is married) should be guided by what his wife will be wearing; she, if in doubt, may call the hostess to find out how she and other close relatives will be dressing. (See Chapter 4.)

CORSAGES

Corsages for the women of the family and boutonnieres for the men, while a pretty touch, are really not necessary. Indeed, in some Orthodox circles they may not be worn at all, as it is considered a form of carrying forbidden on the Sabbath. If in doubt as to the practice, it is best to ask the rabbi, and also the women relatives. Some members of the family may be more strictly observant than others.

46. Appropriate Gifts and Thank-You Notes

GIFTS

Any gift suitable for a thirteen-year-old's birthday is appropriate for a bar mitzvah. Sports and hobby equipment, electronic gadgets, records and books, wristwatches, and jewelry are now more popular than the fountain pen of hoary bar mitzvah jokes. You may ask the boy's mother or father what they think he would like, but if you are at a loss, it is well to remember that presents of cash, checks, or savings bonds are always welcome and avoid frustrating duplication of gift items.

Because of the Sabbath carrying rule, one should not bring a gift to the synagogue. In general, if the celebration is held on the Sabbath, it is best to send your gift to the boy's home, just before or after the bar mitzvah. This avoids unseemly carrying of packages or handling money on the Sabbath day, important in all congregations.

You may, of course, bring your gift to an evening or Sunday party, when these restrictions no longer apply.

THANK-YOU NOTES

A bar mitzvah is the occasion for many gifts. It is essential that every gift be acknowledged in writing by the boy himself, even if he has thanked everyone in person at his party. The youngster should be trained to keep card and gift together carefully until notations can be made in the bar mitzvah book.

The youth will need stationery for his thank-you notes and he will enjoy selecting this himself. Informal notes with his name or monogram on the first page may be ordered at the same time as the invitations, or the very attractive art note folders sold by various charities may be used.

Cards with a printed "thank you" are not correct, even (and especially) if embellished with the young man's picture, although photographers sometimes offer them as part of a photo package.

Black ink is always correct, although a color that matches the monogram or decoration may be used, if it is readable; yellow, pale pastels, gold, or silver are very hard to read.

The note may be of the briefest nature, but it must be handwritten and personalized for each recipient. Four sentences will generally suffice. The gift must be specifically mentioned, but if the gift was money the amount should not be stated. The boy might tell how he plans to use the money.

Some Examples of Thank-You Notes. A typical note might read:

125 Parkway
Philadelphia, Pa.
19103
June 1, 1978

Dear Aunt Min and Uncle Sam,

It was very pleasant to see you again at my bar mitzvah. Thank you so much for your generous check. I am planning to use it to build up my record library.

I do appreciate your thoughtfulness, and hope that we will meet again soon, on another happy occasion.

Cordially, [or Affectionately,]
Barry

A note to a person who did not attend:

Dear Cousin Muriel,

My parents and I were so sorry that you could not come to my bar mitzvah because you were ill. We missed you.

Thank you so much for the beautiful leather wallet. I am looking forward to using it.

I do appreciate your thoughtfulness and hope that you will soon feel better. May we meet at happy occasions!

Cordially,
Barry

When to Send Notes. Gifts should be acknowledged promptly, within two weeks of the bar mitzvah. This task can be accomplished with the least difficulty if a few notes are written each day until they are all finished. As each note is written, the date should be entered in the bar mitzvah book. Reluctant correspondents should realize that the pleasantness, the center of the stage, and the wealth of gifts have their price. An hour a day of letter writing is not too much attention to return to all the friends and family who shared in his happy day.

47. *Unusual Bar Mitzvah Celebrations*

THE BAR MITZVAH RETREAT

An outing to a camp or hotel in the country may be planned for a bar mitzvah, where all the guests will spend the Sabbath together, in retreat style, combining services, Jewish study, singing, folk dancing, *oneg Shabbat*, and escape from worldly cares for twenty-four hours, or even a full weekend.

In keeping with the retreat theme, the party and dress are informal, and food is either homemade by friends in advance or catered by the institution, so that all, including the hostess, may devote themselves to the peace of the Sabbath and the joy of the occasion.

BAR MITZVAH IN ISRAEL

Some families, after considering the amount of money that can be spent in one day on a full round of bar mitzvah festivities, decide instead to make a family pilgrimage to Israel, where the bar mitzvah can take place at the Western Wall of the Temple, as it does for many Israeli youngsters. This is a tremendous experience in living Judaism for the whole family.

Jewish organizations such as the American Jewish Congress have special bar mitzvah tours. The typical AJC arrangements schedule bat mitzvahs on Monday or Thursday mornings only; bar mitzvahs may also be on Saturday. The ceremony takes place promptly at 8:00 A.M.

The degree of participation for boys depends on their preparation. Some read the whole Torah portion and the blessings, others recite only the blessings; it is even possible to have the blessings said for the boy.

Girls are limited to a set prayer after the services on the meaning of bat mitzvah, while the father or another male relative is actually called up to the Torah during the service. There may be several services going on at the same time.

Dress is quite informal: women must have their shoulders and arms covered. Head covering is required for men and married women.

Picture taking is not permitted on the Sabbath.

Families planning such a bar mitzvah should consult both the travel agent and their rabbi well in advance of the date.

48. Bat Mitzvah and Confirmation

The Talmud sets the age of religious and physical maturity for girls at twelve years plus one day, but until the nineteenth century there is no record of a formal ceremony to mark this majority or "bat mitzvah."

In recent years the bat mitzvah has become a more and more frequently observed family celebration in Conservative and Reform congregations. Practice varies as to the degree of participation granted to girls, and the age has gradually moved up to thirteen.

SYNAGOGUE ROLES FOR GIRLS

In some Conservative congregations bat mitzvahs are held only at Friday evening services, when the girl reads part of the service and makes a speech. However, other synagogues have gradually begun to do away with the differentiation between bar and bat mitzvah and allow girls who are qualified by their training to have a bat mitzvah at Sabbath services with the same *aliyah* as boys. In those congregations where women are counted in the *minyan* and receive *aliyahs,* the girls, like the boys, don a yarmulke and *tallit.*

The Torah reading procedure is spelled out in detail in Chapter 44. Everything said there about an individual bar mitzvah celebration for boys applies equally to a girl's bat mitzvah.

The girl's father and older brothers, and any guests to be honored, may be called to the Torah and given other honors in the same manner as for a bar mitzvah.

TRAINING

Synagogues make formal education requirements for girls, just as they do for boys. Plans must be made at least two years in advance for enrollment in religious school. The course of study is usually the same for boys and girls.

Some girls who do not wish to undertake the complete course of Hebrew studies may decide instead to attend confirmation classes and take part in a group bat mitzvah or in a confirmation ceremony. The requirements, in each ritual, vary from group to group. There is no formal recognition of bat mitzvah in Orthodox synagogues. A limited bat mitzvah may be held at the Western Wall in Jerusalem. (See Chapter 47, "Bar Mitzvah in Israel.")

BAT MITZVAH CELEBRATIONS

Most bat mitzvah parties are less elaborate than those given for boys. All to the good! Simplicity is always in better taste than ostentation. Although many parents entertain as lavishly as for a boy's bar mitzvah, no family can be faulted if in their planning they also consider the happy prospect of having to provide a beautiful wedding for their daughter only a few years after her bat mitzvah and limit themselves accordingly.

When a bat mitzvah occurs on a Friday evening, the party is generally held immediately after services; *kiddush,* reception, and dinner are often elaborate functions. One may simplify by having a *kiddush* at the synagogue and then a private dinner for family only, or by having only an "at-home" buffet reception after services. (See also *"Minhah* bar mitzvah" in Chapter 40.)

INVITATIONS

Formal invitations, appropriately worded for girls, are the same as those set forth in Chapter 43. A suitable informal text might be:

> We would be honored to have you share with us the joy of the Bat Mitzvah of our daughter Nancy on Friday evening, the eleventh of June at six o'clock at the Redstone Jewish Center, 340 Circle Drive, Tucson, Arizona. Please join us for services and kiddush afterward.
>
> Marion and Arthur Engel
>
> R.s.v.p.
> 28 Canyon Drive
> Tucson, Arizona 85071

Some very pretty informals are shown in pinks and other pastels, with floral decorations. One should avoid the too-frilly, sentimental styles. The girl should be given a voice in the selection; her tastes are probably more austere than those of her parents!

Informal stationery for thank-you notes may be ordered at the same time.

DRESS

Dress for the Girl.   The choice of costume for a young girl is quite wide, dictated by the time of day, season of the year, and above all, by her physical maturity.

A girl should be allowed to wear whatever will make her happy, within certain basic guidelines. The top must have sleeves and a reasonable neckline (including a back!), pants are a most dubious choice, and any ornamentation should be simple and made of materials that will not rattle or clink on the reading platform. White and light pastel colors are the best choices. A long skirt or dress in peasant or country style is always charming and correct; for morning wear it should be of a cotton or linen print, or some other informal fabric. Even for wear at evening services, anything that resembles a child-size formal evening gown is not in good taste for a young girl.

Above all, the girl should feel comfortable and attractive in her outfit, and have tried it on enough times before the day to have gotten used to the difference between her dress and her ubiquitous blue jeans. If she is planning to wear high heels, she should practice walking in them, and be sure they are comfortable, as she will have to stand for long periods of time on the day.

Jewelry of a modest kind may be worn, although if a girl has a charm bracelet that jingles, she would be best advised not to wear it on this day, when she will be using her hands to point to her reading passage and probably to gesture during her speech.

A head covering is not required for young girls, although flowers, especially wreaths, are sometimes worn in the hair.

Dress for the Family.   See Chapter 45 for a detailed discussion of appropriate dress for synagogue and reception.

The girl's mother should be careful to avoid a competitive feeling in her attire. She should not wear the very same color as her daughter, and she should certainly not choose a "mother-daughter" style, since it should not be her aim to look like her daughter's sister on this day. This is the time for the mother to select a costume that emphasizes her sophisticated maturity in an elegant, refined way.

THANK-YOU NOTES

Like her brother bar mitzvah, a girl owes a personal, handwritten thank-you note to each person who has given her a gift. The notes should be sent out within two weeks after the bat mitzvah. (See Chapter 46.)

SEPHARDIC "BAT MITZVAH"

A few Sephardic synagogues, notably the Spanish and Portuguese Synagogues in New York, have begun to accord some recognition to a girl's coming-of-age. On the Sabbath closest to her birthday her father is called up to the Torah, a special blessing is said for the child, and the rabbi addresses a short sermon to her. The girl remains seated in the women's gallery during this honor. After the service, she will make a speech at a festive *kiddush* for family and guests.

This ceremony may also be held during a Sunday morning service, when Orthodox guests may travel from some distance to the synagogue.

Dress for the occasion is the same as for holiday synagogue attendance.

CONFIRMATION AND GROUP BAT MITZVAH

Some Conservative and practically all Reform congregations have a group confirmation ceremony upon completion of the course of study in the religious school. This graduation ceremony is held on Shavuot. The girls conduct a portion of the morning service and sometimes present a choral reading that the class has written and prepared.

Dress. The style of dress for this occasion is usually decided on by the girls as a group. Sometimes white academic robes are worn, and the girls may wear any spring pastel or a white dress underneath. The hemline of the dress should not show below the hem of the gown. Light stockings and white shoes are the only correct footwear with a white robe. Some congregations use floral wreaths as headdresses for the girls.

Family and guests dress as for synagogue attendance.

Appropriate Festivities. The parents of the class sometimes sponsor a synagogue *kiddush* for all the congregants after services. A girl's family might then invite their own guests to a luncheon at home, or have another party on Saturday night or Sunday.

In some communities a disco dance, for the young people only, is given on Saturday night, sometimes in the synagogue rooms. Such a party is a welcome departure from over-elaborate adult formal dances, but careful supervision will be needed, as well as transportation to and from the dance.

On Shavuot it is customary to serve dairy food, especially blintzes. Usually, the strawberry season begins then. A very appealing buffet for an "at home" can be arranged around these traditional foods.

BOYS' AND GROUP CONFIRMATIONS

Some Reform temples have group confirmation for both boys and girls when they complete their religious school training, also held on Shavuot.

Since most temples set attainment of tenth grade in high school as the age level, the participants in this graduation are generally about fifteen or sixteen years old.

In most temples, a group *kiddush* is tendered for the class. In addition, families may give a party afterward. Most families choose an informal reception or luncheon.

Invitation and thank-you procedures are the same as those for an individual bar mitzvah, except that the function would be called "confirmation."

All that has been said about dress and deportment applies to such a party as well, always bearing in mind that the principals are somewhat more mature because they are older.

ENGAGEMENT

My beloved is mine and I am his . . .

—SONG OF SONGS 2:16

49. *Becoming Engaged*

FINDING THE RIGHT MATE

In traditional Jewish literature the idea that marriages are made in Heaven is elaborately detailed. God is portrayed as the great matchmaker. In one Midrash it is told that ever since the seventh day of Creation, God has been busy with matchmaking, a task deemed more difficult than parting the Red Sea.

Forty days before a baby is born, goes another legend, the name of the person who has been ordained by God to be his or her mate is proclaimed in Heaven. This is indeed an arduous labor. Almost as formidable to some is the problem of meeting this divinely ordained "right mate," or *zivuk*, here on earth, once one has grown to marriageable age.

In patriarchal times, Abraham sent his servant Eliezer to find a suitable wife for his son; Isaac ultimately came to love the wife his father's emissary had selected for him. Jacob, on the other hand, chose for himself, and was deceived by his father-in-law. He worked seven additional years for Laban to earn the woman he truly loved, Rachel. Thus an idea of romantic love has been enshrined in Jewish thought from earliest times; in the Song of Songs it finds superb poetic expression.

For centuries, most marriages were arranged by parents, who assumed that if their choices were correct, the children would come to love each other, as did Isaac and Rebekah. The ideal harmonious marriage was regarded as the *shiddukh* (match) of a true *zivuk* (preordained couple).

THE SHADKHAN (MARRIAGE BROKER)

Originally parents arranged these matters through relatives, but by the Middle Ages the *shadkhan* (marriage broker) had become a respected professional, often a rabbi or a scholar. In time, however, the very nature of the transactions caused a decline in the status accorded to the *shadkhan*, for to be successful in matchmaking, one obviously had to be inquisitive, good-natured, meddling, a perpetual gossip, and more or less of an exaggerator.

Despite the current independence of the young, who feel free to choose for themselves, marriage brokers continue to function in the Jewish communities of New York and other large cities to this day, and their services are used by recent immigrants, widows, widowers, and other people who have problems meeting eligible partners, and, secretly, by anxious parents. There is a set fee for the matchmaker's services, outlined in a formal agreement, usually a percentage of the dowry of the bride, although some have a scale of fees for varying types of introductions, plus an honorarium if a wedding comes about as a result.

Most modern young people follow the example of Jacob and seek out mates for themselves (perhaps at today's equivalent of the watering hole!), although all of them have probably had the matchmaking attentions of a friend or relative more than once. To bring a couple together, despite all the jokes that have been made about it, is a great *mitzvah*.

TRADITIONAL BETROTHALS

In the traditional betrothal of old, once an engagement was entered into, the terms were spelled out in a binding contract (*tenaim*) and a formal year of courtship and ceremonious exchange of traditional gifts followed.

Among the Orthodox today, the *tenaim* procedure is still followed in modified form. The concept itself has shaped social attitudes toward courtship and engagement.

The Yiddish colloquial expression *tsayt tsu shraybn tnoyim* refers to having reached a rapprochement in a relationship, sometimes even a business relationship.

MODERN ATTITUDES TOWARD ENGAGEMENTS

Nowadays, an uncommitted, casual courtship period is usual. It is a time for the two to come to know each other well and develop a serious attachment. During this period they might even date other people occasionally. When they are certain that marriage is for them, a formal engagement may begin, to last only a few months before the wedding.

A breakup during courtship, although it is undeniably painful, is not as embarrassing as a broken engagement which, having been publicly announced, must be publicly ended.

EXCLUSIVITY VERSUS
MEETING THE "CROWD"

Couples high in the romantic clouds of early courtship days rarely think of it, but it is difficult, under the artificial conditions set up by meetings in restaurants, theaters, and other places of amusement, to know what a person is really like, and how a shared life would be on a day-to-day basis. One can only judge what living with another person will be like by seeing him or her in his own background and among one's closest friends, involved in real-life activities. For this reason alone, a courting couple would be wise not to spend all their time exclusively together, but also to meet and socialize with each other's friends and family.

MEETING THE FAMILY

Introducing the person you plan to marry to your friends is fairly simple; it is the meeting with parents and other relatives that sometimes seems difficult, especially now that so many single people live away from the family home, at school or in their own apartments. The separation almost rules out, for example, the informal meeting with the girl's parents which used to occur quite naturally when a man called for her.

Eventually, the time will come when each of you will want to introduce this very special person to your parents. If you want to keep it informal and you are a young woman who does not live at home, you might arrange to be called for at your parents' home sometimes, or you might bring your man occasionally to some casual social gathering at which your parents, and possibly other family members, will be present. A man, by the same token, should plan to have his "lady" meet his family on the same informal basis, if they live nearby, before any serious declarations have been made.

When the families live at a considerable distance from their children, weekend visits, once frowned upon by conventional society, have become quite acceptable. An invitation to the family's vacation home for a summer weekend or a winter ski excursion is pleasant and informal.

Although you may hesitate to introduce each other into your circle of family and close friends because this indication of serious intentions may lead to aroused expectations of a wedding (and the ensuing embarrassment should the wedding not materialize), this socializing is really essential in probing the rightness of a relationship beyond the superficial physical attraction.

The desire to make a good impression may make it difficult to be at ease, but good manners, poise, and, above all, spontaneously natural attitudes will help. A false facade of affluence, super-sophistication, or erudition does not deceive people for very long. Such poses may even offend and alienate the very people you hope to impress. This is as true for parents as it is for a young couple.

Telling the Parents.   Whether or not they have met each other's families before, once a man and woman make the decision to marry, the first persons they should inform are their parents. Even though today's emancipated couples may feel they no longer need their parents' permission to marry, they should still seek their approval and their blessing.

A father no longer expects a young man to ask formally for his daughter's hand, but he still does want to meet him for a discussion of his plans for their future. The independent daughter of today often takes part in this discussion, together with her mother, so that they may all consider the couple's prospects realistically.

If a girl's father is not living, the same courtesy is owed to her mother; if she is an orphan, to her guardian.

As soon as possible after they have spoken with the girl's parents, the young man should present his fiancée to his own parents. If it is impossible to arrange a meeting because of the distance, he should write or phone his parents at once, informing them of his intentions, and telling them something about his bride-to-be.

Formal Visits.   The groom's mother is expected to telephone or write a letter to the bride's parents, expressing the family's pleasure at the engagement and welcoming the bride into their midst.

If the two families live near enough to visit, it is then customary for the bride's mother to invite her in-laws-to-be (*mehutonim*) to her home for a friendly informal call, at which the only other people present would be the engaged couple. Preliminary plans for the wedding are usually discussed at this meeting.

Should the groom's mother fail to write or call with the conventional welcome, the bride's mother should not stand on ceremony but take the initiative herself in inviting his family to call.

If the groom's family comes from out of town for the visit, it may be less straining emotionally if they stay at a hotel or with friends, rather than at the home of the bride's family. Her parents may offer to make hotel reservations for them.

This first visit is then formally returned. A young man will no longer be put to a test of talmudical scholarship by his future father-in-law, nor will a young woman be asked to exhibit her skill at needlework by threading a fine needle with the most gossamer of threads, but it is a stressful encounter, nonetheless. Parents may be self-conscious too. Frankness and a cordial, sincere welcome into the family, an expression of pleasure at the happiness of the children, will do much to smooth the meeting.

The importance of social compatibility in the two families is expressed in rabbinical literature, where in discussing the qualities of suitable *mehutonim*, the rabbis remark that they should be people "with whom one can sit down at the table," something we still seek today.

When Distance Is a Problem.   When, as is common today, the families are separated by great distances and the young people live in their own apartments in still another city, this meeting of the two families might take place on a visit to their children. The parents might meet at the girl's residence and then have dinner together at a restaurant as guests of the bride's parents. His parents might return the hospitality at a brunch or tea.

It is not really necessary to match invitation for invitation when distance presents problems; what is important is an open line of communication for the wedding plans and the future living arrangements of the young couple.

STUDENT ENGAGEMENTS VERSUS EARLY MARRIAGE

Early marriage is still much favored in Jewish tradition. Although the bride price and the dowry are things of the past, it is not uncommon for the two families to arrange to contribute to the support of the couple while they complete their education and start their careers. This avoids a long, frustrating engagement and makes the desired early marriage possible. The details should be openly discussed by the parents and the couple, and a realistic plan fully understood and agreed upon by all.

Very often, young women undertake to support the household by working while the husband finishes his studies, so that they can get married earlier. In the past, many a girl has given up her own career to earn only the degree of "P.H.T."—a graduate school acronym for "putting hubby through."

This is no longer so prevalent. Modern couples now take turns going to school and working, or the husband pledges to give the wife her chance when he has graduated. There are, unfortunately, too many instances when these promises are not fulfilled.

A couple undertaking such a plan should be straightforward enough to write out their commitments to each other so that time and life's accidents do not wipe them out of mind. And the women, in particular, should be aware of a legal trend to award financial settlements to the "sacrificing" partner in the event of a divorce. The financial rights of unmarried partners living together in such arrangements have also been recognized in some states.

THE DECORUM OF ENGAGEMENT

By the mere fact of becoming engaged a couple have announced their exclusive interest in each other. Although people expect them to want to be together and to be loving toward each other, an open public display of physical affection is in very poor taste, and, when carried to extremes, offensive to Jewish ideas of modesty and proper behavior between the sexes. There is no need for the engaged to be always kissing, embracing, or fondling before others, and it is embarrassing to the onlookers.

The decision whether to engage in premarital sex after you are engaged is a personal one, and if you decide to do so, you should be discreet about it. A mature person never enjoys the thought that his or her closest personal relationship is the subject of gossip. Moreover, you may offend or hurt your parents, who may be more conservative in their outlook. During the engagement period, you should at least tolerate your family's attitudes, and respect their rules about sleeping arrangements on weekend visits, for example. A defiant, open confrontation seems overdramatic when the wedding is only a few months off.

Before embarking upon a premarital sex life, a young woman should take the precaution of getting proper contraceptive information. She may ultimately need a lawyer as well, should the engagement become a live-together arrangement that later breaks up.

Both parties should be aware that under ancient rabbinic law, open cohabitation with a Jewish person was considered a valid form of marriage. Although the rabbis long ago declared it unacceptable, some may still require a cohabiting couple to secure a religious divorce should they part, before they will officiate at a marriage to another partner (that is, assuming that the first relationship is known).

It is obvious that discretion is the better part, not only of valor, but also of sex!

50. Parties and Showers

ANNOUNCEMENT PARTIES

A big formal party at which an engagement is announced is now rarely given, but some family entertaining at which the grandparents, aunts, uncles, and friends meet the bride and groom is still done, especially when the engagement will be a long one or the wedding will be very small.

If a special engagement party will be given, it is best held at the bride-to-be's home, or at a party in a fine restaurant or private club.

For families with synagogue or temple affiliations, a *kiddush* following a Sabbath morning service is a gracious way to share the happy news and introduce the couple to other family members and the community.

THE FESTIVE ROUND

Everyone, seemingly, wants to honor a couple about to marry. Family dinners and parties given by friends sometimes seem to be a perpetual festive round. It is all very agreeable, naturally, but both bride and groom have so many tiring details to arrange for their wedding and the beginning of their new life together that some discretion in accepting invitations is advisable. Certainly, neither one wants to arrive at the ceremony completely exhausted by all the partying that has already taken place. A good rule might be to avoid any large entertainments during the week before the wedding. The two mothers might spread this word tactfully among the family members, so that the couple will not have to offend a well-meaning relative by declining an invitation.

SHOWERS

Engagement showers are popular in some communities. Although a pleasant custom, they are often much abused.

A shower may not be given by the bride or her immediate family, or the groom's, since it is obviously asking for presents. A proper shower is supposed to be a spontaneous surprise arranged by friends or co-workers. It is usually held about six weeks to a month before the wedding.

People invited should be close friends, relatives, and colleagues of the bride or the groom. Since people receiving an invitation feel obligated to come, and to give a present even if they cannot attend, it is in very poor taste to invite people living at great distances, to send invitations at very short notice, or to make up the list, especially in a place of employment, on a kind of "dragnet" basis that takes in everyone in a department or on a floor without regard to whether or not they know either of the principals well. No one has that many close friends!

Those planning to arrange showers should consult with each other and perhaps join forces in giving a party, for it can be a real hardship to attend three or four showers for the same bride, bringing a gift to each, in addition to a wedding gift.

Showers are often arranged around a theme, such as a kitchen, trousseau, or linen shower with invitations and decorations coordinated to the theme. The party may be a brunch, luncheon, or tea.

Although the members of the immediate family may not give the shower in their names, they may offer their homes or some financial assistance to the person actually arranging the party and also give her a list of family members to invite. The hostess should have a list of items the bride needs or wants, with colors or sizes where pertinent.

One may invite the mothers to a shower, although it is not obligatory. If they are invited, they too should bring some little gift in keeping with the party theme.

In some communities a "greenback shower" or "money tree" party will be given for the bride on the ground that she will then be able to buy larger things she really needs, or that she will be setting up housekeeping in another city and will find it burdensome to transport her gifts there. Not much can be said to excuse this open asking for a money gift before the wedding, except that it is sometimes done.

At most showers, the groom, if he is there at all, makes only a very brief appearance when he comes to pick up his fiancée and escort her home.

The Office Gift. In some offices a small sum is collected from all the bride's (or groom's) co-workers toward a gift certificate or a single large gift, which is then presented by the closest colleagues at an informal lunch gathering or at coffee or cocktails after work during the week. This is a pleasant way for all to honor a colleague about to be married without making the gift or the party burdensome.

Gifts. Shower gifts, while conforming to the shower theme, are generally inexpensive, since all the bride's friends and relatives will be giving her a wedding gift later.

Colleagues invited to a shower might join together to give a single larger gift if they do not expect to be invited to the wedding.

If a person who does not know the bride well is invited, she is under no obligation to attend or to send a gift, although she should, as a courtesy, reply to the invitation.

The gifts are usually hidden in ingenious ways until the bride arrives, as the shower is supposed to be a surprise. The packages are all opened at one time, usually after all have arrived, but before the refreshments are served. The guest of honor expresses her thanks personally for each gift, so thank-you notes are not necessary, except for gifts sent by those who could not attend. A thoughtful hostess will prepare several shopping bags in which to carry all the gifts home.

The honored guest should write a note thanking her hostess for the party.

Showers for Bride and Groom. A growing custom is that of giving a shower to which the groom and the male members of the wedding party (who are so often neglected in the prewedding social round) are also invited. The party is usually held in the evening or on a Sunday, and might be a picnic or a buffet supper. House gifts such as garden tools, closet accessories, photo equipment, or books, records, and tapes—in fact, anything that could be used by either of the two—are appropriate.

OTHER PARTIES

Bridal teas, rehearsal parties, bachelor dinners, and bridesmaids' parties are other popular prewedding festivities. Customs vary with the community. When a large rehearsal party is given (rare in Jewish practice), it is usually hosted by the family of the groom.

Out-of-town guests are sometimes feted by other members of the family at a brunch or lunch before an evening wedding, or, when it is a morning affair, by a buffet supper before their departure in the evening.

It is not necessary to bring a gift to any party but a shower. Any gifts that are received must, of course, be warmly acknowledged by the bride-to-be.

INVITATIONS

For most informal entertaining, phone calls or handwritten notes are proper. Any appropriate informal notepaper may be used. An invitation to a cocktail party might read:

Dear Gertrude and Aaron,

Our Sarah has become engaged to Jonathan Berger. Harry and I would like you to meet him at a cocktail party at our house on Sunday afternoon, March 15, at 5:00 P.M. Do try to join us then.

Cordially,
Evelyn Pincus

Many charming invitation folders can be purchased at stationery shops and are also correct. The ones specially designed for showers are often quite ingenious.

51. *Formally Announcing the Engagement*

ANNOUNCEMENTS TO NEWSPAPERS

Should an engagement be announced in the newspaper? It is not absolutely essential; in fact, many engaged couples prefer to keep the news strictly private, letting friends and family know in a personal, informal way.

If one desires wider publicity, an announcement may be sent to the local newspapers, Anglo-Jewish dailies, Yiddish papers, and local weeklies. If one seeks publication on a specific date, at least three weeks' notice should be given.

The form of the announcement is the same as that for a wedding story, except that the details of the wedding itself are not given. For special name situations and details as to pictures, etc., see Chapter 65 for the section on wedding announcements.

FORMAL ANNOUNCEMENTS

Formal engraved or thermographed announcements are not generally considered correct. However, if the members of a large family live all over the world, as is quite common today, a couple may decide to send out a card instead of undertaking the onerous chore of writing notes to all. The card should be smaller than a wedding invitation and should give the news very simply:

Daniela Blum
Jonas Kornfeld
Engaged   March 1978

Both families may send these out.

52. Courtship and Engagement Gifts

COURTSHIP GIFTS

When a relationship becomes serious, a man generally gives his fiancée-to-be more important gifts on significant occasions, such as her birthday or Hanukkah. A charm bracelet or pendant, or a fine gold watch, in ascending order of importance, are the expected gifts in most circles. Objects of a very personal nature such as lingerie, or expensive accessories such as furs, are in most questionable taste.

A woman should not accept expensive gifts if she has any doubts about her own intentions. If she, too, feels that this engagement is likely to lead to marriage, she may wish to give her fiancé some special gifts in return. A gold watch or cuff links, or a fine briefcase, are popular choices. In Orthodox communities, where people do not carry keys in their pockets on the Sabbath, a gold tieclip made to hold a gold-plated key-blank is a popular gift.

When the engagement is announced, the parents or grandparents may give ceremonial objects (especially family heirlooms) as gifts, such as a Kiddush cup, a lace Sabbath scarf, or a silver cover for a prayerbook or Bible.

THE ENGAGEMENT RING

Must there be an engagement ring? Although to some no engagement seems official without a solitaire sparkling on the ring finger, many a modern bride decides against it. The convention used to be that the ring should be the finest the young man's means permitted, but no sensible young woman would want her fiancé to go into debt to buy her an expensive ring. Many couples, especially those who are still in school, or just starting their careers, decide together that the money would be better used toward the purchase or outfitting of their first home.

A family heirloom ring is often used; the man would have it reset, if that is needed, at his expense. Or a more modest birthstone ring may be selected.

A very beautiful, less formal engagement ring is the "dearest" ring, which is set with tiny stones that spell "dear" or "dearest"—diamond, emerald, amethyst, ruby, and so forth.

Whatever is decided on, the young woman should be consulted. The ring should be chosen with the wedding band in mind, since they will be worn together. Often the two rings are selected at the same time.

An engagement present for a man might also be set with his birthstone.

The engagement ring band is usually too narrow for engraving. The wedding band is engraved, and about one month should be allowed for this before the wedding. A typical inscription contains the pair's initials (groom's first) and the date—"J.K. to D.B. 6/11/79." The groom's ring would be similarly engraved with the bride's initials first—"D.B. to J.K. 6/11/79."

53. *When an Engagement Is Broken*

Although one enters an engagement with the thought of eventually marrying, circumstances sometimes develop that ultimately lead a couple to part. One quarrel need not signal a broken engagement; patience and forebearance are in order. But if differences cannot be reconciled, ending the engagement, although painful and embarrassing, is far better than ending an unhappy marriage with an acrimonious divorce a few years later.

When an engaged couple decides to part, they must, of course, notify their parents at once. They will take steps to cancel any wedding plans that may have been set in motion, including recalling invitations. (See Chapter 63.)

Legally the engagement ring belongs to the girl, but it is considered rather grasping to keep it, and she should at least offer to return it, especially if it is an heirloom. If the young man insists that she keep it, she may continue to wear it, but not on her engagement finger.

She may keep any other gifts she has received from her ex-fiancé, the family, or friends, although she may wish to return them to make her decision final and complete.

If the engagement is broken so close to the wedding date that wedding presents have been sent to her, they should be returned to the senders, with a brief note. No lengthy explanation of the reasons for the break are needed. The note mailed with the gift might read:

Dear Sharon:
  You'll be sorry to hear that Jonas and I have broken our engagement. I'm returning your thoughtful gift with much regret.

                                                      Sincerely,
                                                      Daniela

Friends and family can be told the news in the same concise way. One should not go into lengthy recriminations or repetitive discussions of the breakup.

If a formal announcement has been sent to the newspapers, the family may wish to announce the termination of the engagement, although it is not strictly necessary, and it should not be done in haste, for lovers' quarrels are often patched up. A one-sentence notice will suffice:

> Mr. and Mrs. Norman Blum of Teaneck, N.J.,
> announce that the engagement of their daughter
> Daniela to Mr. Jonas Kornfeld has been broken
> by mutual consent.

54. *On a Woman's New Name*

The name question is one the engaged couple should decide early. Time was when a woman had no questions about what to call herself after she married: convention dictated that she take her husband's name and keep it for the rest of her life, barring a divorce. A divorced woman was saddled with a combination of her "maiden" name and her married name until she married again. And thus Sally Levy, a girl who had struggled until her mid-twenties or thereabouts to become a person in her own right, disappeared, to become Mrs. Morris Schwartz, or Mrs. Levy Schwartz (divorcée), or Mrs. David Klein (a second marriage), always a kind of addendum to the man under whose "protection" she lived.

Many women still follow this system of naming, but the increasing number of working women and the rise of feminist awareness are bringing about a sweeping change. More and more women now retain their own names after they marry and are never known as "Mrs. Morris Schwartz"; others keep their own names only in their professional role and are known as "Mrs. Morris Schwartz" socially.

Another feminist variation is the joint use of a hyphenated name: both use the name Levy-Schwartz, and are known as Mr. and Mrs. Morris Levy-Schwartz. The complications of such a naming system, especially when there are children, make it of dubious practicality.

If a woman has decided to keep her own name after marriage, or the couple decide on a hyphenated name, this fact is included in the newspaper release announcing the wedding. They can advise their friends and relatives informally if there is no newspaper publicity.

THE USE OF MS.

The use of Ms. instead of Mrs. or Miss is widespread and is proving itself a convenient honorific in business correspondence; it is a correct form of address regardless of a woman's marital status, which is basically a private matter. Ms. is used with a woman's given name, as Ms. Sally Schwartz, *never* Ms. Morris Schwartz.

INTRODUCING YOUR HUSBAND WHEN YOU KEEP YOUR MAIDEN NAME

A woman who continues to use her maiden name after her marriage should be especially punctilious about mentioning her husband's full name when she introduces him at a social gathering where people know her and not him. Most people will assume that both have the same surname, and if Dr. Alice Taylor does not introduce her husband, Michael Harris, by his full name, he may be introduced around as Michael Taylor, to everyone's embarrassment.

INTRODUCING LIVE-TOGETHERS

Unmarried live-together arrangements have become more open and accepted, but people are still sometimes embarrassed at introduction time for lack of a convenient noun that expresses the relationship. The word "lover" seems too blatant, and "roommate" too collegiate—especially when the terms concern a parent! Saying "This is my son's friend, Alice," or "I'd like you to meet my mother's friend, Mr. Taylor," seems the simplest, most direct way to handle such encounters. It does not announce the live-together situation, yet it does indicate a more than casual relationship between the two people.

You can hear young people refer to their "man," "woman," "lover," "old man" or "old lady," and so on, but such terms seem too casual and fleeting for social situations formal enough to require introductions. If none of these terms seems adequate and you know one of the two people well, you may ask "How do you want me to introduce Alice [or Mr. Taylor]?"

JOINT SAVINGS ACCOUNTS

Once the engagement is announced and a date for the wedding set, money gifts often start to arrive, sent to the bride-to-be. It is convenient to open a joint savings account with the title "Daniela Blum and/or Jonas Kornfeld," in which these gift checks may be deposited. If the woman decides to retain her maiden name, this can continue to be their savings account after they are married. If not, the changeover to a "Mr. and Mrs." account is quite simple after the marriage.

55. Just Before the Wedding

MIKVEH AND SECLUSION OF THE BRIDE

Traditional brides go to the *mikveh*, the ritual bath, for the first time a few days before the wedding, to observe the ritual purification required of all married women after their menstrual periods. After the visit to the *mikveh*, the bride does not see the bridegroom again until the wedding. (See Chapter 2.)

Among Sephardim, the bride is accompanied to the bath by her friends, and a small party (for women only) is held at her home afterward, to celebrate her approaching nuptials.

Practically all Jewish brides, whether or not they go to the *mikveh*, observe this custom from seclusion of the groom, for a period varying from one day to a full week. Who knows how many potential quarrels and broken engagements resulting from prewedding jitters have been averted by this custom?

OYFRUF

The wedding celebration actually begins in synagogue on the Sabbath before the wedding, when the bridegroom is called up to the Torah (*oyfruf*), among the Orthodox, amid showers of raisins, almonds, and sweets.

It is customary for the groom's family to tender a special *kiddush* after the services. The bride and her family usually attend, although, among some traditionalists the bride herself does not, because of the custom of seclusion.

When the wedding will take place in a city far from the groom's home and it has not been possible for his family to entertain the bride's people before the day, the *oyfruf* is sometimes held in the synagogue with which the bride's family is affiliated, and this Sabbath becomes an occasion at which the groom's parents are able to fete their new relatives-to-be.

In some communities, the bridegroom may also be called up to the Torah on the Sabbath after his wedding.

WEDDINGS

Kol sasson v'kol simha . . . [May there soon be heard] the voice of rejoicing and the voice of gladness.

What occasion in Jewish life is more joyous than a wedding? How we rejoice that two who were separate and alone will now be one and together! The wedding embodies all our dreams of romantic love in a future-oriented event. We recognize that it is probably the most significant single life change a man and a woman can embark upon together. Even more, we feel, deep in our Jewish bones, that it is the fulfillment of a highly desirable goal.

56. *The Judaic Concept of Marriage*

Marriage is the ideal state, the sages teach us, and was ordained at the moment of Creation. It is a holy act in itself, since it results in the creation of life.

Judaism sees as the purpose of marriage not only the continuance of society, but also the enjoyment of true companionship. It is so perfect and desirable that the relationship between God and the People of Israel is often referred to as a marriage, the Sabbath or the Torah as a bride.

Celibacy is regarded as unnatural and undesirable; sexual desire (within marriage) is neither evil nor shameful, but a natural part of life, meant to be enjoyed.

Because it is a contract which can be dissolved through divorce, marriage is not considered a sacrament in the Christian sense, but a sacred relationship of the highest order—*kiddushin,* or "sanctification." The marriage ceremony surrounds the legal formula of the contract with benedictions that invoke the blessing and sanction of God.

The rationale of the traditional wedding ceremony involves not the concept of "giving away" a bride, but of bringing the partners together under the bridal canopy [*huppah*]. The very words of the blessing used when their child is named include as a goal for parents leading the boy or girl to the *huppah* as a joyous bride or groom.

Helping the couple to rejoice on their wedding day is one of the most important of *mitzvot*, and Jewish weddings from the earliest time on have been celebrated with ornate dress, feasting, music, dancing, jesting, even with juggling, in celebration of the founding of a new home and a joint life—"the building of joy." Assisting in arranging a match or a wedding is a blessed good deed, especially if the bride or the groom is an orphan and bereft of the care of parents.

Even in biblical times the groom and the bride were regarded as king and queen on their wedding day: all of their wishes were granted to give them joy; they wore crowns as part of their costume, were seated on thronelike chairs at the reception, and were raised aloft on the chairs as part of the joyful dancing.

Tradition has it that on their wedding day all the past sins of the bride and groom are forgiven, and among the Orthodox the day takes on some of the characteristics of a minor Yom Kippur. The bride and groom fast before the wedding, the bride dressed in holyday white as a symbol of spiritual purity, and the groom dons a white *kittel* (the ceremonial gown worn on Yom Kippur) for the *huppah*. In order to prolong the fast through as much of the day as possible, it became the custom among the Orthodox to be married in the late afternoon.

So paramount is the joy of a wedding that no other festivity is permitted to encroach on it. Many communities still observe seven days of feasting after the wedding ceremony. (See Chapter 70 on *Sheva Brokhes*.)

The outward trappings of a Jewish wedding may differ in different parts of the world and at different periods in history, but the essence of the wedding celebration resides in these attitudes underlying the basic rituals and legal formulas. The overlay of local custom is often regarded by the uninformed as an essential rite in itself, and thus, the trivial, the ostentatious, or the borrowed non-Jewish rite are often confused with the fundamental Judaic elements of the marriage service.

57. Planning the Wedding

PREPARATIONS FOR THE WEDDING

Although the joy of the wedding day seems to pour forth spontaneously, such occasions do not happen without a good deal of long-range planning. The more formal the wedding, the further ahead must preparations be made.

Although the final choice of type, time, and place of the wedding is customarily exclusively the bride's domain, most young couples make the basic decision together as to the kind of wedding they desire, sometimes even before they consult with their parents. They and their families may agree that no celebration is too much for this gala day; on the other hand, a full-scale formal wedding may seem to be more of an ordeal than either one of the partners can endure.

Good judgment and restraint must rule in deciding how much may sensibly be spent on one night's feasting. A thoughtful girl will take her parents' finances into consideration when making her plans. With imagination and taste in planning, a huge expense is not necessary.

No family should go into debt to provide a wedding far beyond their usual scale of living; to do so is the ultimate in ostentation and bad form. Moreover, one is not required to have a large, showy wedding merely because the family is well-off and can afford it. A young couple who truly desire a small informal wedding should not be pressured into a complicated "showpiece" to gratify their parents' desire for opulent display. To calculate that the gifts to the couple will recoup the outlay on the wedding, as, regrettably, some families do, is utterly vulgar.

The best place for a meaningful wedding is either the bride's home (or the home of a close friend or relative) if an intimate informal wedding is desired, or the sanctuary of a synagogue or temple for a formal wedding. If the party is small, the ceremony can be held in the small chapel of a large synagogue.

When the number of guests is more than the synagogue caterers can accommodate, or if there is no caterer, the family may decide on a hotel or club for the wedding. They should not overlook the possibility of combining a synagogue ceremony with a hotel reception, thus blending religious significance with lavish rejoicing. If they choose a hotel or club for both the ceremony and the reception, the rabbi of their synagogue should be asked to officiate, if he will.

In deciding on the type of wedding they desire, the family should bear in mind that the amount spent on invitations, music, flowers, wedding clothes, and food and drink increases almost geometrically with the size, time, and formality of the affair. All of these factors should be carefully weighed on the basis of firm estimates. The total difference in cost between an informal cocktail or luncheon buffet and a formal seated banquet can be considerable. What will make the wedding truly memorable is not the amount of money spent on it, but the depth of sincere feeling that marks every step of the ritual and the rejoicing.

SETTING A DATE

Once the type of wedding has been decided on, the first step in realizing the wedding plans is to choose a date when weddings are permitted in Jewish law. This should be done at least three months ahead of time, if any degree of formality is desired, as caterers, stationers, and florists require considerable advance notice. At certain popular times of the year (June, long holiday weekends, school vacation periods, and the like) it may be difficult to reserve one's first choice of date and place, and an alternate possibility should be kept in mind.

Days When Weddings May Not Be Held. Weddings may not be performed on the Sabbath, on the major holidays (Rosh Hashanah, Yom Kippur, Passover, Shavuot, and Sukkot), or on Tishah b'Av, in all three branches of Judaism. All these days begin and end at sundown.

In addition, Orthodox and Conservative practice does not permit weddings during the three weeks between the seventeenth of Tammuz and the ninth of Av (generally falling during July and/or August), and during the *sefirah* period between Passover and Shavuot, with the exception of Lag b'Omer (generally this period covers seven weeks of April and May). The reason is that these are regarded as periods of national mourning.

These two forbidden periods are not observed in Reform congregations. Among Sephardim, marriages may be held after Passover, starting the day after Lag b'Omer. In Israel, Lag b'Omer is a very festive holiday and, therefore, a popular day for weddings.

Siyyum Days. *Siyyum* days (on which fasting is not permitted) may be selected: a Rosh Hodesh day or one of the minor historic holidays, such as Hanukkah or Purim, for example. Such dates eliminate the traditionally prescribed prenuptial fast.

Wedding Dates and Mourning. A wedding may not be scheduled to take place during the time that either partner is observing the thirty days of mourning for a brother or sister, or the one year of mourning for a parent. In Reform congregations only the thirty-day rule is followed when mourning parents.

Some exceptions to the one-year rule may be allowed in Orthodox practice, but each case must be decided in conference with a rabbi.

According to custom, a wedding may not be postponed after the date is set, even if a death in the family occurs, because nothing is permitted to interfere with this highest of *mitzvot*. A wedding takes precedence over all other celebrations and may even interrupt the mourning period. The wedding is held as planned, but the festivities, particularly the music, are curtailed.

DOUBLE WEDDINGS

In traditional practice, one *simha* or happy occasion must not be merged with another, and so double weddings are not usually held. By extension, there is a reaction against the sentimental custom of selecting a birthday or a parent's anniversary as the date for the wedding. The rejoicing for each occasion is to be savored separately, so as to make the most of each happy moment in life.

SELECTING THE TIME OF THE WEDDING

Once a date has been set, there is still a choice of times for a wedding that has a direct bearing on both the cost and the formality of the occasion.

The most formal time for a wedding in the Jewish tradition is Saturday night. It is usually also the most expensive; since it is a much desired time, caterers naturally tend to prefer very large parties and to press for their most sumptuous package, complete with white-gloved wine waiters and Viennese table dessert service at the close of the evening.

Because sunset is so late in the spring and summer, many synagogues discourage Saturday evening weddings at that time of the year. The ceremony cannot be held until about one hour after sundown, and thus the music and dancing may run on until very late at night, with resultant overtime fees for musicians and catering staff.

Weddings are sometimes held on weekday evenings, when they may begin at about six o'clock and end at a reasonable hour. Tuesday is particularly favored by traditionalists, because on that day of Creation God twice said, "It is good." A weekday evening reception is usually less elaborate.

Sunday afternoon, starting at four or four-thirty, is considered to be the most fashionable hour, formal, but less pretentious than an evening wedding. Sunday noon has the appeal of potential simplicity and of maximum convenience for guests and wedding party.

Both of these Sunday hours are good choices for a home wedding, since the reception may be a less elaborate buffet and a seated, served meal is not *de rigueur*.

CONFERRING WITH THE RABBI

It is important to confer with the rabbi as soon as the date and location have been tentatively decided on. Usually the place chosen is the synagogue or temple with which the bride's family is affiliated.

The rabbi will give religious sanction to the marriage, ascertain whether the chosen date is acceptable, and indicate whether he is willing to officiate at a hotel, club, or caterer's hall, if that is the place that has been selected.

Some rabbis will perform marriages only in their own synagogues or in private homes. To cope with this problem, many large catering establishments provide a marriage chapel and an officiant (who is not necessarily a rabbi, although qualified to perform marriages).

Shortly before the wedding, the rabbi or the caterer's officiant will require from the bride and groom the information necessary to complete both the secular marriage certificate and the *ketubbah* (Jewish marriage contract). This will include their Hebrew names and the Hebrew names of their parents.

INVITING YOUR OWN RABBI OR CANTOR

Sometimes a couple wishes to invite a rabbi or cantor who is a friend to officiate at the synagogue or chapel. The tactful way to handle this is to suggest dividing the parts of the marriage ceremony with the resident rabbi or cantor. By assigning them some part in the proceedings you can avoid offending them, yet reserve the major part of the service for the officiants you prefer. This should be settled (preferably by the clergymen themselves) at the preliminary planning stage to avoid embarrassing discords just before the wedding takes place.

PROBLEMS ARISING FROM DIVORCE

If either partner was previously married and divorced, an Orthodox or Conservative rabbi will ask to seek the Hebrew *get* (bill of divorcement). Reform rabbis accept the civil divorce decree as the equivalent of a *get*.

If the previously divorced partner did not secure a religious decree at the time of the divorce, it may be necessary to go through certain formalities before an Orthodox or Conservative rabbi will consent to perform the wedding ceremony. Divorced persons should allow sufficient time for this procedure in making plans for a religious wedding, unless it is to be held in a Reform temple. (See Chapter 78.)

PROBLEMS ARISING FROM DIFFERENCE OF RELIGION

Most rabbis will not perform the ceremony when one partner is not Jewish (a mixed marriage). Some Conservative and all Reform rabbis will officiate if the non-Jewish partner undergoes conversion before the wedding. This may take several months of preparation.

If the non-Jewish partner does not wish to convert but a religious ceremony is desired, it will be necessary to find a clergyman who will officiate at a mixed marriage, or participate in an ecumenical service. This is not always easy; a survey in 1978, for example, discovered only 157 Reform rabbis (of 1268) who said they had performed mixed marriages, with another 300 willing to do so, if certain conditions were met by the couple.

Should the religious solution to these problems seem too onerous to the bride and groom, they may forego a religious ceremony and have a civil marriage performed by a judge or justice of the peace, either at a hotel or club, if a large wedding is planned, or at home or in the judge's chambers for a private ceremony. A large reception may be held after the ceremony for friends and other family members.

ELOPEMENTS

There are times when a couple, overwhelmed by the intricacies of planning a full-scale wedding, or simply desiring to do away with what they regard as needless rigamarole, go off by themselves to be married at the City Hall or by a local justice of the peace, presenting their parents with a *fait accompli.* When both are Jewish, the parents, if they are at all observant, may insist on a religious ceremony, regardless of the fact that the civil ceremony has already been performed.

Parents who raise objections and insist on a *huppah* are not being conventional or stuffy; according to religious law, a civil marriage between Jewish persons is not valid without the religious ceremony. The parents are motivated by a religious conviction, which can be very strong even in people who are ordinarily not very observant. The graceful and properly respectful course for the young couple is to go through the religious ceremony with a good heart, making their parents completely happy on this eventful passage in all their lives.

If getting married is good, affirming it once more under the *huppah* cannot be bad! The bride and groom may be happier about it if they remind themselves that in some countries the two ceremonies are separated by law, and personages as great as Napoleon, or as fashionable as Princess Caroline of Monaco, have had two wedding rituals separated by a day or more in time.

A reception may be held after the *huppah*, if all agree. It need not be elaborate, but some rejoicing is called for. (See Chapter 60, "Delayed Receptions.")

CAN THERE BE A RELIGIOUS WEDDING WITHOUT A CIVIL CEREMONY?

The legal answer is no. Some couples, especially elderly pairs who do not wish to marry for estate or financial reasons, feel uneasy about living together without at least a religious ceremony. They sometimes ask a rabbi to perform a religious ceremony without going through the legal formalities and registration of a civil marriage.

In most states it is illegal for a rabbi to perform such a ceremony, as he is required by law to observe the civil statutes governing marriage.

THE LEGAL FORMALITIES

Every state has its own legal requirements for the issuance of a marriage license, which must be presented to the rabbi before the religious ceremony begins. Inquiry at the county clerk's office or a check with the almanac will clarify these requirements and the time sequence that must be followed to fulfill them. Usually the bride and groom must make application for a marriage license together.

Very young couples would be wise to obtain their birth certificates and have them available when they apply for the license to avoid a panicky embarrassment as to proof of age.

DEALING WITH THE CATERER

If the wedding will be too large to be held at home, and a synagogue or temple is to be used, with a catered reception afterward, a careful preliminary conference with the caterer is indicated.

Most traditional synagogues require that one use their official caterer in order to safeguard the *kashrut* of the facility. The family should have decided on some budget limit before meeting with the caterer and go over the possibilities available to them in that budget range. At this point, it is important to keep firmly in mind what is essential to a gracious celebration, what is lavishly festive but perhaps not necessary, and what is purely ostentatious and in poor taste.

The Basics.   The basic ingredients of the celebration are wine (champagne, if possible) to toast the couple, a festive meal for the guests, and music for dancing and general rejoicing.

Pleasant additions are flowers for the pulpit, centerpieces for the tables, colored satin yarmulkes, and a decorated wedding cake. Elaborate floral decorations, exotic, out-of-season dishes, lavish dessert service, favors for the guests, and so on are not really necessary. The family should select only those services they feel they want and can afford and reject any embellishments beyond that.

Preceremony Cocktail Reception.   In many synagogues and temples the rabbis have done away with the once-mandatory preceremony cocktail reception, and rightly so. Too often, after such a reception, the guests assembled in the sanctuary in a condition hardly suited to a highly serious religious occasion. Caterers with their own private chapels still offer this reception, but it is in dubious taste, besides being an unnecessary expense.

Ceremony Practices to Be Avoided.   If the wedding will not be held in a synagogue or temple, where the religious ceremonial will be carefully observed, the couple should ask for detailed information as to how the ceremony will be conducted. Some caterers go to great (and often ridiculous) lengths to produce a theatrical wedding procession. A study of the traditional usage, as described in Chapters 68 and 69, will discover many uniquely Jewish customs that enhance a wedding and make it memorable without turning it into a musical comedy spectacular.

Making an Informed Decision.   In deciding on a caterer, it is perfectly proper, and makes good sense, to ask the banquet manager whether you may observe the completed preparations for a reception just before the wedding takes place. You would not, of course, actually attend any reception tendered by others.

Rooms in a restaurant should be checked for the privacy they afford the party. If there will be more than one function held in a catering hall, the privacy element also becomes important.

Two great helps in selecting a caterer are the recommendations of friends and one's own recollections of having been a guest at such functions.

The cost of a large wedding can run into many thousands of dollars, even when done with simplicity, and, setting starry-eyed sentiment aside, the parents and the bride should be most practical in shopping for what may well turn out to be one of the largest single purchases they will make, aside from a house to live in. They should receive from the caterer a written itemized estimate, indicating the charges for each category, so that they will be able to make an informed decision as to the services they select, and will later be able to check the bill knowledgeably.

A good caterer will provide a dignified, festive reception in which every detail is taken care of almost invisibly. After selecting a menu and a color scheme and giving the caterer the seating plan, the bride and her family need have no other concerns of hospitality, certain that the function will run off smoothly and elegantly as planned. As one bride's mother remarked, "It's a wonderful, plushy feeling!"

KOSHER FOOD AND WINE

When the reception and dinner will be held outside the synagogue, some more traditional rabbis may refuse to officiate at the synagogue ceremony unless they are certain that the food to be served elsewhere later will be kosher. Most will refuse to officiate outside the synagogue if the reception and dinner will not be kosher.

Champagne and all other wines served at Orthodox kosher collations must be kosher, that is, bottled under rabbinical supervision, although there is no restriction on liquor. Conservative practice now permits the use of nonkosher wines. Reform groups have always allowed the use of any wines the party chooses.

CHANGING THE WEDDING RITUAL

Getting married is one of the most important and meaningful steps in a person's life. A young couple enters the world of maturity by marrying, and in their choice of wedding they signify their group affiliations and their attitudes.

In certain circles it has become chic to rewrite the wedding service, to hold the wedding ceremony at some unconventional hour (dawn, for instance), or in some unusual place such as a mountaintop or a deserted seashore, and to dispense with certain rituals as "enslaving" or "male chauvinist." The demand for change often causes family friction and heartache, but is defended by its proponents as "liberating" or "more meaningful."

Poetry and readings from other exotic religions are often interpolated;

each participant may be asked to read an original passage, or odd bits of ritual from other faiths may be added.

At the extreme radical fringe are those who would do without formal marriage of any kind and attempt to set up a "wedding in the eyes of God." Such ceremonies are often of questionable validity if no legally authorized officiant is present.

With rare exceptions, no rabbi will allow any substantive changes in the ritual and the legal formula of marriage, which has been painstakingly developed over the years to provide the maximum legal protection for both husband and wife. The purpose of the ceremony is, first, to make crystal-clear the rights and obligations of both parties to the contract, and then to sanctify the relationship with the blessings. This holy bond joins both functions in the most dignified, impressive, and beautiful manner.

Some rabbis will allow the addition of personal readings after the ring ceremony, or as a supplement to the wedding blessings. The readings should be carefully chosen to avoid the banal or the over-sentimental. (See Chapter 68.)

Affirmatively proud Jewish men and women have no need to abandon the traditions of centuries. When they think through their objections to a conventional wedding, they often find that what they are fighting hardest is not Jewish tradition, but the accretion of caterer's useless and expensive embellishments that have turned weddings into extravaganzas. Study leading to a full understanding of the traditional text of the wedding service will quickly reveal its profundity of thought and its high poetry when properly rendered in English.

For thousands of years, in countries all over the world, Jewish men and women have pledged their loves and lives to each other with the same formula under the *huppah*. A bride and groom who seek deep meaning and true feeling on their wedding day may find it in the thought that their vows reach back through the centuries in an unbroken chain to Isaac and Rebekah.

A HUPPAH *UNDER THE OPEN SKY*

In the European tradition, the ceremony was actually held outdoors in the evening, so that the stars would be visible, a reminder of God's promise to Abraham to make his descendants "as numerous as the stars of heaven" (Genesis 22:17).

Hasidim still follow this practice strictly, either using a caterer's hall that has a special skylight in the ceiling area over the *huppah*, or the terrace of the penthouse suite of a hotel, the inner courtyard of the synagogue of their *rebbe* (spiritual leader), or in some neighborhoods, particularly in New York

City, arranging to have a street closed to traffic during the time the cere-mony takes place there (usually outside the reception hall).

A modern variant of this custom is the garden wedding. An imaginative and resourceful couple might even be able to secure the permissions neces-sary to have their *huppah* in a lovely park, arboretum, or botanical garden. They might also consider using the grounds of the synagogue, if these are appropriate, instead of the sanctuary, or the grounds of a country hotel, in-stead of the ballroom.

Garden weddings are usually held at noon or early in the afternoon, al-though on long summer days a very beautiful effect may be obtained by holding the ceremony at dusk and taking advantage of the long twilight and sunset hours to enhance a candlelit party.

Garden receptions can run the gamut from a charmingly simple informal country style to a formal buffet under a tent for a large group of guests, complete with ornate flowers, a portable dance floor, and an orchestra.

Whichever scale is chosen, the originality and beauty of such a wedding cannot be surpassed, provided, always, that the weather cooperates.

ELEGANT SIMPLICITY

Given a choice between spending a small fortune on a spectacular wedding or using a generous money gift for the furnishing of their first home, many a young couple would opt for simplicity. The "do-it-yourself" wedding, held in a home, the hospitality suite of a fine hotel, or the social rooms of a syna-gogue that does not require the use of a caterer is becoming more and more popular, especially in the face of soaring caterer's and florist's charges.

In such a setting it is possible to cut costs, without sacrificing true ele-gance, by limiting the guest list to the people who really know and care about the bride and groom, and by using a party cook or a combination of purchased prepared food and homemade delicacies. A seated, served meal is unnecessary, although some small tables for dining may be set up if the space permits. (See Chapter 6, "Buffet Service.")

Instead of a shower, today's young brides and their friends sometimes hold a "cook-in," at which they bake and prepare food well in advance and freeze it all for the reception. Those with gardens may contribute flowers and greenery for decoration. This is a devoted gift of time and self, a true expression of the *mitzvah* of causing the bride and groom to rejoice.

For the reception itself, money is well spent on extra professional help to serve and clean up afterward, on one superlative centerpiece for the buffet table, on many candles and candelabra, and on the finest dishes, linen, glassware, and silver (which can be rented for the day).

Instead of purchasing costly custom-made wedding finery that is usually worn only once, or renting expensive outfits, the bride and her friends might well make their own less opulent dresses or select eminently wearable ensembles from today's range of dressy but informal clothes, freeing the men also to dress according to their fancy. Money spent on the very best clothing that can be made or bought in this category is well spent, because the fine attire will be worn many times after the wedding. (See Chapter 67, "What to Wear.")

Music can be provided with records and a good sound system, also rentable. Friends may be asked to bring their instruments and play. There is a world of classical selections available on records for the ceremony, and for reception background music. Later on, if there is room for dancing, disco music can be used.

The finest foods and wines can be served, and still such a wedding will cost only hundreds, not the many thousands of dollars that large elaborate weddings run to nowadays. The occasion will have a warm charm, good feeling, and originality that no ornate, packaged opulence can provide.

58. Paying the Expenses of the Wedding

SHARING THE COST

Traditionally, most of the cost of the wedding has been the responsibility of the bride's parents. However, the two families may decide to share the wedding costs when the guest list is very large, and particularly if the groom's list is much longer than the bride's. The matter may be brought up by either family when the wedding plans are first discussed and lists are being made up.

When the bride's family pays for the wedding expenses, the decision is theirs as to the sum they will spend on the wedding and the type of reception planned. The groom's parents may not demand a certain style of hospitality, and even offering to share the cost must be done tactfully, to avoid implying that one family is not sufficiently generous, or is not able financially to meet the standard of living of the other.

The groom's family may offer to assume the costs of some specific items. A gracious way to handle this would be to offer a gift of the flowers or the champagne and liquor.

When a caterer has given an all-inclusive estimate on a per-person basis, the families sometimes share by deciding how many guests each will pay for. When the bride's family pays for the wedding, they have the final decision on the size of the guest list.

A financially independent bride and groom may pay for their wedding themselves, sharing the expenses, if the cost would be difficult for the bride's family to assume, or if her parents are deceased.

WHAT THE BRIDE PAYS FOR

In the customary division of the wedding expenses, the bride and her family are responsible for the following:

Invitations and announcements (if used) and the addressing and
  postage for mailing them
Rental fee for the place where the ceremony and reception will be
  held and all incidentals, such as chairs and all other rented items
Synagogue fees for sexton, organist, choir, and other music for the
  wedding ceremony
Floral decorations for the ceremony and the reception
Bride's and bridesmaids' bouquets and corsages for mother and
  grandmother, and father's boutonniere (but see note on Flowers in
  this chapter)
Transportation of the bridal party by limousine from home to
  synagogue and synagogue to reception (if necessary)
Gratuities for special-duty traffic policemen, if needed, and for parking
  attendants
The bridal gown
The bride's trousseau
Gifts to bridesmaids
Hotel bills for out-of-town bridesmaids who cannot be accommodated
  at the house or with relatives
All the expenses of the reception, including gratuities for checkroom
  attendants
Bridal photographs (see "Wedding Pictures" in this chapter)
Groom's wedding ring (if used)
Bride's gift to the groom
A substantial wedding gift from her parents
Fees for bridal consultant and social secretary, if used
Gift to synagogue or charity in honor of the couple

WHAT THE GROOM PAYS FOR

Once they have signed the marriage contract, the groom is responsible for all the bride's expenses. First among these would be transportation from the place of the wedding to the locale of the honeymoon, or to their new home. Other traditional wedding expenses of the groom are:

The engagement and wedding rings

Fee for the marriage license

The rabbi's fee

Flowers for his mother and grandmother, boutonnieres for himself, his father, and the ushers (See note on Flowers in this chapter)

Gifts for the ushers

Hotel bills for best man and ushers if they are from out of town and cannot be put up with friends or relatives

A wedding gift for the bride, usually a piece of jewelry to treasure

His own wedding outfit

A substantial wedding gift from his parents

The cost of the wedding trip (if not a gift)

Gift to synagogue or charity in honor of the couple

The home into which they will move and most of its major furnishings

FEES FOR RABBI AND CANTOR

Some synagogues, and also those caterers who provide their own wedding officiants, have a set all-inclusive fee for the use of the chapel and the services of rabbi and cantor. (This fee sometimes goes directly to the synagogue; if the rabbi is a friend or relative, it would be gracious to give him a present in addition.)

When there is no such set fee, the groom must decide what honorarium to present. If one is uncertain how much to give and feels it may embarrass the rabbi if he is asked, one may consult a member of the synagogue staff, the secretary perhaps, or the sexton.

The fees, in envelopes, may be given to the rabbi and cantor privately after the ceremony, or mailed to them with a note of thanks. Such a note should also be enclosed with any gift being given to a rabbi or cantor who is a personal friend.

When a rabbi is invited from out of town to officiate, his travel expenses and hotel bill are paid by the family that invited him.

PARENTS' GIFTS

Traditionally, Jewish parents make a handsome wedding gift to their children to help them start their household or their professional careers. The gifts should, naturally, be relative to their means and may be discussed between the two families, but the utmost tact is required to avoid quarrels and invidious comparisons.

The bride's family may rightfully consider the cost of the wedding itself as their major gift and make a smaller additional present. The groom and his family should take this into consideration. Family attitudes vary. Some do not discuss the gift, preferring to surprise their children on the wedding day. On the other hand, when the gift is a major sum, one that they may count on toward the down payment on a house, major furnishings, or the purchase of a car, it is more thoughtful to discuss it in advance, so that the couple know exactly what their expectations are. When the cost of outfitting professional offices is involved, a major family conclave is in order. Above all, each member of the family must avoid seeming to make a demand or belittling another's gift. The underlying assumption should always be that the parents are doing their best for their children.

A NOTE ON FLOWERS

The extent to which flowers are used and the division of the cost varies in different communities. It used to be customary for the bride to assume the cost of bouquets and corsages for her attendants and herself, and the groom for his party, as noted above. However, most grooms now send at least the bridal bouquet as their gift to their brides, and some assume the entire cost of the flowers, apart from the reception and ceremony decorations, as their share of the expenses.

Floral Decorations. Lavish floral decorations, such as a floral *huppah*, or flower- and greenery-garlanded aisles and reception rooms, are very beautiful and in the hands of a good florist can transform any room into a verdant bower, complete with orchid-bedecked waterfalls and splashing fountains. The bride who desires an unforgettable wedding ceremony may decide to lavish money on this ephemeral loveliness. But even flowers can be overdone; very often the flowers turn out to be one of the most costly elements in the wedding plan. One should not exceed one's budget for this effect merely because the florist or caterer urges it.

Some synagogues do not permit a floral canopy, and have a very handsome embroidered or brocade *huppah* of their own. This should be carefully checked when planning the decorations.

In an ornate synagogue or temple one or two large bouquets for the reader's platform, and possibly a garland for the canopy, are sufficient, especially if candles are used as described in Chapter 69, "Candlelit Processions." Similarly, a pleasant reception room is tastefully enhanced by floral centerpieces and candles on the buffet and bridal tables, with simple flower-decorated candles needed for each dinner table only if the room is very large.

Plastic flowers and greenery should never be used.

Color Schemes.   The maximum decorative effect will be achieved if a color scheme coordinated with the dresses of the bridal party is used for all the flowers, the tablecloths, and the skullcaps for the men (if used). Colors that are appropriate to the season, such as autumn reds and golds, or spring pastels, are always effective. Good taste would decree that one not use the traditional Christmas colors (green and red together) or the Easter color (lavender), and their flowers, the poinsettia or the Easter lily.

White, to seem truly bridal, should appear only in the bride's bouquet, gown, and veil, although one sometimes will see an all-white wedding.

Giving the Floral Decorations Away.   Some brides donate all the flowers used for decoration at the wedding to a hospital or home for the aged, a very pleasant form of the charity that should be part of every *simha*. Alternatively, they may arrange with the caterer to put some marker (a star on the chair, or a note under the plate or the like) at random at one place at each table. The person who sits at this place takes the table flowers home as a gift from the bride.

TIPS TO PROFESSIONALS

In planning a wedding, the bride and her family will deal with a number of professional suppliers of service. One may expect varying degrees of assistance from them; some should be tipped if the service they render is beyond the usual. These would include the bridal consultant, the sexton (*shammash*) if he is not included in the overall synagogue fee, caterer's help at a home reception, the head driver of a limousine service, florist's delivery help.

WINES AND LIQUOR

Champagne, at least for the wedding toast to the bride and groom, is traditional for weddings. One may properly serve only champagne at a home reception, but at more elaborate weddings there is usually a full bar at the reception in addition to the champagne, and at a seated dinner, wines may be served with each course as well as champagne and after-dinner brandy and cordials.

The cost of this wine and liquor is also a customary expense of the bride's family, but many grooms offer to provide the liquor as a cost-sharing gesture.

WEDDING PICTURES

Wedding pictures, especially "candid" photos, can be taken only once, so a careful plan for the photographic work is essential.

It is best to use professional services. If you rely on a friend's offer to take the pictures, the end may be hard feelings if you are not satisfied with the result, plus the inevitable disappointment that there is no adequate pictorial record of this once-in-a-lifetime occasion.

It may even be an imposition to ask a friend to take the pictures, as his camera duties are bound to interfere with his pleasure as a guest. More than one bride has found that champagne and photography do not mix well.

Several wedding photographers should be visited, their work examined, and prices compared. A good photographer will present an organized plan for catching the many interesting moments of the occasion. Good taste should rule here, too. If the sample albums contain shots that seem offensive, such as the "cute" idea of showing the groom adjusting the bride's garter, be sure to tell the photographer you do not wish to have them. Such photos are not only embarrassing, they are offensive to Jewish mores.

Photos During the Ceremony. Even if the synagogue permits candid photography during the ceremony (which, fortunately, is very rare), no bride should permit it. The solemnity of this important moment should not be marred by the antics of a photographer darting up and down the aisle popping flashbulbs in everyone's eyes. If a few ceremony pictures are desired, they may be posed after it has taken place, before the reception.

The cost of the wedding pictures is often shared by both families, who then plan the picture-taking together. The album is, naturally, kept by the bride and groom. The parents may either make up duplicate albums, or have a smaller set of selected prints made to keep as a memento.

When the bride's family plans and pays for the whole cost of the wedding photographs, it is a gracious gesture to ask the groom's family what pictures they would particularly like to have taken. They then pay for any prints they order for themselves.

Formal Bridal Portraits. Although many young women do don their bridal array to pose for portraits well in advance of the wedding day, so as to have the pictures available for use with the newspaper accounts of the wedding, there is in many Jewish families an almost superstitious horror of really wearing the wedding clothes before the actual day. Some bridal shops will arrange for formal portraits to be taken in the shop after the final fitting of the gown, or the bride may have one more try-on at home, with the photographer in attendance.

The bride and groom must make the decision whether to take such formal portraits in advance or to have formal family pictures taken on the day of the wedding.

If a bridal portrait is not available before the wedding, the newspapers may be given a formal engagement portrait, or any other current photo that pleases the bride. (See Chapter 65.)

MUSIC FOR THE RECEPTION

As soon as the general plan for the wedding has been set, the question of music for the reception should be settled. Even if there is to be no dancing, there should be some background music. An accordionist, or a pianist and violinist playing light classical music and requested old favorites and serenading the new couple will add greatly to the festivity.

A formal wedding reception calls for dance music played by a dance band of three or four pieces. In a very large reception hall a full orchestra may be needed. The caterer may allow you to use only musicians from his list and usually will require that any other instrumentalists brought in be members of the musicians' union. If you have free choice, it is important to engage the dance band early, as groups in demand are often booked far in advance during busy wedding seasons.

There are well-known Jewish wedding bands in large metropolitan areas that are willing to travel out of town, if engaged well ahead of time. They usually have an extensive repertoire of Israeli and traditional Jewish music.

When engaging musicians it is important to have a clear understanding as to how much actual music will be provided, and what overtime charges there will be if the festivity runs on past the usual time. (See Chapter 68, "Appropriate Music.")

RESPONSIBILITIES OF THE DIVORCED FATHER

How much, or indeed, whether, a girl's divorced father will contribute to her wedding expenses is an individual problem, to be settled by discussion between the parents. A good deal depends on the amicability of the relationship between the father, the mother, and the girl, on whether the father has been paying alimony or had made a generous financial settlement at the time of the divorce. He may feel no obligation at all, or he may want to make some contribution to the cost; occasionally the father will give the reception or pay for the honeymoon.

Unless a girl and her mother have had very little or nothing to do with the father, he should be notified of the coming wedding, certainly be invited to it, take part in it, and be allowed to share the cost, if he wishes.

The same applies to the divorced parents of the groom.

THE TROUSSEAU AND HOME FURNISHING EXPENSES

Traditionally, the groom was expected to pay for all the costs of fitting out the new home, apart from the household items in the bride's trousseau. Trousseaux are less elaborate today, and the present-day trend, now that so many young women work and have independent incomes, is toward a sharing of the home furnishing expenses by bride and groom.

59. *Planning the Invitations*

WHOM TO INVITE

The size of the guest list is decided on by both families. It is customary for the groom's family to be allowed half of the invitations.

Some families send invitations to all on their lists, even when they live at a great distance and will not be able to attend. In this way they dispense with separate announcements altogether, letting the invitation serve as the announcement. Included in this list should be all relatives of the groom, the bride, all close friends of both families, longtime business associates of the parents and of the bride and groom. One may also wish to include old family servants and neighbors.

It is the bride's responsibility to see to the preparation, addressing, and mailing of the invitations. The groom's family must provide their complete mailing list, giving full names, clearly spelled out, as they are to appear on the envelope. Since no abbreviations are used, the name should be given not as "Mr. and Mrs. J. D. Levine" but as "Mr. and Mrs. Joseph David Levine." ZIP Code numbers should be included with all street addresses. Missing numbers can be checked in the post office ZIP Code directory.

Because people often feel obligated to send a gift when they receive a wedding invitation, one should not send them to casual acquaintances and business contacts.

The invitation itself is a memento of the occasion and should be mailed to the groom's parents, all other members of his immediate family, and members of the wedding party.

An invitation should be sent to the officiating rabbi and his wife, and to the cantor and his wife, if a cantor is used, unless one does not know the officiants at all.

Invitation Exceptions. It is not necessary to invite the young children of guests unless they are very close relatives and their presence is truly desired. Nor is it necessary to invite a partner for each unmarried person invited to the reception. If you wish unmarried guests to bring a friend, you may enclose a note reading "Please bring an escort" (or "a friend").

A guest should not ask to bring a friend to the reception unless the friend is a substitute for some person invited with him (husband, wife, child), or some other guest already on the list; however, an engaged person may ask that his affianced be included.

Invitations to Those in Mourning. Persons in mourning may be invited to a wedding and may accept the invitations, as the *mitzvah* of attending takes precedence over mourning. They may choose to attend only the ceremony, drink a toast to the couple, and leave early, thus abstaining from the full rejoicing of the reception, if they do not feel equal to it.

Mourners may even serve as members of the wedding party; since they are actually waiting on the bride and groom, they may take part in the entire festivity. In Orthodox practice, mourning may also be broken and the rejoicing shared if the mourner serves a dish or a drink at the reception (thus assisting the bride and groom). Pouring some of the wine or cutting the hallah would be such a ceremonial service.

These exceptions do not apply to the *shivah* (formal mourning) period, when the mourner has the duty to abstain from all worldly pleasures.

MAKING UP A MASTER LIST

When there is a long list and the ceremony, reception, and dinner will be treated as separate functions, it is most convenient to break the list down into several categories:

1. Those invited to the ceremony and reception only (R)
2. If the dinner will be a separate function, those invited also to dinner (D)
3. Those who will receive announcements only (if they are to be used) (A)

When the guest list is very large, it should be written up on index cards showing the full name and address of each guest. For elaborate functions, different-colored cards may be used for each category, or the cards may be marked in colored pencil. The cards for each group of guests are alphabetized and filed separately. Another file box may be set up for acceptances and regrets, so that an accurate count may be made quickly.

At Orthodox and Hasidic weddings there are often separate pre-ceremony receptions for both bride and groom. The invitation to the ceremony includes this reception, to which all are invited. Additional dinner cards are used for those invited to the nuptial feast.

At smaller weddings, and at those where the ceremony and reception are held in the same facility, only one list and one invitation are needed, as all guests are invited for the whole celebration.

THE BRIDE'S BOOK

A shorter guest list may be written up alphabetically in a bride's notebook, in which columns are ruled to check off acceptances and regrets, gifts received, and their acknowledgment. The list may be divided into three groups—bride's family, groom's family, and friends. Such a bride's book is a useful family record and address list that will be consulted many times after the wedding. (See Chapter 71.)

A Typical Page in a Bride's Book

Bride's Family Name and Address	Invited to:	Accept (A) or regret (R)	Gift	Note sent
Mr. and Mrs. Joseph Berman 14 Evergreen Terrace Teaneck, New Jersey 07666	D	A	silver tray	10/14/79
Mr. and Mrs. Benjamin Lowe 85 Midway Avenue Detroit, Michigan 48214	D	R	—	—

You may want to include the names, addresses, and telephone numbers of stationers, caterers, florists, and other services used, with notes as to quality of performance and prices charged. The menus served and the recipes for special dishes prepared by friends could also be noted. This becomes a valuable record for use in planning future parties.

WHEN TO SEND OUT INVITATIONS AND ANNOUNCEMENTS

Formal invitations to a wedding should be sent out to arrive about four to six weeks before the date. Time for engraving or thermographing must be allowed as well, and the order should be placed at least eight weeks ahead, so as to leave sufficient time for addressing the inner and outer envelopes, assembling the cards and stamping them, and the mail delivery itself.

Envelopes may be picked up at most stationers as soon as the order is placed, so that addressing may be begun beforehand. It is a good idea to order some extra envelopes in case a mistake is made while writing the addresses.

Announcements are not sent out until after the wedding takes place, but it is best to address them at the same time as one is working on the invitations, so that the announcements are ready to mail the day after the wedding and will arrive promptly, before the news is stale.

60. *Formal Wedding Invitations*

SELECTING THE INVITATION

A formal wedding, especially if held in a synagogue or temple, requires a formal invitation which must be handled in a time-honored, rigidly conventional way.

The very best paper and engraving or thermographing that one can afford is indicated. Engraving has become so costly because of the expensive handmade copper plate needed that many families now choose the raised process, thermography, which requires no plate.

This process also makes it possible to reproduce hand-lettered Hebrew, with all its beautiful calligraphic ornamentation. (See "Hebrew Texts" in this chapter.)

Thermographed formal invitations must follow the conventions established for engraved invitations. The infinite variety of "original" styles shown, featuring monograms, garlands, pictures of the happy couple, sentimental quotations superimposed on full-color flowers, flashy envelope linings, and unusual colors are not correct for formal invitations. A bride planning an informal, offbeat wedding may consider some of these variations, but she should remember that fashions change, but the classical form is always timelessly correct.

All invitations should be on folders, not cards. The most formal size is one that folds in half again to fit an envelope about five by seven and one-half inches. Slightly less formal is the smaller size that fits this envelope without a second fold. The size chosen should be large enough to accommodate the wording without crowding.

The lettering style chosen may vary from script, a perennial favorite, to the very slender, severely simple modern styles. The ink may be black, dark brown, or dark blue; the paper, cream or ivory. Pure-white paper is rarely used now in quality engraving; similarly the plate-marked folder seems to have given way to the borderless style.

Some stationers show contemporary invitations in pastel colors combined with darker harmonizing inks, giving a slightly less formal effect but following the conventional word and line arrangement.

If an ink color other than black is selected, one should make certain that there is a matching ink available to be used for addressing.

Formal invitations require two envelopes, the inner protective one ungummed, and the outside mailing envelope with a gummed flap. There are a few very large invitations shown, designed to be folded only once, which are so heavy that only one envelope is used, with some resulting loss of elegance, despite the large size.

A protective tissue is provided for each invitation to keep the type from smudging.

CONVENTIONAL FORMAL INVITATIONS

General Rules.   A wedding invitation is issued by the parents of the bride (or traditionally, by both sets of parents), except for the special cases considered in this chapter.

The spacing and wording of the text follow set rules. All numbers (except for very long addresses) are spelled out, as is the time of the ceremony. No abbreviations are permitted, except for certain honorifics, such as Mr., Mrs., Dr., and Jr. If the names are short, the title Dr. may be spelled out.

The British spelling with a "u" is used for the words "honour" and "favour." Invitations to a wedding held in a place of worship "request the honour of your presence," since this is a formal religious setting. For less formal weddings at home, or on the invitation to dinner or a reception, the host will "request the pleasure of your company."

A response may be requested by the abbreviation "R.s.v.p." or the phrase "The favour of a reply is requested." One may also use "Please reply" or "Please respond." This line may be put on the reception card, or on the invitation itself if all are being invited to the reception and no enclosures are used. It appears in the lower left corner.

The hour of the ceremony is spelled out; half hours are styled as "half after four o'clock."

It is not necessary to mention the year in the date, but if it is used, it must be spelled out as either "One thousand nine hundred and eighty-one" or "Nineteen hundred eighty-one." The date is written out as "Sunday, the eleventh of June."

When the Wedding Is Held in a Place of Worship. The formal wording reads:

> Dr. and Mrs. Theodore Holt
> request the honour of your presence
> at the marriage of their daughter
> Elisabeth Ariella
> to
> Mr. Zachary Goldblum
> on Sunday, the eleventh of June
> at half after four o'clock
> Congregation Shearith Israel
> Two West Seventieth Street
> New York

With this text, a reception card with the "R.s.v.p." is used. (See "Enclosures" in this chapter.)

Combining Ceremony and Reception Invitation. To avoid the need for enclosures when all the guests are invited to the entire function, a few lines may be added to the formal text. It would then read:

Congregation Shearith Israel
and afterward at the reception
Two West Seventieth Street
New York

R.s.v.p.

or,

and at the reception
following the ceremony
[etc.]

When the Wedding Is Held at Home or at a Hotel or Club.   The second line of an invitation to a wedding not held in a place of worship reads "request the pleasure of your company." "R.s.v.p." or its equivalent is used in the lower left corner. If the wedding will be held in a place other than the home, the address to which the response should be sent is also given, as

at the Pierre
New York

Please reply
70 Hicks Street
Brooklyn, New York 11201

Reception cards, or the special line "at the reception afterwards," are not needed, as it is assumed that a collation will be served when the "R.s.v.p." appears.

Combining Reception and Wedding Invitations at Different Addresses.   When the ceremony and reception are at different addresses, the invitations may be merged like this:

at half after four o'clock
at Congregation Shearith Israel
Two West Seventieth Street
New York
and afterward at
370 Central Park West

Please respond

or

and afterward at
The Essex House

Please respond
370 Central Park West
New York City 10025

TRADITIONAL JEWISH INVITATIONS

Using the Names of Both Sets of Parents on the Invitation.   Although conventional (non-Jewish) etiquette authorities and stationers give all prominence to the bride's parents as the hosts and assert that the names of the groom's parents should not appear on the invitations at all, there is no reason why discord should develop between families because of this convention. The Jewish viewpoint is that both families have an equal part in the honor of the wedding, since they are giving their children to each other to be wed and a merger of the two families takes place.

Following the continental European custom, one may use the names of both families as sponsors of the marriage and prepare a traditional Jewish invitation. If the groom's parents earnestly desire to have their names appear on the invitation, no family friction need develop over feelings of being slighted, especially if they are sharing the cost.

A formal invitation using the names of both families would read:

Mr. and Mrs. Joel Green
and
Rabbi and Mrs. Aaron Blum
request the honour of your presence
at the marriage of their children
Zipporah
and
Raphael
Sunday, the eleventh of June
[etc.]

R.s.v.p.
Mrs. Green
10 Hunts Lane
Chicago, Illinois 60601

A less conventional wording for a wedding held at home or in a hotel or club could be:

Mr. and Mrs. Joel Green
and
Rabbi and Mrs. Aron Blum
invite you to share in the joy
of the wedding uniting their children
Zipporah
and
Raphael
on Sunday, the eleventh of June
at five o'clock
Lakeside Country Club
Chicago, Illinois

R.s.v.p.
Mrs. Green
10 Hunts Lane
Chicago, Ill. 60601

Still another arrangement, which indicates the family connections clearly, is the following:

Mr. and Mrs. Joel Green   and   Rabbi and Mrs. Aaron Blum
request the honour of your presence
at the marriage of their children
Zipporah   and   Raphael
[etc.]

When these texts are used with a Hebrew page, the form comes close to the traditional Hebrew style which gives the names of both sets of parents in the lower corners of the invitation.

Note the use of "and" instead of "to" and the use of given names only for the bride and groom.

Hebrew Texts.   Traditional Jewish wedding invitations often have elaborate Hebrew texts in addition to the English. Verses from the marriage blessings set amid many calligraphic embellishments are used, in addition to the names, day, time, and place. The lettering is most beautifully done by a *sofer*, a Hebrew scribe who specializes in the writing of Torah scrolls and in ornamental calligraphy. Such craftsmen can be found in the Orthodox communities of New York City and other cities with large Jewish populations. If one decides to use a hand-lettered Hebrew text, the invitation must be reproduced by thermography, and thus the English page would have to be done by the same process.

The arrangement of the two texts really looks best when they are placed side by side on the two facing inside pages of the folder. One may also arrange them on pages one and three, and then decide which text is to come first, Hebrew or English. Either choice is correct, depending on which language one chooses to emphasize.

Another pleasing variant is to use a Hebrew quotation and its translation, such as

קול ששון וקול שמחה

kol sasson, v'kol simha . . .

the voice of rejoicing and the voice of gladness . . .
—from the Wedding Blessings

or

דודי לי ואני לו

dodi li v'ani lo . . .

My beloved is mine and I am his . . .
—Song of Songs 2:16

These are set in harmonizing typefaces, on page one, about one-third of the way down the page, with the formal English text on page three of a small folder. In the large size, the quotation is placed across the width of the last half of page four with the English invitation text on page one as usual. When the sheet later is folded twice, the quotation appears as an ornamental cover.

SPECIAL NAME PROBLEMS

Father's Title. If the girl's father has a title, such as Justice, Rabbi, Doctor, Senator, etc., the title may be used in the invitation, as "Senator and Mrs. Herman Bloom."

Bride's Title. If the bride is a doctor, or has some other professional title or name, her parents do not use her title in an invitation or announcement they issue, since they refer to their daughter by her given name only, but if the couple themselves issue the invitation or announcement, the title may be used, as:

Dr. Evelyn Fisher
and
Mr. Howard Fine
announce their marriage
[etc.]

מזל טוב

אורי

טובה

Figure 8. Hebrew wedding invitation, hand-lettered by a *sofer* (scribe). Note the elaborate ornaments over many of the letters and the decorations around the words *Mazel Tov* at the top. The English text was printed on page 2 of this four-page folder and the Hebrew on page 3, so that the pages face when folded.

בראשון בשבת באחד עשר לחדש תשרי שנת
חמשת אלפים ושבע מאות ארבע

Figure 9. Decorative cover for a wedding invitation. A specially designed page, based on the Jewish Zodiac, which includes the Hebrew names of the bride and groom under the figures of Adam and Eve. © King David Publishers Inc.

Some conservative authorities used to suggest that a woman not use her title if her husband did not also have one, but in more modern practice a bride need not be bound by this unless there are personal considerations involved, or if she does not always use her title professionally.

Sometimes a bride who is well-known by a professional name may wish to include it in her invitation or announcement. This is done by putting it in parentheses under her full name as:

> Deborah Weinberg
> (Dee Wayne)
> and
> Richard Goldstone
> announce their marriage
> [etc.]

When the Parents Are Divorced.   A divorced mother issuing the invitation in her own name usually calls herself "Mrs. Grace Levy." A few still use the older form, "Mrs. Goldman Levy" (her maiden name plus the name of her former husband).

> Mrs. Grace Levy
> requests the honour of your presence
> at the marriage of her daughter
> Eve
> [etc.]

If both parents, even though divorced, have decided to issue the invitations together, their names would appear separately as

> Mrs. Grace Levy
> Mr. Howard Levy
> request the honour of your presence
> at the marriage of their daughter
> Eve

The "R.s.v.p." should indicate clearly that the responses go to Mrs. Levy.

If the bride is living with her divorced father, it is he who usually issues the invitation, as Mr. Harold Levy, to the marriage of "his" daughter.

When the Mother Is Widowed.   A widow properly continues to use her late husband's name, calling herself "Mrs. Edwin Gold," not "Mrs. Rose Gold."

When a Parent Is Remarried. When the bride's mother is remarried, the invitation may read

Mr. and Mrs. Charles Newman
request the honour of your presence
at the marriage of Mrs. Newman's daughter
Anne Martin
[etc.]

An informal invitation that avoids using so many surnames could read:

Muriel and Charles Newman
request the pleasure of your company
at the marriage of Muriel's daughter
Anne Martin
[etc.]

Note that the bride's surname, now different from her mother's, is given in this form.

If it is the father who has remarried, the invitation reads "at the marriage of his daughter Anne." However, if the bride has been living with a step-parent for some time and she feels truly the daughter of both, the invitation may be to the marriage of "their" daughter Anne (Martin), the surname being added when it is different from her stepfather's.

When the Invitation Is Issued by Others. The bride's father may issue the invitation if he is widowed.

If a bride has no living parents, or, after her parents are divorced, lives with other relatives, not either parent, the invitations are sent out by the persons with whom she makes her home.

Dr. and Mrs. Walter Cohen
request the honour of your presence
at the marriage of their granddaughter
Anne Martin

or

Rabbi and Mrs. Abraham Weiss
request the honour of your presence
at the marriage of their sister
Grace Weiss

The bride's surname is used to show whose sister she is.

If there is no relationship (as in the case of foster parents), the title "Miss" is used before the bride's name.

The Bride's Own Invitation. A bride may issue the invitation in her own name if she has no close relatives to act as hosts, or if she is an older woman who has been independent of her family for some time. The form reads:

> The honour of your presence
> is requested at the marriage of
> Miss Abigail Sherman
> to
> Doctor Martin Burns
> [etc.]

R.s.v.p.
Miss Sherman
Forty Ring Drive
Washington, D.C. 20008

Note the use of "Miss." Also, the wording could be "and" rather than "to Doctor Martin Burns."

PRIVATE CEREMONY, LARGE RECEPTION

When a couple desires a very intimate wedding ceremony, in the chapel or the rabbi's study, or before a judge or justice of the peace, and a large reception afterward, they may reverse the usual arrangement of the invitations, and use the large folders for the invitation to the reception, with a separate card or note enclosed for those invited to the ceremony.

A ceremony card could read:

> Ceremony
> at half after four o'clock
> in the Chapel
> Temple Emanuel
> Atlanta

or, more formally

> The honour of your presence
> is requested at the marriage ceremony
> at half after four o'clock
> [etc.]

Alternatively, the bride's mother may invite a few ceremony guests by phone or in person.

The invitation to the reception itself would then read:

Mr. and Mrs. William Franks
request the pleasure of your company
at the marriage reception of their daughter
Annabel
and
Mr. Gabriel Solomon
on Sunday, the fifteenth of July
at six o'clock
The Hyatt Regency
Atlanta

R.s.v.p.

Note the use of "the pleasure of your company," as the reception is a social occasion, and "and" rather than "to" the groom, since the wedding will have taken place by the time the guest arrives.

WEDDINGS IN A FOREIGN COUNTRY

Customs vary in many parts of the world, and if the wedding will be held in an unfamiliar country, the parents of the bride or the groom should not hesitate to ask their future in-laws about their role in the ceremony, proper dress, special customs, the hospitality expected of them, and the like. An embarrassing breach of etiquette can be avoided by a few questions.

When the bride's family is giving the wedding abroad, the invitations are usually printed in the language of the country, even though they are being mailed overseas to the list supplied by the groom. In Israel and some Spanish-speaking countries a bilingual form may be used.

Announcements are not generally used abroad; therefore the groom's list should include all the people whose names would ordinarily be on the announcement list.

Foreign invitation style generally includes the names of the groom's parents, sometimes with a parallel form for each family on the two facing pages of a large folder.

INVITATIONS TO A DELAYED RECEPTION

There are occasions when a wedding ceremony takes place overseas or in a distant city and the young couple do not return to their home community until after the honeymoon. A reception may be given after the wedding trip and the invitations issued by either the parents of the bride or the groom, or both families together. An invitation sent by both families would read:

In honour of
Mr. and Mrs. Daniel Wise
Mr. and Mrs. Aaron Grey
and
Mr. and Mrs. Nathan Wise
request the pleasure of your company
Saturday, the eighth of September
at eight o'clock
The Emerald Room
Hilton Inn
Pittsfield, Massachusetts

R.s.v.p.
Mrs. Wise
Foxhollow Lane
Lenox, Massachusetts 01240

An informal invitation may also be used, especially if the occasion is a visit by the newlywed couple to the home city of the groom, in an area so distant that most of the family could not attend the wedding. His parents may send out their visiting cards or an informal folder with the notation "To meet Mr. and Mrs. Daniel Wise" written above their own names (or inside the folder), and the day, date, and time below, adding an "R.s.v.p." if they wish.

ENCLOSURES

Reception and Dinner Cards. In Jewish practice it is not customary to invite guests to the ceremony only, as feasting and rejoicing are an integral and important part of the wedding ritual. Thus special invitations to the repast following the ceremony are usually not needed.

Reception and dinner cards may be used, however, to divide up a large guest list when a buffet reception is tendered to all after the ceremony and then a smaller dinner is given for the members of the immediate family and the bridal party, or when, as is common at ultra-Orthodox and Hasidic weddings, there is a reception before the ceremony for all the guests and a dinner after it for only part of the group. Occasionally, when the repast will be served in a place different from the ceremony, the length of the addresses makes a separate card for the reception necessary for the best appearance of the invitation.

Such cards are made up in the same typeface and ink on matching card stock and enclosed with the invitation. They may read either

Reception
immediately following the ceremony
The Pierre

R.s.v.p.
90 Central Park West
New York City 10025

(note that the address may be given if it is not a very well-known hotel or synagogue) or

The pleasure of your company
is requested at dinner
immediately following the ceremony
Lakeshore Country Club
Glenwood

Please reply

Response Cards.   Although most conservative authorities still consider the enclosure of response cards to be incorrect, they are more and more widely used, and have the value of convenience, especially when the guest list is very large and one must keep track of many replies.

The family should decide whether to use response cards on the basis of practicality. They are expensive to make up, since a printed self-addressed envelope and first-class return postage must be included. If one feels they are truly necessary, an old custom should not stand in the way of modern convenience.

When used, response cards are made up on matching card stock, in the same typeface and size as any other enclosures, and with matching imprinted envelopes addressed to the host. First-class postage is affixed by the host. The card generally bears the legend

The favour of a reply is requested
before May 25

When the response card is used, the corner "R.s.v.p." on the invitation is not necessary.

The bride who decides not to use response cards can feel secure that she is both traditionally correct and frugal at the same time.

Travel Directions.   A printed card with travel directions to suburban or country locations is often enclosed; it may include the train or bus schedule for the convenience of guests. The paper used should match the invitation as closely as possible.

ADDRESSING ENVELOPES AND ASSEMBLING INVITATIONS

Addressing Procedures. The addressing must be done by hand in black ink, or a matching ink if a color has been used for the text. Abbreviations are not used except for Dr., Mr., Mrs., Jr. Initials are used only when one does not know the full name. The word "and" is written out.

The mailing envelope would read:

Dr. and Mrs. Joseph Jacob Levine
95 Lake Shore Drive
Chicago, Illinois 60640

Note the preferred indented form, which looks very handsome on a large envelope. The block form is also correct.

The inside envelope reads:

Dr. and Mrs. Levine

No given name is used, and the names should be centered.

The expression "and family" is not used. If there are young children who are also to be invited, their names may be included on the inside envelope, thus:

Dr. and Mrs. Levine
David and Alisa

Family members over eighteen should receive separate invitations. All the daughters or all the sons of one family who live at home may be sent one invitation. For two sisters one writes "The Misses [or "Misses"] Susan and Ann Levine" on the outer envelope and their address, and on the inner envelope simply "The Misses Levine" [or "Misses Levine"]. Similarly, for two brothers the outer envelope would read "The Messrs. [or "Messrs."] Jonathan and Benjamin Levine" and the inner, "The Messrs. [or "Messrs."] Levine."

A person who has a Ph.D. and who usually uses the title may be addressed as Dr.

A couple who are both M.D.s are addressed as "The Doctors Ratner."

A widow is properly addressed by her late husband's name as "Mrs. Saul Sherman," but a divorcée is addressed as "Mrs. Janet Sherman." A single woman may be addressed as "Ms."

One invitation may be sent to a couple who live together without being married. It is addressed to both with the names in alphabetical order as:

Miss [or Ms.] Alice Brown
Mr. Joseph Siegal

The inside envelope would read:

Miss Brown
Mr. Siegal

If a married woman retains her maiden name for her social as well as her professional life, the invitation is addressed to "Dr. Joseph Jacob Levine and Ms. Grace Hoffman" (both names on one line). The inside envelope would read "Dr. Levine and Ms. Hoffman." If you are not certain that she keeps her maiden name even for social occasions, you may address the envelope, as for any other married couple, to "Dr. and Mrs. Joseph Jacob Levine."

See "Forms of Address" in Chapter 8 for the usage when the woman has the title of office.

Addresses are never typed.

Return Addresses.   Post office regulations require the use of the sender's return address on the mailing envelope. In the past this was usually embossed or imprinted on the rear flap. Computerized mail handling, however, is making the front left corner return address a post office requirement. As this rule becomes firmly established, the practice of having it imprinted in this corner of an invitation envelope will be accepted, even though most authorities have regarded this as not quite correct. Using a sticker in the corner is also permissible, although certainly not very attractive.

Assembling Invitations.   The invitations will be delivered flat, scored, but not folded. All must be folded in half along the score line, text side out, except where facing English and Hebrew pages are used. The smaller size folder is inserted into the inner envelope folded side up, with the text facing the flap. The protective tissue is placed on top of the text. The larger size is folded in half once more, text inside, with a half tissue separating the two halves of the text, then inserted with the fold up.

Enclosure cards are placed inside the fold, next to the text in a large invitation, facing the same way. In the smaller size they are sometimes placed inside the fold (where there is a risk that they may not be seen), or, more commonly, on top of the text, facing the same way.

The inner envelope is placed inside the outer envelope with the flap closed and the inscribed side facing outward.

It is advisable to assemble a complete invitation with all its enclosures (especially if one is using the large size) and have it weighed at the post office, so that the correct postage will be applied and delivery assured. Stamps should be very carefully placed in the upper right-hand corner. Using a new commemorative stamp is a nice touch.

61. *Informal Invitations*

Small informal weddings do not require engraved invitations, although the alternative, handwritten notes can be an onerous chore. The bride's mother may telephone friends and relatives, or invite them in person, but it is better to write if one can, as a specific place, day, date, and time are involved. The bride may ask her maid of honor or bridesmaids to assist her and her mother in writing the notes.

The invitations are issued by the same persons who would be sending them if they were the formal engraved ones, that is, by the bride's mother, close relatives, or the bride herself, if she has no close relatives.

Such invitations may be sent on very short notice, if necessary, but the customary two weeks in advance should be observed whenever possible.

The note should be written in black or blue-black ink on the best white paper and could read:

May 15, 1980

Dear Edith,

    Our daughter Sarah will be married to Gordon Abrams here at home on Sunday, June second, at noon. We do hope you will be able to join us on this happy day and rejoice with us at luncheon after the ceremony.

Cordially,
Helen

If the reception will be held in a different place from the ceremony, one could write

. . . will be married to Gordon Abrams in the Chapel of Congregation Shearith Israel, Beverly Hills . . . and rejoice with us at a luncheon at the Sheraton immediately after the ceremony.

62. *Responding to Invitations*

FORMAL INVITATIONS

It is an honor to be invited to a wedding and every wedding invitation requires the courtesy of a prompt reply (whether an acceptance or a regret). Since the guest will be invited to some sort of collation after the ceremony (or, in Hasidic practice, before it) his hosts must know the number of people for whom they will have to provide.

When the invitation bears a corner "R.s.v.p." and there is no response card enclosed, one writes a formal reply, on the best conservative notepaper, using black or blue-black ink, following the style and spacing of the invitation exactly:

> Mr. and Mrs. Joseph Jacobs
> accept with pleasure
> Doctor and Mrs. Cohen's
> kind invitation for
> Sunday the eleventh of June
> at noon

Only the date and time need be repeated.

A regret follows the same form, the second line reading "regret they are unable to accept." No explanation is necessary, although one may give a reason in this form:

> Mr. and Mrs. Joseph Jacobs
> regret exceedingly that
> their absence from the city
> [or "a previous engagement"]
> prevents their accepting
> [etc.]

It is pleasant to add the Hebrew greeting *"Mazel Tov"* or in Hebrew מזל טוב at the top of such a note, or to write it at the top of the response card, if it is used.

Response cards should be returned promptly.

INFORMAL INVITATIONS

The response to an informal invitation is addressed to the person who issued it and is made in the same kind of handwritten note:

May 17, 1980

Dear Helen,

Mazel Tov! We will be delighted to attend Sarah's wedding on Sunday, June 2. Until then,

Love,
Edith

A regret should include a reason and felicitations to the couple. A typical note might read:

May 17, 1980

Dear Helen,

Harry and I are delighted to hear of Sarah's forthcoming marriage. Unfortunately, we will be unable to attend because my nephew's Bar Mitzvah will be held on the very same Sunday. Nothing else could keep us away.

We send Sarah and Gordon our very best wishes for long life and much happiness together. We hope to see them soon in their new home.

Mazel Tov to all!

Love,
Edith

If one does not know the host intimately, one may use last names in the signatures, as "Edith Weiss."

FOREIGN-LANGUAGE INVITATIONS

You may respond in English to a foreign-language formal invitation to a wedding abroad, using the proper form for an acceptance or regret. If the invitation is in the two-panel style for both families, you respond to the family you know, presuming it is they who invited you.

RECALLING AN ACCEPTANCE

When a guest who has accepted an invitation finds that an unforeseen circumstance, such as sudden illness or a death in the family, makes it impossible for him to attend, he has an obligation to notify the host as expeditiously as possible, by phone, telegram, or in writing. A valid reason must be given. It is inexcusable to recall an acceptance because a more attractive invitation has come up. It is even worse to back out of attending without having the courtesy to notify the host.

63. *When Plans Must Be Changed*

WHEN A WEDDING IS CALLED OFF

There are some rare occasions when, after the invitations have been sent out, a wedding is called off. In that event, the guests must be notified as quickly as possible. This may be by phone, telegram, or handwritten notes, or, if there is time, by printed cards.

If the wedding will not take place at all, one might write:

> Dr. and Mrs. Morris Cohen
> announce that the marriage of their daughter
> Evelyn
> to
> Mr. Jonathan Taylor
> will not take place

If handwritten, these notes should be done in black or blue-black ink on folded white or ivory notepaper.

It is not necessary to give a reason.

Telegrams are sent in the name of those who issued the invitation, as:

> The marriage of our daughter Evelyn and Mr. Jonathan Taylor will not take place. Dr. and Mrs. Morris Cohen.

If the invitations are to be recalled by phone, the calls may be made by friends or relatives of the bride's mother, who, by adopting a formal, al-

though cordial tone, may be able to keep questions and conversations to a
minimum. It is simplest to say something on the order of: "This is Marian
Berger, Mrs. Cohen's sister. She has asked me to call you and tell you that
her daughter Evelyn's wedding, which was to be on Sunday, has been can-
celled."

A DEATH IN THE FAMILY

In the event of a death in the immediate family, the wedding need not be
called off (in Orthodox tradition *may* not be called off), but the family may
decide to have a very quiet wedding instead of the lavish formal affair. This
may necessitate recalling the invitations.

If there is time to print a card to recall the invitations, it might read:

> Dr. and Mrs. Morris Cohen
> regret that because of a death in the family
> the invitations to their daughter's wedding
> on Sunday, the eleventh of June
> must be recalled

If the time is too short for printing, guests may be notified by phone or by
written notes.

64. Wedding Announcements

The use of announcements is optional. If one decides to use them, formal
announcements are sent only to those relatives and friends who were not
invited to the wedding.

Announcements may be ordered at the same time as the invitations and
made up on the same quality paper and in the same typestyle.

The year must be given and it is written out. Either form shown below is
correct. The name of the synagogue or temple where the wedding took
place may be given if one wishes, and the city and state.

Dr. and Mrs. Theodore Holt
have the honour of announcing
the marriage of their daughter
Elisabeth Ariella
to
Mr. Zachary Goldblum
on Sunday, the eleventh of June
One thousand nine hundred and eighty-one
New York

The second line may read "have the honour to announce" or "announce the marriage of."

A bride and groom living independently of their parents may announce their marriage themselves as:

Miss Abigail Sherman
and
Doctor Martin Burns
announce their marriage
on Sunday, the eleventh of June
Nineteen hundred eighty-one
Chicago, Illinois

Announcements are sent out the day after the wedding, or as soon as possible thereafter.

Although no response to a wedding announcement is necessary, it is pleasant to send a congratulatory note expressing your good wishes to the people you know, either the newlyweds or the persons who sent out the announcements.

65. Press Releases

Local newspapers will print every announcement story (usually with the bride's picture) that they receive in time; however, big-city newspapers, such as the *New York Times*, will publish the items only if the family has some social prominence.

At least three days' advance notice is required, plus the time for mailing. A local weekly would require advance notice timed to their weekly deadline.

A release may be sent in English to a Yiddish newspaper. They will usually translate it.

Some newspapers have standard forms to be filled out for announcements, which the society editor will supply on request. Although the society desk may take the information over the phone, it is best to rely on the accuracy of the written word, and send in the completed form or a full story.

A TYPICAL ARTICLE

A typical wedding story follows. Not all wedding releases will have all the paragraphs included here. The release should be typed and double-spaced. If several copies are needed they should be Xeroxed, and a copy should always be kept by the sender for reference.

Name and address of sender

FOR RELEASE JUNE 11, 1979 [the wedding date]
    ELISABETH ARIELLA HOLT
    WEDS ZACHARY GOLDBLUM

Miss Elisabeth Ariella Holt, daughter of Dr. and Mrs. Theodore Holt of Pawling and New York City, was married today (June 11, 1979) to Zachary Goldblum, son of Rabbi and Mrs. Issachar Goldblum of Hartford, Connecticut. The noon ceremony at Congregation Shearith Israel here [or "New York" if sent to out-of-town papers] was performed by Rabbi A. Lopes Cardozo. A reception followed at the Hotel Pierre.

The bride [or "Mrs. Goldblum"; she is no longer Miss Holt] is a graduate of Miss Hall's School and Vassar College, and is assistant curator of the Museum of Contemporary Crafts here. Mr. Goldblum is a graduate of Cornell University, where he was elected to Phi Beta Kappa, and of the Harvard School of Business Administration. He is a senior research analyst with T. R. Price Company of Baltimore, Maryland.

The bride's father is head of orthopedic surgery at Columbia Presbyterian Hospital; her mother is a well-known writer of children's books under the name of Marian Kent. Rabbi Goldblum is head of the Connecticut Board of Rabbis; his wife is on the executive board of the New England regional conference of the League of Women Voters.

The bride wore a gown of antique ivory satin and her grandmother's rosepoint lace veil. She carried a bridal Bible with a marker of white orchids. Her attendants were her sister, Mrs. Sarah Fine, matron of honor, Miss Abigail Holt, another sister, and Miss Eva Goldblum, sister of the groom, who were bridesmaids. The groom was attended by his brother, Joseph Goldblum, who was best man, and by Marvin Goldblum, another brother, and Edward Silver, who were ushers.

After a wedding trip to South America, the couple will live in Baltimore.

If the groom has a record of service in the armed forces, the data should be added to his biography.

A description of the dress of the bridal party may be given after the list of attendants, if desired. Some newspapers do not publish any details of dress, even the bride's.

Giving the street address of the bride's family, or of the new residence of the couple, is optional. In these days of high crime, it is perhaps best omitted, as it is a lead for thieves to a home where there may be many wedding gifts, jewelry, and furs left unattended during festivities and a honeymoon trip.

Policy as to publication date varies with papers. Some local newspapers will publish the story prospectively on the day of the wedding, stating that "the wedding . . . *will* take place, etc.," but the *New York Times* and other large national dailies will print the story only after the wedding has actually taken place. Thus the Monday edition usually has all the Jewish social notes, since most Jewish weddings are held on Saturday night or Sunday.

The release is generally addressed to the society editor, but if the wedding is newsworthy enough to warrant straight news or press association coverage, it should be sent to the city editor.

If enough advance notice is given, the paper may send a photographer to cover the wedding of a prominent couple.

Identifying the Release.   In the uper right-hand corner of the page, the name, address, and telephone number of the person responsible for the story must appear. This enables the editor to verify the story or ask for additional information. Unidentified stories are often not used.

Any member of the family, or a secretary, may prepare and send out the release. It is not done in the bride's name, although she may prepare the story for the person who is sending it for her.

Sending Pictures.   The picture sent out with the press release should not be a finished portrait but a black-and-white "glossy" which the photographer is usually very glad to supply for newspaper use, as he will get a photo credit.

The photo should be identified with a caption on a sheet attached to the back and folded over the front. The wording "Miss Elisabeth Ariella Holt, whose marriage to Mr. Zachary Goldblum took place June 11, 1979" is typed on an 8½- by 11-inch sheet of paper, below the middle, then the sheet is pasted on and folded so that the caption and most of the page of paper cover the picture. You may also, very lightly, write the name in pencil on the back of the photo itself, in case the caption and picture should become separated. The photographer's name appears on the back as well.

The picture, the release sheet, and a protective cardboard are placed in a mailing envelope and send to the papers of your choice, marked "Special— Society Editor." Even better than mailing is delivery by hand, if it is at all possible.

The picture may not be used. Whether it is or not, it will not be returned.

The groom's picture is rarely used, unless he is very prominent, or he appears in a picture of the couple taken at the wedding by the news photographer.

Mentioning a Previous Marriage. If you have been married before, it is best not to omit the information. It is usually mentioned at the end of the story: "This is Mr. Jacobson's second marriage. His previous marriage ended in divorce"; or

"Mrs. Levy's previous marriage to Albert Goldman was ended by divorce. She has one child by the marriage, Jonathan Goldman"; or

"Mrs. Sherman [the bride's new married name] is the widow of the late Julius Blake of Miami Beach."

NAME PROBLEMS IN PRESS RELEASES

The family situations that require special forms in invitations and announcements are also special to news releases, but handled a bit differently, as the names of both sets of parents always appear.

Deceased Parents. The word "late" should be used to refer to a deceased parent or parents. Even if the bride or groom no longer lives with the surviving parent, the name must be mentioned in the release. If both parents have died, the announcement may be made by a close relative, friend, or guardian, but here also the names of the parents must be given. Thus:

Miss Madelyn Kahn, daughter of Mr. [or Mrs.] Jacob Kahn and the late Mrs. [or Mr.] Kahn, was married today to [etc.].

Some identification of the deceased may follow, if desired.

Mrs. Kahn was an interior decorator and a well-known collector of porcelains and enamels.

If the father is deceased and the mother has remarried, the announcement might read:

Miss Evelyn Marshall, daughter of Mrs. Saul Black of Blackberry Hill, Cranston, and the late Aaron Marshall of Philadelphia, was married today to [etc.].

If it is the groom who has lost a parent, the same information would follow his name, as:

. . . was married to Mr. Martin Weiss, son of Mrs. Arthur Weiss of Brookline and the late Mr. Weiss.

Divorced Parents.   When the parents are divorced, the name of the father must appear in the release, even if the parents are remarried.
If the mother is not remarried, the wording is:

Miss Anne Levy, daughter of Mrs. Grace Levy [or, Mrs. Goldman Levy], was married today [etc.]. The bride is the daughter also of Mr. Philip Levy of Cleveland, Ohio.

If the mother has remarried, the names appear as:

Miss Barbara Miller, daughter of Mrs. Simon Katz, was married today [etc.]. The bride is the daughter also of Mr. Abraham Miller of Baltimore, Maryland.

If it is the parents of the groom who are divorced, a similar sentence is used in giving the groom's parentage.
The word "divorce" need not be used, as the form of the names makes it quite clear that the parents are divorced.
When the child of divorced parents was adopted by the stepfather in childhood and now bears the same family name, the name of the divorced parent need not figure in the story.

Legally Changed Name.   If the groom has changed his name from that of his parents, the fact may sometimes be mentioned, as: ". . . the wedding of Miss Muriel Blake to Mr. Robert Beaumont, son of Mr. and Mrs. Abraham Schoenberg. Mr. Beaumont changed his name legally." However, since a person has a simple right to change his name if he wishes, there is no need to use the last sentence. The notice states that he is the son of the Schoen-bergs, and the reader will assume that he changed his name, whether through the courts or not.

66. *The Wedding Party*

THE ATTENDANTS

A Jewish wedding may have as few or as many in the bridal party as the bride wishes. Since both sets of parents, and sometimes the grandparents, take part in the procession and ceremony, bridesmaids and ushers are mainly ornamental.

You may choose to have no attendants other than your parents and grandparents. At most weddings, however, it has become customary to have at least a maid or matron of honor and a best man to assist and wait on the bride and groom, the hope being that the attendants will remain calm and collected as the tension mounts for bride, groom, and parents.

A decision as to the size of the bridal party should be based on the size of the place where the ceremony will be held, on the degree of formality you seek, and on the number of relatives or close friends you desire to honor.

Choice of Attendants.   Relatives or very close friends are customarily the attendants. The bride's sister would serve as maid or matron of honor, and the groom's brother as best man, although a best friend may be chosen instead.

It is gracious to ask the groom's sisters to serve as bridesmaids, and if there are to be ushers, the brothers of the bride might similarly be honored.

Bridesmaids.   There is no obligation to "return honors" and choose for the bridal party friends at whose wedding the bride has served as an atten-dant, especially if you decide to keep the bridal party small. Explanations are not necessary.

Since the attendants must pay for their own outfits, including shoes, ac-cessories, and gloves, it might be kinder not to "honor" those friends for whom this would be a financial burden.

The Maid (or Matron) of Honor. The matron of honor precedes the bride down the aisle in the processional. She helps the bride finish dressing and will hold the bride's bouquet during the ceremony. She may be entrusted with the groom's ring to hold until it is needed in the ceremony.

If there is also a maid of honor, she may either precede the matron of honor or walk alongside her, as the bride decides. The honor attendants will also have the duty of straightening the bride's veil and train when she turns to go back down the aisle in the recessional on the arm of her husband.

If there are many bridesmaids, the chief honor attendant is responsible for seeing that they are all on time, have their proper accessories and flowers, and assemble promptly for any pictures that will be taken on the wedding day.

Junior Bridesmaids. Sometimes young girls between the ages of ten and fourteen may serve as junior bridesmaids. Occasionally, one is chosen as "maiden of honor," if there is no adult honor attendant. The junior attendants precede the bridesmaids or the maid or matron of honor.

A very charming effect can be obtained by having only junior attendants dressed in very simple long dresses, carrying single flowers or tiny nosegays with streamers. It is important to set a girlish tone in the dress of junior attendants, and above all, to avoid using a cut-down imitation of an adult's formal gown.

The Best Man. The best man precedes the groom in the procession. He carries the ring for the ceremony, helps the groom finish dressing, and sees to all the details of transportation to and from the wedding and the reception. He may assist the groom in managing the details of the wedding trip, making reservations, safeguarding tickets, hotel room keys, and the like.

He is in charge of the ushers, if there are any, and sees to it that they have been outfitted properly and have the necessary hats, collars, ties, and gloves. He checks to see that all have arrived on time and that they gather promptly for picture taking.

Ushers. Ushers have no specific duties in seating guests at a house of worship, as guests may sit where they wish as long as they conform to synagogue rules. The ushers function purely as an honor guard during the procession. They may assist the best man in arranging wedding day transportation details. At receptions where there is mixed dancing, they serve as attentive extra men, dancing with as many of the women as possible, so that all will be able to take part in the rejoicing.

Children. Very young children, aged from four to seven, may serve in the wedding party if they are very closely related to the bride or groom. They may be flower girls, ring bearers, or train bearers.

Having children in the bridal party, charming as they are, can become a problem when the wedding is to be held in the evening and the festivities will run on till very late hours.

Housing for Out-of-town Attendants. Members of the bridal party are expected to pay for their own transportation to and from the city where the wedding takes place. The bride's family arranges for the bridesmaids' transportation to and from the ceremony and reception. They also pay for hotel accommodations for those bridesmaids who cannot be put up with relatives or friends. The groom's family does the same for the ushers and the best man if they are from out-of-town.

Wedding Party Gifts. The bride and groom each give gifts to their attendants. The gifts should all be alike and are usually of silver or gold. If they can be engraved with the date and the recipient's initials, they will have lasting value as mementoes of the occasion.

Wedding Rehearsals. Elaborate wedding rehearsals are rarely held before the wedding. Instead, the wedding party is expected to assemble at least an hour before the wedding to go over the procession procedure with the person in charge of the wedding ritual, usually the sexton or the caterer's assistant. The order of the music and the cues should be checked at this time.

The bride does not take part in the rehearsal, or even appear to watch it. She does not see the groom until the moment of the ceremony, except at the most informal of home weddings.

67. What to Wear

THE BRIDE'S ATTIRE

A Jewish bride may dress in white or off-white, no matter what her age, and even if it is not a first wedding, for the white is a symbol of the spiritual purity of this solemn day. Except in some Reform groups, she must also wear a veil and headdress, with a face veil conforming to the formality of her dress.

Formal Weddings. For a formal wedding, her gown should be full length and may even have a train. It should be in a fabric appropriate to the time of year. Lace, satin, embroidered sheers, taffetas, or silk-like knits will do for any season; velvets and brocades are suitable for fall and winter months.

Long or three-quarter sleeves are best, since they eliminate the need for gloves and the complications they create during the ring ceremony.

Many fine stores will alter wedding dresses that are too décolleté for the traditional bride. At Bergdorf Goodman in New York, for example, the head fitter takes pride in their ability to add sleeves, fill in a neckline, or line sheer parts of gowns so that the change seems not an alteration, but part of the original design. This shop will also make to order the extra head covering needed by an Orthodox bride for the *bedeken;* fabric and trimming that match the dress are used.

Bridal shops in Orthodox communities specialize in styles that meet all these requirements without alteration.

The Veil. The veil worn with a long gown may reach to the floor; if there is a train, the veil must be as long as the train. With summer gowns, or when a very simple, uncluttered effect is sought, a fingertip-length veil may be worn.

The headdress may be tulle veiling draped over the head and secured with a pearl crown or a floral spray or wreath (generally artificial, to avoid wilting), or a lace or fabric pillbox or cap to which the veiling is attached, with the face veil separately arranged in front.

A crown or tiara effect is the traditional favorite because in ancient times both bride and groom actually wore elaborate crowns on their wedding day.

The Bride's Handbag. The bride does not carry a handbag during the procession or ceremony, of course, but she will need a handbag, sometimes even two. She will want a small, dressy white bag in which to carry her personal needs—lipstick, comb, tissues, and the like.

Some bridal dressmakers will make up a draw-string bag in material and trim matching the bride's gown, which the bride uses for safekeeping of the many envelopes containing money gifts that will be presented to her during the reception.

The bride who does not fancy this should delegate one of her parents to hold all the gifts she passes along. She may also hand them to the groom, who can keep them safe in his inside jacket pocket.

Informal Dress. For an informal wedding the bride may wear either a street-length or a full-length dress, and a fingertip- or shoulder-length veil.

A short face veil, usually about a yard square, can be worn with a short dress. With informal long dresses, one might wear only a circular or trian-gular lace shawl, arranged so that there is a fold in front that may be used as a face veil for the ceremony.

Large picture hats are best left to attendants or the mothers, as they rarely work well with the necessary veiling.

Shoes. Shoes for any style of wedding dress should be of silk or satin, dyed to match exactly (all whites are not the same shade). The bride should be most careful that the shoes are comfortable, as she will be standing and dancing for many hours. She would be well-advised to wear her wedding shoes for a few hours at a time at home for several days before the wedding to break them in a bit.

Something Borrowed. In some communities it is possible to rent wed-ding gowns and some of the accessories. There is no reason but sentiment not to rent a gown if the cost of the new outfit a bride has her heart set on is far beyond her means; however, the dress must not be too elaborate to be worn at a simple wedding. Careful attention should be given to the fit of the dress.

Similarly, a bride may use a dress lent by a friend or relative, provided it fits, and she does not mind the fact that the proverbial "something bor-rowed" is the gown itself. In ancient times, brides all wore borrowed dresses at the joyous weddings held after the Yom Kippur fast ended.

Jewelry. Some brides wear no jewelry at all on their wedding day, in keeping with the fast-day theme, except for the engagement ring, worn on the right hand for this day. The wedding gift of the bridegroom may also be worn, if it is appropriate (for example, pearls, or diamond or gold earrings).

Heirlooms. A beautiful veil may well be a wearable, treasured heir-loom if it has been properly stored, but it is difficult to keep a wedding gown packed away and wearable, especially as fashions and tastes change. A bride should never be pressed to wear an antique gown or veil if she feels it is not really becoming, or is forcing on her a wedding style that she does not desire.

Some families have ornate silver- or ivory-bound prayerbooks or Bibles that are used for weddings. With a floral marker these make very effective heirloom additions to the bride's ensemble without dictating her choice of costume.

THE MOTHERS' ATTIRE

The bride's mother has first choice of color and style for the gown she will wear; the mother of the groom should consult with her before ordering her own gown. Both mothers should wear dresses of the same length and general style; the degree of formality should correspond to that of the bridal gown. If the bride will be wearing a street-length costume, the mothers must do the same.

Almost any color is appropriate except white, black, or bright red. Usually pastels are favored, but there is no rule except selecting what is most becoming and harmonious in the overall color scheme.

The headdress may be anything from an evening hat to a twist of veiling, a flat bow, or a mantilla, but both mothers, especially if they are to walk together in the procession, should agree on a general style. Small, light hats are most comfortable for the many hours they must be worn on the wedding day.

Shoes should be of a lightweight material dyed to match the ensembles, and above all, be comfortable.

Gloves are optional, although they add a great deal to the total elegance of any ensemble. If gloves are worn, they are removed for the receiving line.

Handbags appropriate to the costume are used, but are not carried in the procession, under the canopy, or in the receiving line.

DRESS FOR THE BRIDE'S ATTENDANTS

Once the bride and the mothers have decided on their costume, the clothes for the honor attendants and bridesmaids are selected. They should harmonize in style and length with the bridal gown.

Most brides dress all their bridesmaids alike, with a different but related outfit for the maid or matron of honor, but it is also possible to select a basic color scheme and allow a variety of styles and tints to suit individual figures and complexions.

Bridesmaids need not wear a headpiece if they are unmarried, but the ensemble effect is usually better if some uniform style of headdress is chosen and all are turned out alike.

The attendants should all meet with the bride, after she has chosen the shop where the clothes will be ordered, to be fitted for their dresses together, and to make their selections together when they have a choice of individual style. A good bridal shop will offer the services of a consultant to coordinate all the details of matching shoes, gloves, headdresses, and other needed accessories.

Originality is the fashion with many young brides today, especially for informal weddings, and while they may relish complete freedom in choosing an individualistic style for their own weddings, it is still true that startling, overornate, or flashy effects are not in good taste.

One charming picture for informal weddings is made by garbing the attendants in long rustic dresses in different dainty prints, or in varying long flowered skirts with flowing peasant blouses of harmonizing pastels. These are outfits that might even be made by the bridesmaids themselves, and best of all, can be worn again after the wedding.

DRESS FOR THE GROOM, FATHERS, BEST MAN, AND USHERS

The degree of formality of the bride's gown determines the dress worn by the men of the wedding party. All dress alike, with the exception of the groom's boutonniere, which is usually a spray of lilies of the valley, sometimes a gardenia or a large carnation.

When the bride wears a long formal wedding gown and veil, the occasion ranks as a formal wedding. For a day formal wedding (before 6:00 P.M.), conventional dress for men is either a cutaway (morning suit) or oxford jacket with striped trousers, ascot or four-in-hand tie, gray waistcoat, and other accessories to match.

For an informal evening wedding (after 6:00 P.M.), dinner jackets, black tie and vest, and suitable accessories are worn. Formal evening weddings call for white tie and tails.

At daytime weddings of slightly less formal degree, dark business suits may be worn by the men. They may also wear them at informal evening weddings, although black tie is more suitable if the bride is wearing a long dress.

Summer Weddings. For a summer wedding, white jackets and black formal trousers, beige summer suits, or blazers and white flannels are correct and very good-looking. Informal dress of a more picturesque variety sometimes leans to flowered shirts with matching vests and trousers of colorful fabrics. The choice again depends on what the bride is wearing.

Rented Outfits. Formal clothes are often rented, and it is essential to make the arrangements about a month in advance to allow for necessary fitting and alterations. The groom, the two fathers, and the best man and ushers should all be outfitted by the same rental agency to be sure of having matching outfits.

A perfect fit in jacket collars, and trouser and sleeve length, should be insisted on. The back of the suit will be seen for a long time while the men are standing at attention, and a gapping neck or ill-fitting tails become very noticeable. Trousers should break slightly over the instep and be of current length, the jacket collar must hug the neck, almost completely covering the shirt collar, and the tails of a tail coat or cutaway should end just below the back of the knee.

Innovative Men's Styles. Men's formal wear has undergone many changes in recent years, from the introduction of soft-collared ruffled shirts and silk knit turtlenecks to a wide spectrum of colors in both morning suits and evening wear.

To a conservative eye, nothing is as correct or as universally becoming as conventional formal dress, but a groom nowadays has considerable latitude in selecting his style of dress, provided it harmonizes with the bride's choice, both in formality and color.

A thoughtful groom will bear in mind that the two fathers, who may be considerably more mature-looking than the groom and the best man, will also have to wear the colorful raiment he has chosen as most flattering to himself. Above all, the young men should avoid looking like the chorus boys in a musical comedy wedding, or a nightclub singing group.

A compromise may be struck at an informal wedding. The groom and best man may decide on some original effect, such as satin peasant tunics and black formal trousers, or velvet suits and elaborate ruffled shirts, while the fathers wear conventional dark suits or black tie.

Hats. Hats are a most important part of a man's turnout, since, except for Reform congregations, they are worn throughout the ceremony, and at traditional receptions, all through the repast as well.

For the best appearance, the type of hat to be worn must be uniform for the entire wedding party. With formal wear, all may wear top hats; with business suits, homburgs or fedoras, all in the same or very similar colors. With summer dress, panama hats are appropriate.

The party may also opt for colored satin or velvet or ornately embroidered white satin skullcaps, especially if they usually go hatless, or if they are wearing the very latest in colorful formal wear.

In Hasidic circles, the fur-trimmed velvet hat, the *shtrayml,* represents the height of formal dress for men.

Accessories. Gloves are still sometimes worn with formal attire, although not rigidly required. The groom and the best man remove at least the right glove for the ceremony.

Shoes should be either black dress styles, or for summer wear, white, with matching silk socks. Comfort is a factor for men, too, at weddings where they have to stand for so long, and new shoes should be broken in a bit at home before the wedding.

Ties vary with current modes. Whatever is conservatively fashionable and elegant should be chosen.

Jewelry should be simple and real. Studs may be silver or gold, pearl or onyx. Cuff links should match. Colored stones should be avoided.

Now that men wear perfumes, they should be careful to choose one that is discreet, and use it sparingly on a day when they will be meeting a great many people at handshake distance, in a room already filled with flowers and the perfumes worn by all the guests.

DRESS FOR GUESTS

Guests dress according to the time of day and the formality of the occasion. Weddings occurring after 4:00 P.M. and going on into the evening hours can be a problem, as they are neither daytime affairs nor yet full-fledged formal evening occasions. Dressing as for a cocktail party or a theater gala is often the best choice.

Women Guests. Women are always correct to wear street-length dresses except for the full-dress evening wedding. For late-afternoon weddings, either cocktail dresses or long dinner gowns are appropriate. Formal evening gowns are correct for a Saturday evening wedding, but women guests should be wary of extreme décolletage. A scarf, stole, or jacket that will cover the shoulders for the ceremony is a judicious addition to a sleeveless or décolleté gown. Skirts with exaggerated, immodest slits are in questionable taste.

Any becoming color or print may be chosen. Usually a woman guest does not wear white because it seems to compete with the bridal gown, but when off-white and winter white are very much in fashion, she may decide to wear an ensemble in such shades, as long as it does not make her look like a bride herself.

If the ceremony will be held in a place of worship (except for Reform temples) a married woman will need a hat or head covering of some kind for the service. At an Orthodox or Hasidic wedding the women do not remove their hats during the reception or repast. Unmarried girls may wear hats or not, as they think most becoming.

Men Guests. Men may wear dark suits at informal weddings, or in summer, any combination of light, dressy summer wear. A full-scale formal wedding on Saturday night calls for formal dress, although there are many comfortable "soft" variants worn by men today. Sunday-morning wear is usually a dark business suit.

Hasidim, especially the groom and the fathers, wear fur-trimmed hats and black frock coats, or the long caftan, as festive garb, no matter what the hour or the formality of the occasion.

Male guests will need a head covering, at least for the ceremony (except at Reform temples), and may choose appropriate hats, or carry a skullcap if they do not ordinarily wear hats.

The host usually provides ornamental skullcaps for all the male guests, and sometimes white lace scarves or caps for the women guests. These are kept as mementoes of the occasion.

When in Doubt. If in doubt as to the formality of the wedding, a woman guest may call the hostess or the bride and inquire, unless, of course, she does not know her at all. Conservative, dressy attire suitable for High Holiday synagogue attendance, or in the evening, for a dinner dance, is usually just right.

A married man should dress to the same degree of formality as his wife.

"Traditional Dress." Occasionally one receives an invitation with the legend "Ladies are requested to dress in accordance with Jewish tradition." One should make an effort to comply with this request, as it is obviously most important to the family. (See Chapter 4.)

Children. Children should be dressed in their holiday best, as for synagogue attendance or festive party-going. As for teenagers, they are a law unto themselves. A parent can only forbid the ubiquitous blue jeans and trust to their young people's desire to look "dressed-up" within their own fashion rules. The sections on dress in Chapter 45 may serve as a guide.

"A JEWISH FOUR O'CLOCK"

Years ago, no Jewish function ever started on time. Weddings, in particular, with long preliminary formalities and a smörgåsbord and cocktails before the ceremony, were notorious for having the *huppah* a good deal later than the announced time. Guests arrived correspondingly late.

This casual timing is a thing of the past. One can no longer be "fashionably late" to a wedding; it is rude not to arrive on time. Most synagogues and temples schedule the *huppah* no later than half an hour after the announced time; some wait only fifteen minutes. At Orthodox and Hasidic weddings, where there is still a lengthy preliminary reception, the time of *huppah* is stated separately on the invitation, and here, too, the ceremony starts on time.

Traveling to and from suburban areas on a Sunday requires additional time. Should you be unavoidably detained by traffic or inclement weather, and arrive to find the ceremony has already started, slip into a back seat as quietly as possible and make no attempt at apologies afterward, for certainly the hosts and the bride and groom will have been far too occupied to notice the late entrance!

Members of the wedding party have absolutely no excuse for tardiness. They should plan to be very early, rather than merely prompt in arrival. A wise bride and groom assemble the attendants well ahead of time at their homes or at the chapel, to finish dressing together.

68. Wedding Traditions

Little girls are encouraged to daydream about their weddings and to play-act their fantasies. As brides they often plan their real weddings in the same way. The question a young woman has to decide is whether she wants a ceremony that resembles the finale of a musical comedy or a Jewish modification of a High Church Anglican wedding, or whether she wants one that embodies cherished Jewish traditions. Actually, apart from the required legal formulas, there are no rules for the ceremony but those of custom, good taste, and personal preference.

Many of the traditions of a Jewish wedding ceremony had their origin in biblical times, as far back as the first wedding mentioned in the Bible, that of Isaac and Rebekah. When, for instance, Rebekah saw Isaac, her promised bridegroom, approaching her across the fields, she covered her head and veiled her face out of modesty, a Middle Eastern custom that has given us the bridal veil (Genesis 24:65).

The deception practiced on Jacob at his first wedding, when he found that he had married Leah instead of Rachel, is said to be the incident that later inspired the *bedeken* ceremony (described below) still followed in traditional circles.

The *huppah,* the bridal canopy, symbolizes the tent within which the newlyweds dwelt. It first came into use during the Middle Ages, when weddings were held in the marketplace, under the stars; the *huppah* served to create a separate, special space for this sacred ceremonial.

The prescribed ritual of a present-day traditional wedding incorporates, actually or symbolically, the three ancient Jewish methods of establishing a marriage: the delivery by the groom to the bride of a contract and her acceptance of it, the presentation to her of an article of known value and her acceptance of it, and sexual intercourse.

During the ceremony, the groom presents the bride with both a wedding band and a contract (the *ketubbah*). Immediately after the ceremony the couple retire to a private room (*yihud*) for a symbolic consummation of the marriage. (See Chapter 69.)

WITNESSES AND MINYAN

Witnesses are essential to all three parts of this ceremony, and thus we have the origin of the Jewish wedding party, which may be as numerous as the bride and groom desire, or be strictly limited to their parents, with all the assembled guests constituting a body of witnesses.

It is also necessary to have a *minyan*, hence the smallest wedding should include ten men among the assembled family and guests. If special circumstances make this impossible, a rabbi should be consulted as to the permissible exceptions and changes in the ceremony.

THE WEDDING RING

The wedding ring has become the traditional object of value ceremonially presented by the groom to the bride to signify their marriage. To prevent any misunderstanding as to its value, tradition decrees that the ring must meet three standards: it must belong to the groom, be made of solid metal, usually gold, with no holes piercing it, and have no precious stones set in it.

The wholeness of the ring is thought to represent the wholeness achieved through marriage and the hope for an unbroken union.

The bride who desires a more ornamental ring may use a simple gold band for the ceremony and later wear a carved or stone-set ring. Some select an elaborate wedding band to mark a wedding anniversary or the birth of the first child, wearing the new ring in addition to the ring used in the ceremony.

DOUBLE-RING CEREMONIES

Most Orthodox rabbis will not perform a double-ring ceremony, although the groom may, if he wishes, wear a ring after the wedding. Conservative and Reform rabbis will incorporate the groom's ring and a marriage formula spoken by the bride into the wedding ceremony if the couple wish. This ring is a gift from the bride to the groom.

SIGNING THE MARRIAGE CONTRACT
(KETUBBAH)

Before the public ceremony takes place, the rabbi meets the groom in the room where he is readying himself, presents him with the contract he has prepared for him, and formally asks him whether he is willing to undertake the obligations stated in the *ketubbah*. The groom usually signifies his assent in the traditional manner, by taking up a handkerchief or some other object given him by the rabbi and returning it to him. This action, called *kinyan*, is performed in the presence of witnesses, who will later sign the *ketubbah* with the groom.

The witnesses are usually synagogue functionaries, since tradition requires that the witness be a man who observes *kashrut* and keeps the Sabbath. To avoid embarrassing people by asking questions about their observance, modern rabbis use the *shammash* and other officials as witnesses.

In some Conservative and Reform synagogues the rabbi also goes through the same procedure of assent with the bride before the ceremony.

Among Hasidim, and the ultra-Orthodox, the signing of the contract is the occasion for a jubilant reception for the male guests (*mekabel ponim hoson*), marked by spirited singing and dancing. The groom attempts to deliver a learned discourse to prove his scholarship; his friends do their best to interrupt him by their singing and jesting.

GREETING THE BRIDE

Many brides and their attendants prefer to finish dressing at the place where the wedding will be held, donning headdresses and veils, arranging their bouquets, and posing for formal portraits in the bride's room.

The bride may or may not receive guests at this time; practice varies widely. Some regard this as the peak moment of prewedding nerves for the bride, and keep all but the wedding party out of the room. For others, the seclusion also lends to the theatricality of the bride's first appearance in the procession. At the other extreme are Hasidim and the very traditional Orthodox, who formally seat the bride in a throne-like chair banked with the bridal bouquets, where, surrounded by all her young friends, she presides over a reception for the women guests.

Whichever practice is followed, the bride does not usually see the groom before the ceremony.

BEDEKEN—THE TRADITIONAL VEILING OF THE BRIDE

The emotional climax of an Orthodox or Hasidic wedding occurs at the end of the prenuptial reception, when the groom, having finished the ritual of signing the wedding contract, comes to claim his bride. Surrounded by his singing and dancing friends and escorted by the two fathers, the groom approaches the bride, looks directly at her, and signifies that this is indeed the girl who was promised him by drawing the veil down over her face. The rabbi recites the blessing given Rebekah by her brother: "O sister, may you grow into [become the mother of] thousands of myriads" (Genesis 26:40).

The veiling of the bride indicates that she is consecrated to her husband-to-be. From this moment until the wedding ceremony is over, the bride's face will remain veiled. Some Hasidim now add still another veil to the ones she is already wearing, so that the girl's features are completely hidden from view.

THE BRIDAL CANOPY (HUPPAH)

The ceremony is performed under a *huppah*, the bridal canopy, usually made of velvet or satin, ornately embroidered and stretched between four staves. It is an honor for a man to hold one of the poles aloft at a friend's wedding.

When the wedding takes place in a synagogue, the *huppah* is placed before the Ark; some synagogues set up an elaborately draped, fixed canopy, which may be decorated with a few garlands or bouquets, if desired. A floral *huppah* is sometimes used. (See "Flowers" in Chapter 58.)

Some Reform congregations do not use the *huppah* at all, some only when it is requested.

Among Sephardim, a large *tallit*, held by members of the wedding party, is stretched over the bride and groom during the ceremony.

Under the *huppah* (or on the platform) is placed a small table covered with a white cloth, holding the two Kiddush cups and the wine which will be needed for the ceremony.

APPROPRIATE WEDDING MUSIC

Music during the wedding ceremony may be provided by an organ if the synagogue has one, or by a choir, a classical trio, or the musicians hired for the reception (when it is in the same place).

Not enough is generally known about truly Jewish music for weddings. Orthodox and Hasidic groups use only their own melodies, which are most appropriately moving and joyful. There is also a wealth of Israeli, folk, liturgical, and modern specially composed music for Jewish weddings, including some exceptional settings of passages from the Song of Songs.

Unfortunately, acculturation, ignorance, and apathy have led far too many to accept the two most widely used conventional wedding marches of non-Jews. Both are inappropriate. One, the march from *Lohengrin,* is the creation of Wagner, a notorious anti-Semite, and celebrates a mystical Christian wedding that was never consummated; the other, from *A Midsummer Night's Dream,* part of a pagan ceremony, is the work of Mendelssohn, an apostate Jew. Apart from any questions of insensitivity, these two works are so cliché that any couple seeking a distinctive wedding would do well to consult the rabbi, the cantor, the choir director, or the various councils of rabbis for suggestions as to appropriate Jewish music for the ceremony. Some less trite classical music would also be preferable to the continued use of the conventional selections.

The Union of American Hebrew Congregations (Reform) and the New York City Cantors' Assembly (Conservative) have published specially commissioned music for weddings, and there are a number of good recordings of traditional Jewish wedding music. Jewish bookstores sometimes have sheet music for traditional and Hasidic music.

Vocal solos of a secular nature are never allowed to interrupt the wedding service in a synagogue, although they are sometimes permitted while people are assembling before the service begins. Orthodox synagogues may not permit female voices.

CHARITY

It is customary to give charity as part of the thankfulness aroused by a joyous occasion. Many families give donations to the synagogue or other organizations in honor of the bride and groom.

At many Orthodox and Hasidic weddings one may see women at the door, extending an open purse, or a man making the rounds at a reception, holding out a yarmulke for donations. They are not seeking personal charity, but following the ancient custom of asking for contributions to help pay for the wedding of a poor bride or an orphan.

Only a small donation of a few coins is expected. It is ungracious to refuse to give or to resent being asked, as the "beggar" is enabling the giver to perform a great *mitzvah*. Those attending an Orthodox or Hasidic wedding would do well to provide themselves with a pocketful of change in preparation for these requests.

69. *The Wedding Ceremony*

THE WEDDING PROCESSION

To lead their children to the *huppah* has always been considered the greatest joy for parents. How much more so for grandparents who live to see their grandchildren wed! Therefore, all the forebears are given honored places in the festive entourage that since ancient times has escorted bride and groom to the wedding canopy.

Unless the rabbi enters the platform from a side door, the procession will be led by rabbi and cantor, chanting a hymn of welcome.

Grandparents may come next—first the groom's, then the bride's—or they may come first in each family's entrance, just before the attendants. If there is only one elderly grandparent, he or she should be escorted by an usher, son, or grandson.

The groom's party is first in the procession. If there are attendants, the ushers lead, followed by the best man. Last is the groom, escorted by his mother on his right and his father on his left.

The groom, his parents, and the best man take their places under the *huppah*, usually at the rabbi's right. The ushers line the aisle.

The bride's party follows in the same order. First come the bridesmaids, if any, who take places in the aisle opposite the ushers, then the maid of honor, flower girls, if any, and finally the bride, escorted by her mother on her right and her father on her left. She usually stands at the groom's right.

The bride always enters with her face veil lowered—in all branches of Judaism.

The bride's parents stand under the *huppah* facing the groom's, with the maid of honor and the best man behind the couple. If there is not enough room for all under the *huppah*, either the parents or the attendants may stand just outside the canopy. The grandparents may be seated on side benches or in the first row, or they may stand on the platform if they wish.

Circling the Groom.   In very traditional ceremonies, the bride, led by the two mothers, who sometimes carry candles, circles the groom seven times before taking her place at his right under the canopy. The number of circuits may vary, but seven is usual, by analogy with the seven heavens and the seven wedding blessings. In mystical symbolism, the bride is thought to be entering the seven spheres of her beloved's soul.

This impressive old tradition has spread to Conservative synagogues, and most rabbis will add it to the ceremony if asked, although Sephardim do not follow this practice.

Varying the Escort.   If there is only one parent, he or she may escort the bride or groom alone, or be joined by a close relative or friend. If the widowed parent has remarried, the stepparent may appropriately be part of the procession.

When the parents are divorced, they ought to try to bury whatever bad feelings there may be for the sake of the happiness of the child, who is, after all, the offspring of both. Even when a divorced person has married again, he or she may escort his child to the *huppah* together with the former spouse, always provided that some amicable relationship still exists among all three. Their child will be between them, in more than one sense.

If either bride or groom is orphaned, close friends or relatives may be asked to be the escort. Only at the very smallest of wedding ceremonies, in a rabbi's study, for example, do the couple merely take their places before the officiant without attendants.

In some Orthodox and Hasidic communities, the two fathers escort the groom and the two mothers escort the bride. At such weddings, the ushers, if there are any, are paired, and likewise the bridesmaids, to avoid unseemly mingling of the sexes.

At some Reform weddings the procession follows the order of a Christian wedding, with only the father of the bride escorting her to the *huppah*, where the groom, who has entered with the rabbi, is waiting. At such weddings, the mothers and grandparents are seated in the first row on each family's side of the sanctuary. The father hands the bride to the groom, who has stepped down from the platform to meet him, then takes his seat with his wife in the front row.

When the Father Is a Rabbi.   A rabbi-father whose son or daughter is being married may escort him or her to the *huppah* while some other clergyman or the cantor begins the ceremony; then he may join in the service under the canopy and share in its completion.

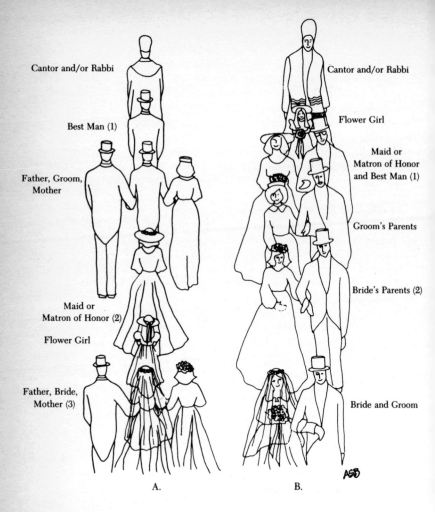

Figure 10. A. The Basic Procession. (1) Grandparents, then ushers, if any, come before the best man. (2) Grandparents, then bridesmaids, if any, come before the maid or matron of honor. (3) For Orthodox weddings, see "Varying the Escort" in this chapter. B. The Recessional. (1) Paired attendants, if any, follow. For Orthodox weddings, see below. (2) At Orthodox weddings, the two fathers follow the bride and groom, then the two mothers, then paired ushers, last, paired bridesmaids. The best man leads ushers, the maid or matron of honor leads the bridesmaids.

Figure 11. Under the *Huppah*. (1) rabbi (2) cantor (3) groom (4) bride (5) groom's parents (6) bride's parents (7) best man (8) maid of honor. Flower girl and grand-parents (if any) are seated on a side bench or in the first row.

Candlelit Processions.   Lighting many candles is a Jewish symbol of rejoicing. In the old European tradition, when weddings were performed outdoors under the evening sky, all members of the wedding party carried candles, as did many of the guests, to provide light for the ceremony.

This picturesque custom may be followed in a modern procession by using flower-trimmed candles instead of bouquets or corsages for the bridesmaids and the two mothers. The two fathers and the ushers may be given plain tapers to carry. Braided Havdalah candles may be used. These are so handsome they need no adornment.

Great care must be taken to avoid fire, and some synagogues will not allow candles for this reason. The rules should be checked with the sexton before orders for candles and flowers are placed.

The candlelit procession is most effective in a garden setting, or in a very large synagogue that is not too brilliantly lit. In a more intimate setting, where there is not room for a full procession, the rooms and tables may be decorated with many stationary candles for a similar celebratory effect.

THE WEDDING SERVICE

The service opens with a blessing of welcome chanted by the rabbi or cantor as the bride enters. The service incorporates two ceremonies that were once separate in time: the betrothal (*erusin*), and the *nisuin* or marriage vows.

In the *erusin* portion two blessings are recited, one over the wine, symbol of joy, and one proclaiming the sanctity of marriage. The rabbi hands the first cup of wine to the groom, who takes a sip from it. The maid of honor or the bride's mother raises the bride's veil so that the groom may look at her once more; then he hands the bride the cup so that she may sip from it.

At this point the bride may pass her bouquet to the maid of honor to free her hands for the wedding ring.

The Marriage Formula.   The best man now hands the ring to the rabbi, who, in states where it is required, will ask in English, "Do you take this woman to be your wedded wife?" The response is given in English by the groom, who then takes the ring from the rabbi.

Placing the ring on the right index finger of the bride, the groom repeats the marriage formula:

Harey at mekuddeshet li b'taba'at zo k'dat Moshe v'Yisrael

and in English,

Behold thou art consecrated unto me with this ring according to the
law of Moses and of Israel.

This sentence legalizes the marriage in Jewish law and is the one essential part of the ceremony.

The ring is placed on the right index finger because it is regarded as the seat of the intelligence. It is the finger one uses to point with when reading from the Torah, hence it symbolizes informed consent.

The bride may, after the ceremony, place the ring on the ring finger of her left hand. In the Reform service the ring is immediately placed on the left ring finger.

Double Rings.   If a double-ring service is permitted, the groom's ring is now given to him by the bride, with much the same ceremony.

Some rabbis will permit the bride and groom to add personal readings about their love and devotion and the meaning of marriage at this point.

The Sermon.   In synagogues where it is customary for the rabbi to preach a marriage sermon, he now adds a short address to the couple in English (or the language of the congregation).

The Marriage Contract.   After this, the marriage contract (*ketubbah*) is read in the original Aramaic and then in English, in Conservative and Orthodox ceremonies, and presented to the bride. This important document belongs to the bride and must always remain in her keeping.

Reform congregations dispense with the reading of the *ketubbah* during the service. In some Conservative synagogues an English summary of the Hebrew is read instead of the whole document. Actually, the properly translated text is a moving description of the devotion expected of partners in a marriage, and it should not be slighted.

In one translation the bridegroom makes the following declaration to the bride:

I faithfully promise that I will be a true husband unto thee. I will
honor and cherish thee; I will work for thee; I will protect and support thee and will provide all that is necessary for thy due sustenance,
even as it becomes a Jewish husband to do.

The bride, in this version, plights "her troth unto him in affection and sincerity, and takes upon herself the fulfillment of all the duties incumbent upon a Jewish wife."

There has been an attempt by some to approach modern feminist attitudes by writing an "equalized" *ketubbah*. Whether such a contract meets the standards of rabbinical law is a question best decided by a rabbi.

You can order an illuminated, hand-lettered *ketubbah* from a calligrapher to frame and hang in your new home as a cherished heirloom-to-be.

The Seven Wedding Benedictions.   The chanting of the seven wedding benedictions follows.

The groom, and then the bride, partake of the second cup of wine. The bride's veil is thrown back over her headdress to reveal her face after this final sanctification.

In addition to the blessing over wine, these benedictions include praise for God as Creator of the world, of man, and of woman, a prayer for the restoration of Zion and one for the happiness of the young couple, and praise for the Creator of rejoicing, gladness, "mirth and exultation, pleasure and delight, love, brotherhood, peace and fellowship."

The reading of parts of this concluding service may be delegated to guests whom one wishes to honor.

Distributing Honors During the Wedding Service.   At some Orthodox and Hasidic weddings, it is customary to honor dignitaries among the guests, especially if they are rabbis, by giving them a part in the ceremony. A guest may read the *ketubbah;* more usual is the division of the Seven Benedictions among several guests.

In modern variations, close family or friends may be asked to read the blessings in the poetic English translation. Appropriate poetry or prose readings may be added at this point.

The more who participate, the more honor to the couple.

A relative who is a rabbi or cantor may be allowed to officiate together with the rabbi of the synagogue.

Other honors that may be given to an older relative are saying the blessing over the hallah and cutting it at the reception, or leading the special wedding Grace after the meal.

Breaking the Glass.   The ceremony ends with the breaking of a glass by the groom, who crushes it under his right foot, amid cries of *"Mazel tov!"* from the guests.

The breaking of the glass, a universal Jewish symbol of marriage, is explained by some as a reminder that even in happy moments we must be aware of the seriousness, indeed the fragility of life. Over the ages, however, this act has come to be taken as a symbol of the destruction of the Temple and of mourning for Jerusalem.

A very thin, inexpensive glass is used. To avoid accidents from flying splinters, the glass is placed in a paper bag before the ceremony, ready at hand for the rabbi. The practice of some caterers, who use a flashbulb in place of a glass because it makes a very loud noise when broken, is deplorably vulgar and should be avoided.

In some synagogues the Priestly Blessing is invoked just before or just after the glass is broken.

The groom may or may not kiss the bride, depending on the custom of the community. Among the Orthodox it is never done.

THE RECESSIONAL

The bride takes her bouquet from the maid of honor, and amid a joyful burst of music, the married couple turn and lead the recessional, the bride on her husband's right arm. They are followed down the aisle, in the reverse of the processional order, by the bride's parents, the groom's parents, the maid of honor and the best man, the paired attendants, and finally the rabbi or cantor.

Children and aged grandparents who have entered in the processional and were later seated at the sides of the platform need not take part in the recessional. When they do, they take their respective places in reverse order of their entrance.

In Orthodox and Hasidic recessionals, after the couple the mothers walk together, followed by the fathers, then the maid of honor, the paired bridesmaids, the best man, and the paired ushers. It is not uncommon among Hasidim to see the groom's young friends jubilantly dancing and even turning cartwheels up the aisle in front of the newlyweds as they leave the *huppah* together.

YIHUD

In traditional practice, the bride and groom now retire to a private room, where they break their fast together. This first light repast taken together is held to be symbolic consummation of the marriage *(yihud)*. It is customary to serve them a rich golden chicken broth as a symbol of a rich life to come.

During this brief seclusion the bride also removes all the extra veiling she has worn, retaining only the cap or headdress. The Orthodox groom, if he has worn a *tallit* (prayer shawl) and *kittel* (ceremonial gown) under the *huppah*, now takes them off.

In Conservative congregations, the same seclusion is followed, although food may not be served to the couple. The bride may remove her veil and head covering altogether if she wishes, and the groom puts aside the hat he wore for the ceremony.

When the couple emerge to make their entrance at the reception, they are greeted with fanfares, singing, dancing, and general rejoicing.

If it is necessary to travel to another location for the reception, bride and groom ride to the place alone in the limousine or car in which the bride came to the ceremony.

THE WEDDING OF A RABBI

A rabbi actually serving a congregation may choose between being married at the synagogue with which the bride's family is affiliated or his own. If the bride's place of worship is selected, the clergy of that institution would officiate.

Should the couple decide to be married in the rabbi's own congregation, the ceremony must be performed by some other clergyman, either his superior, his assistant (if he has one), or a friend who is the rabbi of another congregation.

The groom wears the usual dress appropriate for the hour and formality of the wedding.

In a small congregation the rabbi is expected to invite all the members to attend his wedding, either by an informal announcement from the pulpit before the wedding, or more formally by sending invitations to all on the mailing list.

A reception must be tendered to all. This is usually a gift from the members of the congregation and is generally elegant but simple. The bride's family hosts a more elaborate luncheon or dinner after the reception for close family members and friends.

INFORMAL WEDDING CEREMONIES

In a less staged informal wedding, held in a home, hotel, small synagogue chapel, or garden, the ritual under the *huppah* remains the same, but the processional and recessional are much simplified or dispensed with.

Members of the bride's family greet the guests as they arrive. When all are present, the groom, escorted by his parents, and then the bride and her parents, may simply walk down an aisle cleared by their guests to take their places under the canopy where the officiant is waiting. When the ceremony is over, the couple usually turn in their places to receive the felicitations of all.

The couple would then leave for the seclusion of the *yihud*, if that custom is observed, while the reception begins without them. If there is no *yihud*, the newlyweds could lead the way to the reception room to begin the feasting.

For an intimate wedding, formal seating for the ceremony is not necessary, although if the group is too large to permit the guests to sit informally or stand comfortably during the ceremony, the room may be cleared of all furniture and rented chairs may be arranged in rows with an aisle.

Flowers, candles, and music all may be used to add to the festivity of the day.

MEMORIAL PRAYERS

At some traditional weddings a memorial prayer for a departed parent may be offered just before the ceremony begins. Many people find the custom to be emotionally disturbing at a festive gathering and so it is often said at another time.

Some dispense with the publicly uttered prayer, but have it said privately for the bride and groom and surviving parents in another room before the ceremony proper begins. The prayer may also be added to the services on the day the bridegroom is called up to the Torah (*oyfruf*), when it is probably least disturbing and most appropriate.

In some communities it is also customary for an orphan to visit the grave of a deceased parent shortly before the wedding to say memorial prayers.

70. The Reception

THE RECEIVING LINE

Pro and Con. At the most formal of Conservative and Reform weddings a receiving line has been regarded as a necessary courtesy to the guests, and no food is served until all have passed through the line. At large weddings, with each guest stopping to shake hands and say a few words to each person in the line, the procedure can take more than an hour and be extremely fatiguing to all. A receiving line is now less frequent for this reason.

In less formal modern settings the receiving line is dispensed with. Generally a brief cocktail hour is held while the bride and groom are in seclusion, and the parents circulate among the guests to greet them.

The Formal Receiving Line. If a formal receiving line is to be held, the bride's mother, as hostess, is first in line, then the father of the groom, the groom's mother, and optionally, the bride's father. In another arrangement, the bride's parents, as hosts, stand together, first in the line, then come the groom's parents.

After the parents come the bride, to the right of the groom, the groom, the maid of honor, and if there are any, the bridesmaids. The ushers and the best man do not stand in the receiving line.

The father of the bride may, instead of taking a position in the receiving line, act as host by circulating among the guests, seeing that each is introduced, and directing them to the refreshment tables if some collation is being served.

A receiving line is most appropriate when a brief reception is tendered to all the guests at the place where the ceremony is held, with a separate, more intimate repast to follow later. One may then be certain that all the guests have been greeted during the shorter time that all will be together.

Complicated Relationships. When the parents are divorced but have not married again, they may, for the sake of a harmonious wedding, stand together in the receiving line. If either of the parents has married again, it is not really appropriate for them to stand together in the line, but this problem can be avoided because the father's place in the line is optional. Any new spouse of either parent attends the wedding as a guest and does not receive, except in the case of a stepmother who is the hostess.

What to Say. Appropriate greetings to bride, groom, or parents are "Mazel tov," "Kol hakovod," and to the parents and grandparents, "May you have much *nakhes* [joy, gratification]."

The response to all is the same: "Thank you so much," or some variant of "We're so glad you could come to our wedding."

Kissing the Bride. The bride must expect to be kissed, but only those who are really close should claim this privilege.

At ultra-Orthodox weddings men do not kiss the bride unless they are older, close relatives.

Of course, with kissing *tantes* even the groom may receive a hearty buss now and then!

WHEN THERE IS NO RECEIVING LINE

The bride and groom make a formal entrance to 'a fanfare of music when there is no receiving line, and are seated at the bridal table immediately.

Since the meal is not served until they are seated, and no one should begin to eat until they do, they wait to circulate among their guests and greet them until after they have partaken of the first course, and after their first dance together, if there is dancing.

At a buffet reception they take some food as soon as they enter, so that the guests may partake, and then they may circulate among their guests informally.

THE BRIDAL TABLE

In the usual formal arrangement, the bridal table is a long one, at which all sit on one side, facing the room. The bride and groom are at the center, the bride on the groom's right and the maid of honor on his left; the best man is on the bride's right, and bridesmaids and ushers alternate along the rest of the table.

The wedding cake serves as a centerpiece, with flowers and candelabra adding to the decoration of the table.

Even at a stand-up buffet reception, where no formal table for the bridal party is planned, it is pleasant to have a small table set for the bride and groom, where they may be served with some refreshments. The cake is not cut until the bride has finished her repast.

THE PARENTS' TABLE

The parents are sometimes seated at a special table which also includes the grandparents, the officiating rabbi and his wife, and possibly a few other distinguished guests.

The father of the groom sits to the right of the bride's mother, who is the hostess. Opposite her sits the father of the bride, with the mother of the groom to his right. The rabbi is always placed to the left of the hostess, and his wife to the left of the host.

When there has been a divorce, the divorced parents are not seated together unless their relationship is very amicable. If the divorced parent who is not the host has remarried, he and his spouse should be seated at another table with some prominent guests. If this is not possible, it is sometimes better to omit a special parents' table to avoid hard feelings, and seat all the parents among the guests.

It is also possible, when the wedding party is small, to combine the bride's and parents' table. Here the bride and groom sit together at the center (bride on groom's right), with the best man on the bride's right and the maid of honor on the groom's left. The mother and father of the bride sit at opposite ends of the table as host and hostess, with the groom's father in the place of honor on her right, and the groom's mother on the bride's father's right. The others at the table are seated with men and women alternating as above.

SEPARATE SEATING

At Hasidic and ultra-Orthodox weddings, men and women are seated separately, on opposite sides of the room, or when there are many guests, even in separate reception rooms.

A bridal table for the bride, groom, and parents only, may be set up at one end of the room, in the center. Sometimes, when there are two banquet rooms, an honor table is set for the bride, the two mothers, the bridesmaids, and the wives of dignitaries at the women's dinner, and a similar one among the men for the groom, the two fathers, and the honored male guests. When one large dining room is used, two tables may be set this way on opposite sides of the room.

In the course of the evening, the bride will be carried high in her chair to the groom's table to join the rejoicing there for a few moments, and the groom in turn will be carried to her table. Much singing, dancing, and general merriment accompanies each visit.

HANDWASHING AND BLESSING OVER BREAD

At a traditional meal it is customary to begin with *Hamotzi*, the blessing said over the large braided hallah placed on the bridal table. After the blessing, the hallah is cut into portions which are served to the guests.

The Orthodox *seudat mitzvah* (banquet) also includes ritual handwashing before breaking bread at the beginning of the meal, and once more before Grace is said at the end.

At some Orthodox receptions, held in halls especially equipped for this purpose, the ritual washing may be done at wash basins installed in the entry way. A guest who is not observant himself should follow suit in this traditional ritual to avoid offending others.

TOASTS

The best man offers the first toast to the couple when the champagne or punch has been poured for all. The toasted couple, or the bride, raise their glasses, but drink after the others.

The best man may call on others to offer toasts as well; usually the fathers of the bride and groom and the grandfathers toast the couple, but the best man should also informally ask other members of the bridal party beforehand whether they wish to offer a toast, and introduce each one at the appropriate time. At a small reception, he might name a toastmaker for each table, who would present the greetings of that group of guests.

A few spontaneous, loving words about the couple, about the happiness of welcoming a new daughter or son into the family, or the briefest of cheerful anecdotes will suffice.

THE ORDER OF THE DANCING

When music for mixed dancing is provided, it may have begun informally before the bride and groom enter, but there is always the ceremonious moment, usually after the first course has been cleared away, when the bride and groom are called upon to dance together for the first time as husband and wife. This is usually a waltz. They take one turn around the floor together, then are joined by the parents. The attendants join in, and finally the guests.

The bride always dances with both fathers, the groom with both mothers.

Traditional Dances. Circle dances to traditional and Israeli melodies are also done and are very popular. At some time during the evening, bride and groom will be elevated in chairs by the young men, carried about on high, and then seated in the center of a jubilant, dancing ring, reigning as king and queen, to be royally entertained.

Mazinkeh Dances. In the European tradition, one is supposed to marry children off in chronological order; if the younger sister, in particular, marries first, the older one is expected to dance barefoot at her wedding as a sign of forgiveness.

A special significance attaches to marrying off the last, and presumably the youngest, of one's children—the *mazinkeh*. The parents are honored by a circle dance around them as they are seated in their chairs in the center. Sometimes they are presented with bouquets or wreaths during this dance. In this way the new social status of the parents with an "empty nest" is expressed.

CUTTING THE CAKE

When it is time for dessert, the bride and groom cut the wedding cake together, sharing the first slice from the same plate. The cake is then taken away to be cut by the waiters and served to the guests. (This custom is not followed at ultra-Orthodox weddings with separate receptions for men and women.)

The top tier may be removed and saved intact for the bride and groom to keep. This can be put in the freezer and served on the first anniversary, or, together with any leftover cake, it may be kept to serve at postwedding parties.

The time when the cake is being served is a good moment for the bride and groom to circulate among the guests and exchange a few brief words with each, if they have not been able to do so before.

LEAVE-TAKING

Once the cake has been cut, guests may begin to leave. Although it is most courteous to wait for the Sheva Berakhot (Wedding Grace after meals), it is permissible to leave before if the wedding dinner has run on into the very late hours of the night, as often happens at Saturday-evening weddings.

As they leave, guests should seek out the hosts to make their farewells. If they have not had a chance to meet the bride and groom, they must speak to them also before leaving. Money gifts are usually presented at this time, if they were not mailed before the wedding.

Although bride and groom may leave after the cake-cutting if the Wedding Grace will not be said, when it is recited they must stay for the ritual end to the meal. In any case, most couples wait until most of the guests have departed.

A thoughtful couple will phone their parents the next day, or as soon as they arrive at their honeymoon destination, to thank them for the wedding and assure them that all is well. Parents can feel very lonely and left out after the wedding excitement dies down.

"SHEVA BROKHES"

From biblical times on, seven days of feasting were held after a wedding by the observant. At each meal during this week, the seven wedding blessings (Sheva Berakhot) were recited as part of the grace after meals, whenever a "new face" was present, and thus the period came to be referred to in Yiddish as *Sheva Brokhes*.

When these benedictions are recited for the first time at the wedding, a special ritual is followed. It is a great honor to be asked to lead the Grace; in addition, seven different guests whom one wishes to honor may be asked to recite one of the seven benedictions. The hosts generally decide this beforehand and make up a list for the leader.

The hosts usually provide small booklets for the guests containing the text of the Grace in English and in Hebrew. These may be ordered from a synagogue bookshop or a Hebrew bookstore, personalized with the names of the bride and groom and the date of the wedding. There are several different attractive editions available, from a simple leaflet to a lavishly illustrated small book, all attractive keepsakes.

A *minyan* is required for the recitation of all seven benedictions. An abbreviated form may be said if at least three males are at the table.

If the marriage has been between two widowed persons, the wedding Grace is said only on the first day.

At modern traditional weddings, the special Wedding Grace after meals is said only after the wedding feast, but among the Orthodox and Hasidim the entire week of feasting is still observed.

MECHUTONIM: *A SPECIAL RELATIONSHIP*

The parents of the bride and groom have a special relationship in Jewish family life, expressed in the Hebrew and Yiddish terms *mechutonim* (plural), *mechutan* (masculine), *mechtenista* (feminine). For a lack of an equivalent English expression, the word "in-laws" is used for the plural, but there is no word to express the relationship in the singular.

Before the wedding, in-laws are usually elaborately courteous to each other, paying the expected "state" visits and entertaining the bridal couple. After the wedding they may exchange holiday hospitality; when they live nearby and can visit each other fairly frequently, *mechutonim* often develop an extended family relationship, especially once there are grandchildren to dote upon together.

The relationship can be touchy when both sides do not agree on the degree of wedding hospitality to be extended, or their other obligations to each other. Wise parents, faced with such difficulties, will not permit them to mar their relationship with the newlyweds. The continued happiness of the new couple and cordial relations with them should be their chief concern.

71. Wedding Gifts

People invited to a wedding need send a gift only if they accept; those who are close to the family may send a gift even though, for some reason, they cannot be present at the wedding.

A generous wedding gift is a Jewish tradition, and some make a real effort to have the gift "fit the circumstances," meaning the lavishness of the wedding itself. But the circumstances of the giver must be taken into account as well. What is a modest gift for the rich uncle from South America may be an extravagant gesture from the widowed aunt trying to get along on a small pension.

If one is not able to write out a munificent check without feeling it, one does not have to forego attending the wedding. There are any number of tasteful, unique gifts that will not strain a modest budget and that will be much appreciated by the bride and groom.

A wedding gift should be selected with the lifestyle of the couple in mind. If they will be traveling to a distant city to set up housekeeping, the transportation of heavy or fragile gifts may create problems. They may be moving into a tiny apartment, or the bride may have a career that leaves little time for polishing silver or safeguarding delicate china or stemware. She and her husband might be delighted to receive books for their new library, records or tapes for their sound system, or photographic, sports, or camping equipment.

PRIVATE GIFT LIST

A couple hoping to receive gifts they will truly enjoy should make up a list and entrust it to the bride's mother, a close friend, or a sister. A guest wishing to be sure of giving a much-desired gift should ask one of the family for suggestions. When asked, the keeper of the list should not hesitate to name a specific item, and to note on her list who will be giving the gift. One electric blanket is a cherished gift, six, an *embarras de richesse!*

GIFT REGISTRY

Some department stores and specialty shops maintain a bridal registry where the bride may list her silver and china pattern choices so that friends may be sure of giving her what she really prefers.

Her mother or a friend may be asked to spread the word of her registration, but a bride should never allow the store to commercialize the registration by sending out a mailing to her guest list announcing the fact.

Young relatives or friends who may not be very affluent might join forces and each give a place setting of china or silver or a matching serving piece.

MONEY GIFTS

If the couple would prefer gifts of money, the family may very properly suggest a check when asked about a gift. Carpeting, furniture, appliances, and the like are very expensive, and pooled cash gifts make these big purchases easier.

A money gift may take the form of a check, cash, a gift certificate to a favorite store, or a U.S. government or Israeli bond. It is often presented to the bride on the day of the wedding at the reception, made out to both bride and groom. If one is mailing a check, certificate, or bond before the wedding, it should be made out to the bride-to-be in her maiden name and sent to her home.

DELIVERING GIFTS

Wedding gifts have customarily been sent to the bride's home, to arrive before the wedding, but delivery by mail or parcel service is so uncertain nowadays that it has gradually become acceptable to bring one's gift to an informal reception, especially if it is a fragile item.

A friend or family member should be delegated to take charge of packages brought to the reception, noting their receipt in the bride's book and storing them safely until they may be taken home.

A card should be carefully enclosed, under the top layers of tissue and inside the box, to prevent inadvertent loss of the card before the gift is unwrapped.

A visiting card or plain informal card with a brief handwritten greeting and signature is most personal and correct. If you want to use a commercial greeting card, you should add a few words of your own in addition to your signature. You may have your own personal greetings enclosed in a gift package sent from a store by giving the card to the sales clerk at the time you order the gift.

Gifts should not be opened at the reception, to avoid losing cards, breakage, and hurt feelings among those who may earlier have sent gifts to the bride's home, and the inevitable invidious comparisons among the gifts.

KEEPING TRACK OF GIFTS

The bride should list each gift in her bride's book, noting specifically what it is and checking off her thank-you notes as she writes them.

People enjoy having their gifts remembered and she will find that she is referring to the list more than once after the wedding to refresh her memory and enable her to show visitors that their gift is being used.

MONOGRAMS

Monogrammed gifts, if they are to bear the married initials of the bride, should be made up and sent after the wedding.

Since an initialed gift cannot be exchanged, and must, of necessity, arrive some time after the wedding, it might be more convenient, when circumstances permit, to select the gift, pay for the monogramming, and send it unmarked, with a voucher to be used for the engraving or the embroidery, which the bride can then select herself.

EXCHANGING GIFTS

It is a delicate matter to exchange a wedding gift, if you cannot do it yourself. When you ask the giver to exchange a gift which he or she has gone to great pains to select, you may cause hurt feelings. Making the exchange may also be very inconvenient for the giver.

When you can make a discreet exchange yourself, it is perfectly correct to do so, especially if you have received duplicate items. You need not tell people you have exchanged their gift for something else unless they specifically ask about it later. The thank-you note you write is always for the original gift, not the one for which you exchanged it.

DAMAGED GIFTS

When a gift arrives damaged, the couple should deal with it themselves if they can, taking it back to the store it came from. If it is from an out-of-town store, it is best to write first, describing the damage and awaiting instructions. If the guest packed and mailed the gift himself and it was insured, it will be necessary to write the giver, explaining what happened. The original wrappings should be saved in such cases.

If the gift was not insured, or you do not know the source, there is only one graceful way out—the bride must simply write her thank-you note as though the gift had arrived unbroken.

INSURANCE OF WEDDING GIFTS

A floater insurance policy should be taken out to cover all gifts received and stored either at the bride's home, in the couple's new residence, or in transit, if they are moving to a different city. Thieves are known to follow the society news and to prey upon homes that may be replete with valuable gifts still in their unopened cartons. The new home is especially vulnerable while the couple is away on a wedding trip.

TRADITIONAL FAMILY GIFTS

In addition to substantial gifts from their parents of cash, or major home furnishings, the bride and groom may be given certain traditional gifts. The bride or her mother gives the groom a fine *tallit* (prayer shawl) of silk or wool. The bride may embroider a velvet *tallit* bag herself, or order it made. A silver Kiddush cup may be given to the groom by the bride's parents or grandparents. The groom's mother presents her new daughter-in-law with Sabbath candlesticks, the grandparents with a tray for the Sabbath hallah or a fine banquet-sized cloth for Sabbath and holidays. Heirloom ceremonial objects, such as a spicebox, a hallah knife, or a Passover plate, are also often passed on to the next generation as wedding gifts.

RETURNING GIFTS WHEN A MARRIAGE DOES NOT TAKE PLACE

Should a marriage be called off, all gifts received beforehand must be returned, even if monogrammed. A note thanking the giver for graciously sending a present should be enclosed, together with the explanation that the wedding, unfortunately, will not take place. No reason need be given. The man writes these to his family and friends, the woman to hers.

The bride-to-be may keep the gifts only in the unhappy circumstances where the groom dies before the wedding. Even then, she should really not keep the gifts meant for a new household that now can never come to be. Unless the people who gave them to her urge her to keep them, she should return them.

When the marriage lasts only a short time, the gifts belong equally to husband and wife, according to the laws of most states. However, it has been customary for the bride to keep all the wedding gifts except family jewels or heirlooms received as a gift from the groom's family. In the interest of fairness, the other gifts are sometimes equally divided between the two, with the groom keeping any that were specifically given to him. When objects of substantial value are involved, competent legal advice may be in order.

When a wedding is annulled soon after the marriage has taken place, any gifts that have not been opened and used should be returned to the giver, never directly to the stores.

ACKNOWLEDGING GIFTS

Every gift received must be acknowledged by the couple with a thank-you note, even though they may have thanked the senders personally at the reception. The letters should be written as soon as possible after the wedding, within two to three weeks, certainly no later than a month at the latest.

Although this has conventionally been the bride's duty in the past, there is no reason why the groom cannot share this social responsibility, now that so many women continue their studies or careers after marriage.

Acknowledgment Cards. At a very large wedding, where hundreds of wedding presents may be received, an engraved card may be sent out immediately after the wedding on the bride's behalf. Such cards may be addressed by a secretary or by several friends, and are useful to acknowledge receipt of a gift at once.

An acknowledgment card sent by the bride right after the wedding would read:

> Mrs. Zachary Goldblum
> wishes to acknowledge receipt
> of your wedding gift
> and will write a personal note
> of appreciation at an early date.

It can be ordered at the same time as wedding invitations and is usually made up in matching type and card stock.

The bride must remember that she still has an obligation to write personal letters of thanks as soon as she can, despite this acknowledgment.

Thank-You Notes. Thank-you notes should be handwritten on the best quality, conservative notepaper. Informal notes engraved or imprinted with the bride's new name or monogram are a good choice when she will be writing all the letters. These can be ordered to match the wedding invitations.

Printed thank-you cards should not be used. When your guests have gone to the trouble and expense of sending you a gift, a personal response is the only adequate expression of thanks. If you do ten short notes a day faithfully, you can write to one hundred wedding guests in only ten days. Your husband can share the burden (if he does not actually write some of the notes himself), by checking the list, sealing all the envelopes, putting return addresses and stamps on them, taking them to the post office, and looking up all the inevitably missing ZIP Code numbers—no small chores!

Each note must contain a specific reference to the gift, and should be natural and spontaneous in tone. The husband should be mentioned in the note when it is signed by the bride, and vice versa when it is signed by the groom.

You might write:

Wednesday [or date]

Dear Aunt Miriam:

   What a lovely piece of cut glass you sent us! Zachary and I are both delighted to have your fruit bowl as the first piece in our collection-to-be. When you come to visit us you will see it in a place of honor in our new dining room. Do come soon.

Affectionately,
Elisabeth Ariella

When the gift has been sent by a couple, the note would be addressed to "Dear Mr. and Mrs. Weiss" or "Dear Aunt Hannah and Uncle Saul."

The notes are closed "Sincerely," "Cordially," "Love," or "Affectionately," and signed "Sarah" or "Sarah Martin" (depending upon how well you know the giver). When the husband writes, he follows the same closing style, using his name in the signature.

When money gifts are acknowledged, the amount is not mentioned; one should refer to some specific use to which the money will be put.

Wednesday

Dear Mr. and Mrs. Weiss,

   Joel and I were happy to receive your generous check. It will go a long way toward the purchase of the super color TV set we have wanted so much. We will be thinking fondly of you during the many hours we will be enjoying our favorite programs. Do come and visit us soon and see how the set is gracing our living room.

Cordially,
Sarah Martin

72. *Second and Subsequent Marriages*

Whoso findeth a wife findeth a great good.

—PROVERBS 18:22

Since marriage is held to be the most desirable, indeed, the perfect, state of life for men and women, a second marriage is as much an occasion for rejoicing, in Judaism, as a first. No opprobrium attaches to the divorced. They and the widowed are encouraged to remarry as soon as possible after a proper interval. The guiding principle is the thought expressed in the Babylonian Talmud that he "who has no wife lives without joy, without blessing and without goodness."

Second and subsequent marriages may be more subdued because of the inevitable sadness left by the ending of a previous marriage, and because the principals may be more mature, even well on in years. But the mere fact of its being a second marriage is no reason in itself, in Jewish thought, to restrain the rejoicing.

The ceremony may be as elaborate as the bride desires. Some young women, whose first wedding may have been a hasty or defiant elopement, often choose full formality for their second and, they hope, lasting marriage. The implied reconciliation with their parents is also reason to rejoice.

DRESS FOR THE BRIDE

A bride of any age may wear a white or off-white gown, although a more mature woman would probably look best in an ensemble less frilly and romantic than the conventional wedding dress. The soft suit, street-length covered-up cocktail dress, or full-length dinner dress, depending on the time of day and the formality of the occasion, are all correct. Any becoming color, even a soft print, may be chosen instead of white. Shoes should be dyed to match.

The Veil. For traditional ceremonies, a short face veil, at least, will be needed. A pillbox hat, flat bow, or twist of tulle may be used as the headpiece, instead of the usual floral sprays. In Conservative and Reform congregations the bride need not wear a veil, but a hat or head covering is ap-

propriate. When large hats are in style, they may be worn with a soft drap-
ing of tulle instead of a veil.

A young bride may wear a full veil, if she wishes.

Bouquet. A bouquet may be carried. The bridal Bible with a floral
marker is especially appropriate to simpler costumes.

GROOM'S DRESS

The groom dresses according to the formality of the hour and the occasion.
A dark business suit is correct for all but the most formal of evening weddings. Light suits or white jackets and dark trousers are suitable for summer
wear. The groom might make his dress more festive by wearing a dinner
coat, a ruffled shirt, or a silk turtleneck, if that is his style. (See Chapter 67
for "Dress of the Groom.")

GIFTS

Gifts are always given by those who attend the wedding, but at a second
wedding they are usually smaller, since the couple are presumably not
starting a new household from scratch, and the reception is generally not as
lavish as for a first wedding.

Money gifts are perhaps the most useful to the newlyweds and easiest for
the giver, who may be aware that, between them, the bride and groom already have almost everything they need for their home.

CHILDREN

The question of whether children should appear at a parent's second wedding is largely one of age and, when there has been a divorce, of the attitude
of the ex-spouse. If there is no serious opposition from the other parent and
the children are grown-up enough to attend a reception, they should certainly be present and take part in the rejoicing at this new happiness for
their mother or father and the prospective enrichment of their family life.
To bar them from the wedding festivities (as some Sephardim do) can only
emphasize the exclusion from the mother's or father's new life that the child
already fears.

An exception might be made when a child feels a conflict of loyalty because of devotion to the divorced or deceased parent. The child should be
allowed to decide whether he or she wishes to attend, and the decision
should be respected without fuss.

A relative or friend should be delegated to look after young children at the wedding and give emotional support to older ones, leaving bride and groom free to enjoy their wedding day without distraction.

Teenage girls may even properly serve as maid of honor, but this is a delicate question, to be settled between the bride and her daughter or stepdaughter-to-be. The young girl's feelings of awkwardness or ambivalence, if these are problems, should be respected.

Similarly, a grown son may act as best man for his father. While most second weddings are not elaborate enough to call for flower girls and page boys, if there are youngsters of seven or eight whom one wishes to include, they lend a charming note to a simple ceremony.

The emphasis must be on making the children feel attractive, loved, and part of the special happiness of the day.

The wedding trip presents the same psychological and emotional problems, and each couple must work them through on a personal basis. It may be helpful to remember that a honeymoon is not *de rigueur*, and that a family trip, embarked upon when the newness of the living arrangements has worn off a bit, may be a much more rewarding experience for the family unit.

FORMER IN-LAWS

Should the former in-laws of a divorced or widowed person be invited to a second wedding? Unless, in the case of a widow or widower, the first marriage lasted a long time and a close relationship has been maintained with the family of the first spouse, it is most unlikely that they would be invited to the wedding. Where there has been a divorce, it is obviously inappropriate. However, courtesy requires that the in-laws of the widowed should be notified of the impending second marriage by a visit, an informal note, or a telephone call.

If there are children of the first marriage, the grandparents obviously have a very real interest in the stepparent of their grandchildren. An informal social gathering at which the new spouse may meet this branch of the family is a cordial and gracious gesture. The occasion might well be the party most couples give, when the wedding has been very small, for friends and relatives who could not be invited to the ceremony and reception.

PAYING FOR THE SECOND WEDDING

The bride and groom may share the costs, or the groom may pay them all. Parents do not usually pay the expenses, unless the bride is a very young widow or divorcée, or the couple are not financially able to assume the costs themselves.

THE CEREMONY

The ceremony under the *huppah* is the same as for a first wedding. For a large wedding there may be a procession and recessional, complete with attendants, but they are not usual at informal or small weddings. If the parents are still alive, they escort the bride or groom to the *huppah*. If there are no parents, other close relatives or a dear friend may serve.

THE RECEPTION

Once the couple have decided how large and how formal they wish their wedding to be, the details of the reception are the same as for a first wedding. (See Chapters 57, 70.)

INVITATIONS

If the wedding will be small and simple, the invitations may be telephoned, made in person, or by handwritten notes. If a formal invitation is needed, the protocol is the same as for a first wedding, but the wording is slightly different.

If the bride is a young widow or divorcée, the invitations would be issued by her parents. For a large reception following a small intimate ceremony, the card would read:

Dr. and Mrs. Charles Green
request the pleasure of your company
at the wedding reception of their daughter
Marian Brenner
and
Mr. Jonathan Miller
on Sunday, the seventeenth of November
at four o'clock
The River Club
Harbor Drive
Stony Point, New York

R.s.v.p.
19 Maple Drive
Spring Valley, N.Y. 10952

An older bride and groom may issue an invitation jointly reading:

Mrs. David Brenner
and
Mr. Jonathan Miller
request the pleasure of your company
at their wedding reception
on Sunday, the seventeenth of November
[etc.]

A widow, like Mrs. David Brenner in the example above, may use her given name, Marian Brenner, if she wishes.

A divorcée may issue her invitation in whatever name she decided to use after the divorce: Marian Green (her maiden name), Mrs. Marian Brenner, or in the older usage, Mrs. Green Brenner. She would follow the same style in an announcement.

WEDDING ANNOUNCEMENTS

Engraved announcements may be sent to a wide list of friends and family after a small reception; they should be mailed a day or two after the wedding. Their use is optional and many people simply rely on spreading the good news by word of mouth.

The announcements may be made by the parents of the bride, if she is young, or by the couple themselves. The name style of the invitation should be followed.

A news release may be sent to newspapers. (See Chapter 65.)

TIMING OF A SECOND MARRIAGE

According to Jewish law, a divorcée or widow should not marry again for ninety-two days, to eliminate any question as to the paternity of the children born after a second marriage.

Now that civil divorces may be quickly obtained, the same discretion might well be observed, if only to avoid the appearance of a hasty marriage on the rebound.

Formal mourning for a spouse need last only thirty days, but most people find that it takes almost a year to adjust to a new social life. The "decent interval" for a widowed person's second marriage has by custom also been held to be about a year, which corresponds roughly with the time lapse between the funeral and the unveiling of the tombstone, or for the Orthodox with the rule that three major festivals must elapse (Pesah, Shavuot, and Sukkot).

This is, however, a personal matter and one's own emotions and circumstances are the best guide. Certainly, older persons need not unduly delay a second marriage because of a mistaken fear of appearances. They (and their children) should remember that the Bible states that "it is not good for man to be alone."

73. Interfaith Matters

INVITATIONS TO CHURCH WEDDINGS

At church weddings, it is customary among Christians to invite a large group of acquaintances and business associates to the ceremony only.

There is no "R.s.v.p." or response card with an invitation to the ceremony only. Separate cards are generally used for the reception or wedding breakfast invitations.

If, therefore, you receive an invitation without enclosures, "R.s.v.p.," or a reply card, you have been invited to the ceremony only. No response is necessary, as no collation will be served. If you have been invited to the reception, the usual formal acceptance or regret is required in reply.

ATTENDING A CHURCH WEDDING

A church wedding is a religious service (sometimes a nuptial Mass). Women attending a church ceremony generally wear hats; men remove their hats on entering a church. Guests wait to be escorted to a pew by an usher, who will point out the bride's and groom's sides of the church. (The bride's side is usually the left.) You sit with the family and friends of the person you know.

During the service you stand and sit when others do, but should not kneel or genuflect before the altar. It is least conspicuous to sit toward the back of the church. At a Mass, some of the guests may go to the altar rail to take communion. A Jew, of course, should never participate in this religious rite.

A cautionary note—church weddings are held promptly, within five or six minutes of the announced time. If you do not arrive in good time, you run the risk of missing the ceremony altogether.

A conservative dressy outfit is the best choice of attire, as Christian weddings are usually held in the morning or at noon. Unless you have been invited to the reception (which may be formal), this attire is also appropriate for an evening ceremony.

THE NON-JEW AT A JEWISH WEDDING

Relax and enjoy yourself! If skullcaps will be worn by the men, the host will give you one. It will be worn in the sanctuary; afterward, follow the lead of your host on when to put it on. Women will need some head covering in the synagogue, and should follow the lead of the hostess at the reception afterward.

Dress up for the occasion. The usual attire for a Jewish wedding is the most elaborate outfit suitable to the time of day. (See Chapter 67.)

With very rare exceptions, the invitation to the wedding includes some kind of reception, sometimes before the ceremony. Come a bit early and forget your diet for this day.

ATTENDANTS AT WEDDINGS OF OTHER FAITHS

It is an honor to serve as an attendant at weddings. A non-Jew may serve as an usher or bridesmaid at Conservative or Reform weddings, but not at Orthodox ones. Similarly, a Jew may be an attendant at a non-Jewish wedding.

TWO OTHER HAPPY OCCASIONS

74. Anniversaries

Wedding anniversaries are celebrated in many ways, depending on the length of time the couple has been married.

In the early years, most couples mark their anniversary in simple fashion, with gifts to each other, perhaps a bottle of champagne, and a pleasant dinner and night out. As the years pass, more and more festive parties may be given, until the big "milestone" anniversaries—the tenth, twenty-fifth, fortieth, and fiftieth, and, God willing, the seventy-fifth—which generally evoke special celebrations. To have lived together for twenty-five years or more is truly an event for rejoicing in these days of short-lived marriages and "nonmarriage relationships."

The party may be given by the couple themselves or by their children. Sometimes a surprise party is planned. When parents are elderly, it is important not to have the "surprise" be so unexpected that it becomes a shock.

INVITATIONS

Invitations may be as informal as a phone call, a handwritten note, or one of the many attractive cards available at stationers. One may also design a personal informal card and have it reproduced by offset printing.

For the big anniversaries, formal invitations may be engraved or thermographed in silver (for the twenty-fifth), deep red (for the ruby, or fortieth), or gold (for the fiftieth). The addresses should always be in black ink.

When the couple give the party themselves the text would read:

1955   [dates optional]   1980

Mr. and Mrs. Jonathan Berger
request the pleasure of your company
to celebrate their Silver Anniversary
[or Fortieth Wedding Anniversary]
on Saturday the twenty-second of June
at nine o'clock
Valley Country Club
Newton, Massachusetts

R.s.v.p.   Black Tie
10 Edgewood Terrace   [when formal dinner
Newton, Massachusetts 02172   dress is expected]

When a dinner or reception is planned at home the invitation need read only "to celebrate .../ on Saturday the twenty-second of June/ at nine o'clock." The "R.s.v.p.," always included, gives the location.

When the party is given by the children, the wording might read:

In honour of the
Twenty-fifth Wedding Anniversary
of
Mr. and Mrs. Jonathan Berger
their sons and daughters
request the pleasure of your company
on Saturday, the twenty-second of June
[etc.]

R.s.v.p.
Mrs. Daniel Weinberg
95 Brookside Drive
Newton, Massachusetts 02172

The expression "their sons and daughters" is used to eliminate the need for listing the names of all the children as hosts. If there are only one or two, a married daughter and an unmarried son, perhaps, their names could be used in this way.

Mr. and Mrs. Daniel Weinberg
Dr. Joseph Berger
request the pleasure of your company
at a celebration of the
Silver Wedding Anniversary
of
Mr. and Mrs. Jonathan Berger
[etc.]

One may indicate the nature of the party by requesting the guest's company "at a dinner to celebrate" the anniversary.

A very charming popular invitation combines a reproduction of the original wedding party photo on the first page and the formal invitation on the third.

REPLIES

When there is no reply card, one writes the standard formal reply, copying the spacing from the invitation. (See Chapter 62.)

APPROPRIATE GIFTS

Gift giving is synonymous with anniversary celebrations. In the early years of a marriage, presents that fill in gaps in the household furnishings or decoration, or hobby and sports equipment, are popular and welcome.

A gift theme has come to be associated with each anniversary. Party decorations, the cake, and favors may all be planned in keeping with the theme. Gifts may be wrapped in decorative papers that carry out the theme, although the gift itself need not be an object of tin or leather or whatever the anniversary idea is.

A money gift is always appropriate, especially as the years go by and a household has not only every object and appliance a couple could want, but they may even be planning to move to a smaller retirement home or relocating in a different part of the country. How much more pleasing a check can be than yet another silver tray or breakable ornament!

Gift certificates, theater tickets, or a restaurant dinner credit for a "night on the town" are also good choices. The check or gift certificates can be enclosed with an appropriate card. Some stores provide charming ornamental wrappings for their gift certificates.

"NO GIFTS"

Some families, wishing to avoid a deluge of redundant gifts, put the line "no gifts, please" either on the invitation itself or on a separate enclosed slip. Close friends and relatives, unwilling to let the day go unmarked, may make a gift to a synagogue or a favorite charity. The hosts may appropriately suggest this when a guest asks what gift to bring. Such a donation avoids the giving of costly "gimcracks" and accomplishes a constructive, often substantial act of *tsedakah*.

CHARITY (TSEDAKAH)

Tsedakah is a Hebrew word that has many meanings, ranging from justice, loving kindness, and mercy, to charity. It encompasses the modern concepts of caring, giving, and sharing. In times of personal rejoicing, one must remember those less fortunate, and so *tsedakah*, in the form of direct charity to individuals or gifts to organizations, has become an integral part of every Jewish festivity and act of remembrance.

Some thought should be given to *tsedakah* in planning a family celebration. A gift in keeping with the scale of a festivity such as a wedding or bar mitzvah is appropriate; for other occasions, such as a birthday, recovery from serious illness, or an anniversary, a modest donation is usual. Gifts to various synagogue funds, such as the flower or prayerbook funds, or to Jewish organizations, charities, and homes for the aged or convalescent, are all eminently suitable; these institutions are significantly dependent on individual generosity to carry on their work.

Often the gifts commemorating an anniversary or other occasion are listed in synagogue and organization bulletins, honoring both the giver and the recipients.

NEWSPAPER RELEASES

A notice of the anniversary celebration may be sent to the local newspapers, giving all the essential information: full names of the couple, the wife's maiden name, date and place of marriage, names of the children, place and time when the party was held, and so on. Some local papers also add biographical material and will publish a picture of the couple. At least a week's notice should be given daily papers, two weeks to a weekly. See Chapter 65 for details on writing the news story and sending it out.

REAFFIRMATION OF WEDDING VOWS

In some congregations couples reaffirm their wedding vows after having been married for a number of years. The procedures vary with the synagogue and rabbi. The ceremony planned may take place on a Friday evening or Saturday morning or on a Rosh Hodesh. New wedding rings may be exchanged to replace worn old ones. Husband and wife may read selected passages from Psalms and other texts.

A reenactment of the actual wedding is in questionable taste; some rabbis do not permit it. They suggest a service of thanksgiving instead, with appropriate blessings and readings.

An *oneg Shabbat* (Friday evening) or Sabbath Kiddush is usually tendered by the couple after the service, either in the synagogue or at their home.

The couple may dress as formally as they wish. A white dress is always appropriate, but actually wearing one's bridal gown again (assuming it still fits) presents a question of taste best settled on an individual basis. For most women, a lovely new dress suitable to age and figure is a better choice than a sentimental attempt to recapture the past.

NOSTALGIA THEMES

One may develop all the nostalgia one desires in party decorations and favors, reprinting old photos, using decorative objects and themes from the early years. An informal "Fifties" or "Sixties" dance can be great fun, especially if guests are cooperative enough to dress up in period costumes.

A MEMORY BOOK

The old picture album is always a success at smaller parties. A "memory book" is a project that can bring great pleasure to the couple being honored, and their friends as well. Using informal invitations, the children, or the friends who are the hosts, ask each guest to return a note with a recollection of an event or an emotion they have shared during the past twenty-five or fifty years with the guests of honor. These are put together in an album, which can be illustrated with photos, newspaper headlines, programs, and other memorabilia. The album is presented at the party and shared with all. It is a priceless gift.

THE CELEBRATION

A wedding cake, the playing of the wedding march as the couple enter, and champagne for toasts are very much in order at any large party. The person charged with the toasts and congratulatory greetings should be sure to include the Sheheheyanu blessing in his or her remarks. The oldest and the youngest persons present could be called upon to offer greetings, and the couple to respond.

As the anniversaries approach the golden one, it can become a bit sad to contemplate the "empty chairs," but the positive emotion of gratitude for happy years granted always triumphs. Anniversaries may inspire looking back, but they face forward as well.

PRESIDENTIAL GREETINGS

Birthday greetings to all Americans eighty years of age or older and anniversary congratulations to couples married fifty years or more will be sent on behalf of the president from the White House. The request should be mailed to the Greetings Office, The White House, Washington, DC 20500. Be sure to give the full names and addresses of the people to be honored, and the date, and allow at least six weeks' time for the reply.

75. Hanukkat Habayit: *Dedicating a New Home*

You shall write them on the doorposts of your house and on your gates.
—DEUTERONOMY 6:9

Settling into a new home is a joyous event usually accompanied by various housewarming parties. In a traditional Jewish home this housewarming has an element of dedication in that it centers around the hanging of a *mezuzah* (scroll) as well as the reception of friends and relatives extending good wishes and gifts.

With today's upsurge of Jewish ethnic pride, more and more homes have a *mezuzah* at the front door. Conservative and Reform congregations have prepared special home services of dedication and thanksgiving for the occasion. There is a minimum amount of ritual and it becomes an occasion for creativity in preparing readings and songs.

THE MEZUZAH

The word *mezuzah* (plural: *mezuzot*) literally means doorpost in Hebrew, but the term has come to mean the entire parchment scroll and its case that one attaches to the doorpost, and also the small ornamental *mezuzot* that are worn as pendants, following the command in Deuteronomy 6:4–9: "And these words . . . shall be upon thy heart. . . ."

Inside a proper (kosher) *mezuzah* is a parchment scroll, hand-lettered, containing the texts of the Shema (Deuteronomy 6:4–9) and the verses beginning *"Vehayahu shamo'a"* (Deuteronomy 11:13–21).

The tightly rolled scroll also bears a large Hebrew letter *shin*—the *Shaddai* or symbol of the Almighty—so arranged as to be visible through an opening in the face of the container.

The container may be any permanent material and one may buy them in all sizes and shapes, ranging from the smallest pressed-tin ones to works of art in enamel, silver, and gold. Many very beautiful *mezuzot,* including some carved from olive wood, are made in Israel and available in Hebrew gift and bookshops and through synagogue sisterhoods.

Making a *mezuzah* is an exciting arts and crafts activity for a Hebrew school class or a family.

PROCEDURE FOR HANGING A MEZUZAH

A *mezuzah* should be attached to the front doorway, and in more traditional homes to every doorway inside and out, within thirty days after moving into a new residence.

The appropriate blessings to be said before and after affixing the *mezuzah* will be found in the daily prayerbook, and also in leaflets available from most congregations.

The *mezuzah* should be attached with screws, nails, or glue to the doorpost on the right side as one enters, in the upper third of the doorway. The top should slant inward, unless the doorpost is too narrow, in which case it may be hung vertically.

At a ceremonious *mezuzah* hanging, one might invite the rabbi, who would recite the benedictions and appropriate Psalms. The honor of leading this brief ritual may also be given to a parent or older friend or relative.

A woman may hang a *mezuzah.* A couple might want to share the task of hanging several *mezuzot* and include their children also, thus giving each member of the family a ceremonial part in the dedication of their home.

THE HOUSEWARMING

A party may be planned to follow this ceremony, with wine and liquor for a *lehayim*—the traditional toast to life—and the usual range of buffet refreshments for tea or cocktail party.

Popular times are weekday cocktail hours, Sunday brunch, and lunch or cocktail hours. Because of the "work" involved in hanging the *mezuzah* a reception should not be planned for Friday evening or Saturday afternoon unless the *mezuzah* has been hung before the Sabbath.

CHILDREN

A housewarming is best as an informal party at which whole families are invited and special refreshments and activities planned for youngsters, so that the children also may become acquainted with new neighbors.

INVITATIONS

Invitations are usually informal, by phone, note, or card, in keeping with the informal nature of the occasion. "At-home" cards are also correct.

GIFTS

It is customary for guests to bring some small gift for the new home, such as would be suitable for a shower. Plants for the house or garden, records, and other hobby or recreational gifts are also appropriate.

The gift should contain a securely attached card identifying the giver. Often the presents are put on a table in the hall as the guests arrive. They may or may not be opened at the party.

Opening presents is always fun, especially if one can thank the giver in person, and display the card and the gift. If there is a large number of gifts, care should be taken to keep the card and gift together. Even better is the assignment of a person with a steady head and hand to list the gifts and givers as the packages are opened.

Thank-you notes should be sent promptly by the hostess (or host, if it was a bachelor apartment), even if thanks were spoken as the gift was unwrapped.

Occasionally a "housewarming" is given to celebrate and display the redecoration or renovation of a long-established home. In that case, gifts are not expected, although lavish praise for the new look is. Those guests who do not relish arriving empty-handed may bring a present of wine or some gourmet delicacy.

THE TRADITIONAL "THRESHOLD" GIFT

There is a tradition of bringing candles, bread, and salt to the house even before settling in. Sometimes parents or a close friend will bring them on moving day. They express the wish that there may always be light and joy and enough to eat in the house.

Variations on this theme, such as books on breadmaking, pans and equipment, salt mills, and ornamental candles, make interesting gifts.

THE GUEST BOOK

When a family is new to the community, it is a good idea to set up a guest book near the door, where all the guests at the housewarming enter their names, addresses, and telephone numbers as they arrive. This gives the new family a valuable record of their first party, and a most useful guest list for future social occasions.

DIFFICULT TIMES

ILLNESS

. . . refuah shelemah

—TRADITIONAL WISH FOR RECOVERY

76. *Visiting the Sick:* Bikkur Holim

Anyone who has ever languished through lonely hours in a hospital bed knows from experience the importance of a visit to the sick. In the Talmud, *bikkur holim* (visiting the sick) is set forth as a primary religious obligation derived from the precept to love one's neighbor (Leviticus 19:34).

By the Middle Ages this concept had been exquisitely refined in rabbinical writings, and the principles there set down still make sense today. The basic purpose of visiting the sick is seen as cheering the patient, helping him to manage his daily affairs, and praying for his recovery. Above all, the visitor must help the invalid feel that he has not been abandoned in his hour of weakness and pain.

THE HOSPITAL VISIT

Visiting Regulations.   Before there ever were hospitals with set visiting rules, rabbinic writings stated that a visitor was not expected to come during the first three days of an illness unless he was a very close family member, nor, after that, to arrive in the first or last three hours of the day. These maxims are still sensible for home visits.

When the sick person is hospitalized, the visitation rules should be carefully followed. Most hospitals allow rather extended hours in private and semiprivate rooms, with more restricted hours in wards and stringent curtailment for the critically ill.

Usually only two visitors may be with the patient at a time. Most hospitals do not allow children under twelve to visit.

When many visitors come during the same hours, it is correct to telephone the room from the lobby and ask if you may come up, thus notifying the others that someone is waiting. In such situations, limit your visit to fifteen or twenty minutes.

If the illness is so painful or critical that no visitors are allowed, greeting cards, notes, and gifts may be sent to cheer the patient. The more serious the illness, the more comforting such little attentions.

The telephone should be approached with the same discretion as an actual visit. To a seriously ill person, the effort of talking, indeed, the ringing of the telephone, may be very taxing. Unless it is obvious that the patient wants to talk, a phone call should be cheerful but brief.

When a person faces a long confinement, whether in a hospital or at home, frequent short phone calls relaying news of the outside world are great morale builders, making the invalid feel that he or she has not been forgotten.

Smoking is not permitted in most hospitals for patient or visitor, except in certain lounges. In those rare cases where smoking in the room is allowed, a visitor should always ask permission of all the patients in the room before lighting up. The "no smoking" signs posted in various hospital areas should be scrupulously observed.

Hospital regulations generally require a married woman patient to be admitted as "Sarah Meyers" not "Mrs. Abraham Meyers." Any messages, mail, flowers, or gifts should be sent to her under her given name to be sure they are properly delivered.

The Considerate Visitor. Be thoughtful of those who are ill and never visit a hospital when you are suffering from a cold, virus, or other communicable ailment. The one gift you do not want to give the patient is another illness!

To be a truly welcome visitor, ask when to come and what to bring, and avoid, if you can, those hours when husbands, wives, or other close family members might want a few precious private minutes together. Never overstay. Twenty minutes to a half hour is usually long enough, unless the patient is obviously lonely and openly wants the visit to go on.

If the invalid begins to seem weary or uncomfortable, a visitor should leave. The arrival of a meal tray or a nurse with a treatment or medication is also a good signal to end the visit.

Keep the conversation optimistic, good-humored, and concerned with news of family, friends, and colleagues. Coming to the hospital often puts you, the visitor, in a depressed frame of mind and leads the talk to such topics as death and misfortune. This is the time to make a determined effort to think of pleasant subjects and store up some funny or happy anecdotes to recount in order to counteract this natural tendency. Especially avoid dwelling on accounts of other people's sufferings with the same ailment.

Try to keep the conversation calm and controlled. Overhilarious or bois-
terous raillery can be disturbing to other patients in the room and ultimately exhausting to the one who is supposedly being cheered up.

Don't pry into the details of the operation or illness unless the patient
wants to talk about them.

Family members visiting in semiprivate or private accommodations
should be careful about coming early and staying all day. It is inconsiderate
of the other patients and does not allow the sick relative the time alone that
he needs to sleep, rest, and, if need be, give in to the pain of his illness.

"Refuah Shelemah." The traditional farewell for a visit to the sick is
the expression of a wish for a *refuah shelemah*—"a perfect healing." You
say, "May you have . . ." or "I wish you . . . a *refuah shelemah.*" In Yiddish
you may offer a toast to health, if sharing a drink (even a glass of water), by
saying, *"Tzu gezunt!"*

GIFTS FOR THE INVALID

Flowers. There is no denying that fresh flowers brighten up the usual
drab sickroom, but the bouquets often wilt quickly if they need special care.

Most hospitals have very few flower vases and they are always in use;
thus, a smaller arrangement in its own container is a better choice than a
dozen tall gladioli or roses in an elaborate box. Better still is an easy-to-
care-for potted plant that can be taken home. Convalescents with a green
thumb have been known to propagate an impressive indoor display from
the contents of one or two dish gardens. Green plants, moreover, are easier
for those with allergies to tolerate.

When you find the patient's room already full of flowers, it is even more
thoughtful to send a floral arrangement or a plant to the home on the day
the patient will be discharged. Maternity stays, especially, are now so short
that a bouquet at home does much more to brighten the new mother's hours
of rest and relaxation.

When the happy day of leaving the hospital after a long illness comes at
last, many patients send their flowers to the wards instead of taking them
home. It is a gracious way of expressing thanks for recovery.

Other Appropriate Gifts. Many small gift items are more practical
than flowers. Interesting paperbacks (easy to hold), a neck or elbow pillow,
a frilly bedjacket or nightgown, a lounge T-shirt for a man, magazines, craft
projects, toilet waters, fine soaps and lotions to combat hospital dry skin (for
men as well as women) are all appreciated. For someone ill at home, a pillow backrest with arms is a thoughtful gift.

Most hospitals provide rental television sets. A gift of a few days or a week of television is a thoughtful and cheering one.

Gifts of candy or food are appropriate as long as the patient's condition does not preclude enjoying the goodies. Even though the delicious chocolates or cookies are often consumed by other visitors, this itself contributes to a patient's well-being by enabling her to be a hostess even when ill.

A true friend will never bring food gifts obviously not allowed by the patient's condition. No matter how much a convalescent coaxes for an ice-cold martini or a hot pastrami sandwich, a sensible friend will ask permission of the nurse or the family first. One might note that champagne is reputed to be good for almost any invalid who is well enough to sit up and drink it.

The Gift of Self. With master practicality, the rabbinic sages noted that one must not only pray for the sick but must also see to it that their material needs are met and their daily affairs kept in order if necessary. Such attentions require that one give not money, but oneself.

More than a hospital visit, a young mother might value a friend's taking her children on an outing, preparing a meal for them while she is incapacitated, or babysitting so that her husband may visit her.

People who live alone often desperately need someone to pick up their mail or go to the bank. Their pets or plants may need attention. Someone convalescing from a broken arm may need help to answer important letters, or assistance with a shampoo, since hospitals no longer have the many aides who used to do these things for patients.

Such are the acts of friendship that stem from true thoughtfulness. One need only imagine himself in the same situation to think of practical ways in which the invalid can be helped.

VISITING THE CRITICALLY ILL

People often dread contact with the sorrow of a disfiguring or terminal illness, and as a result, the critically ill are sometimes alone and rejected, just when they need emotional support the most. It is precisely these difficult visits that are the most important.

What to Say. Although one should set an encouraging and upbeat tone, one should not obviously lie to someone seriously ill by exclaiming about how well he or she looks. The patient is often well aware that his appearance has been adversely affected by his illness. At such times it makes much better sense to recognize the gravity of the situation by some remark such as, "You look as though you've been through quite an ordeal. This has really been a bad time for you." This allows the patient to voice some of his or her depressed feelings and may lead the sick person to express the resolve to overcome the ailment.

How to Help.   When the patient knows or fears that the illness is terminal, he should be allowed to reveal his anxieties and his needs. One should listen responsively to the emotions expressed. The chance to voice his feelings may be a much-needed safety valve. It may also help a critically ill person to face the need to put his affairs in order. In the true spirit of *bikkur holim*, a friend will assist in every way he or she can.

By your calm pleasant manner, sympathetic ear for the recitation of problems, and the practical offer to run some necessary errand, you can help the sick person to overcome the feelings of helplessness and isolation that are bred by a long hospital stay.

But the visitor should take his cue from the patient. He or she may show by his questions that he wants not sympathy so much as cheerful news from the outside world. Pictures of the new baby, a grandchild's drawing, and other bits of "real life" are especially welcome.

At the first sign that the sick person is growing tired, one should finish the conversation quickly and leave. A kiss or a handclasp and a sincere promise to return make for a supportive leave-taking.

77. *How to Be a Patient*

THINGS YOU WILL NEED

When preparing to enter a hospital for elective procedures, the patient should pack a couple of nightgowns or pyjamas, personal toilet articles, a robe, and comfortable slippers. A woman should take some light makeup. For a man, a shaving kit is essential. When there has been an emergency admission, a member of the family should bring these articles to the patient as soon as possible.

For your own peace of mind, keep only a small amount of cash on hand in small bills and change. Leave all your jewelry, credit cards, checkbooks, licenses, and other valuable papers at home. If you enter the hospital in an emergency situation, turn all these valuables over to a relative or friend for safekeeping as soon as you can.

SHARING A ROOM

Most people find themselves in semiprivate accommodations in these days of sky-high hospital costs. Although this is sometimes trying because the other patients may be either much more ill or, conversely, much further along in their recovery, consideration for each other is the key to making this hospital reality a pleasant experience.

If a roommate makes conditions intolerable, you may quietly complain to the head nurse or your doctor. After all, the purpose of a hospital stay is to get well, and lack of rest and quiet may impede recovery.

You may introduce a visitor who comes regularly, such as your husband or wife. Once introduced, the thoughtful visitor will inquire after the roommate when he comes again. Some families even become quite good friends as a result of this chance acquaintance.

YOU AND THE HOSPITAL STAFF

Courtesy to Professionals. Nurses, interns, and residents are professionals in health care, not servants. They should be treated with appropriate courtesy, and their patience under pressure appreciated. A nurse should not be badgered by the patient (or visitor) for information on her condition. These are questions for the doctor.

Nurses and doctors should always be addressed by name. In fact, it humanizes hospital relationships to try to learn the names of all the people who serve you; most hospital employees now wear name badges, which makes this courtesy easier.

Complaints. There is a dislike of the chronic complainer which leads some people to endure unnecessary hardship in a stoic way. Neglect of legitimate needs, surly or ungentle behavior, and mistakes in medication (they do happen!) should not go unreported. A quiet firm manner in discussing these matters with your doctor will usually correct the situation. If he does not come every day, do not hesitate to report such problems during the "grand rounds" made by the head nurse and the charge physician.

Some hospitals now have patient representatives to help with problems of service and treatment. When you are dissatisfied or perplexed, you may find the "patients' bill of rights" interesting reading.

Tips. One does not tip professional hospital staff; in fact, it is in very poor taste to do so. On going home you may want to leave a large box of cookies or candy at the nursing station for all who have helped in your care.

It is even more gracious to write a note to the hospital administrator or the head nurse expressing thanks for the attention of the nurses, doctors, aides, and housekeeping staff. It will be posted and shared by all.

A longtime patient may want to tip the cleaning staff or the aides if they have given special service and have come in on a regular basis.

SERVICES FOR JEWISH PATIENTS

Kosher food or vegetarian meals are available at most large hospitals on request. But hospitals run under Jewish auspices do not always routinely serve kosher food to all; even in such hospitals it may be necessary to make a special request.

The family should check to be sure the patient understands how to order the food desired, and that it is indeed being correctly served. With elderly patients especially, it is sometimes difficult to get them to eat properly if they are not fully assured that the food is kosher.

Most hospitals have a visiting rabbi to serve the religious needs of Jewish patients, either on special call or on regularly scheduled days. The rabbi will provide prayerbooks and help with personal spiritual problems.

Hospitals with large numbers of Jewish patients often provide religious services by means of closed-circuit TV or in-hospital radio. Where there is a hospital chapel, ambulatory patients may attend services. Again, one must ask about such facilities.

A donation to the hospital religious fund or to the rabbi's synagogue is a suitable way to show appreciation through *tsedakah* (charity) for help rendered and for a speedy recovery.

STAY WELL!

Each person has a duty, the sages tell us, to maintain his good health, to preserve the life that has been granted him. To that end, one may do all that is necessary to keep body and mind sound. One should affirmatively seek health and bodily well-being, and a cure for illness. Judaism does not permit refusing medication and treatment if there is any chance that it will make the patient well.

To the sick person one extends the wish for a *refuah shelemah* ("a perfect healing"), and to the healthy, "Stay well! It's a *mitzvah!*"

DIVORCE

78. The Judaic Attitude toward Divorce

. . . according to the laws of Moses and Israel
—FROM THE MARRIAGE SERVICE

A divorce is never pleasant; on this all religious creeds agree. Catholic dogma regards marriage as an indissoluble, everlasting sacrament. Even in the most liberal of Protestant sects a divorce is still viewed with moral disfavor, as the breaking of a holy vow. In some groups a divorced person may not marry again, or must wait a long period before doing so. Since classical Christianity originally made no provision for divorce, it eventually became a function of the civil courts.

The Jewish viewpoint has always been totally different. To begin with, marriage is an agreement between two individuals that is sanctified by blessings. One of the prime purposes of marriage is companionship. When relations between two people deteriorate so badly that they can no longer live together in loving harmony, Judaism has, from biblical times on, provided the machinery for divorce. No opprobrium, no sin, obtains against those who divorce, although great sadness is felt for the couple who must end their marriage. It is said in the Talmud, "The very altar of God weeps for one who divorces the wife of his youth" (Gittin 90b).

RELATIONSHIP BETWEEN CIVIL AND RELIGIOUS DIVORCES

Because the divorce apparatus of civil law exists outside the rabbinical courts, the religious bill of divorcement, known as a *get* (decree), must be obtained in a separate proceeding. Unlike the civil court, which decides whether there are grounds for a divorce, sometimes in an adversary proceeding, the rabbinical court functions only to ratify the decision of a married couple to end their marriage. The covenant they entered into as individuals can be set aside by mutual consent. The *get* procedure acts to protect the rights of each party to remarry and to assure the legitimacy of the children of such later marriages. It is assumed that remarriage will probably occur, since the married state is the desideratum.

Because people often do not realize that in Orthodox and Conservative practice it is necessary to obtain a *get* even though a civil divorce has been procured, problems may arise in second marriages. Sometimes the first husband, out of spite or negligence, will refuse to give his ex-wife a rabbinical divorce, especially when she has been the one to press for the civil divorce.

At the time one is going through the unpleasantness of a secular divorce, one rarely thinks of future marriageability in a religious sense, especially if there is no actual candidate eagerly waiting for the day when the second marriage will become possible. The civil decree, embodying alimony, tax, property, and child-custody provisions, seems to be complete in itself. But from a traditional point of view, a person who has had a religious wedding ceremony can only complete its dissolution with a religious divorce. Both must be "according to the laws of Moses and Israel."

Some lawyers are not aware of the need for a *get;* others may hesitate to reinforce the powers of the rabbinical courts or interfere in their client's religious life. Nevertheless, they do have some responsibility to suggest to Jewish clients that at least a consultation with a rabbi is in order before making any final legal arrangements.

The thought that one may one day choose to marry an observant Jew, or want to be married in Israel, may seem remote indeed at the moment of a civil divorce, but that is the time when a *get* may most easily be secured as one of the conditions of a civil settlement. If one should seek the religious decree several years after the marriage has been dissolved, the *get* may be difficult or impossible to secure if the husband cannot be found or refuses to cooperate.

Obtaining both decrees at the same time will prevent many acutely embarrassing and possibly insoluble problems later.

THE IMPORTANCE OF A RELIGIOUS DIVORCE

The consequences of failure to secure a *get* can be serious indeed. Only the Reform movement recognizes a civil decree as final for religious purposes. In both Conservative and Orthodox groups, a previous marriage to a Jewish partner must have been ended by a *get* before a rabbi will consent to marry either of the parties to a second spouse.

A divorced person without a *get* may not marry another Jew in Israel, where all marriages and divorces are governed by religious law.

Women are particularly vulnerable, since a rabbinical divorce proceeding can only be initiated by a man, except in very special circumstances; thus if a woman seeks to regularize her position, she is dependent on the man's goodwill for the decree. To a lesser extent, the man who desires a *get* needs his ex-wife's cooperation, but if she refuses to go through the proceedings, he can always arrange a *get* by proxy.

A woman who marries again without first securing a *get* is regarded by traditionalists as entering into an adulterous union, for in their eyes she is still married to her first husband. Any child of the second union, moreover, is regarded as a *mamzer* (illegitimate to the tenth generation, therefore not a permissible spouse) by traditional communities all over the world. In some observant communities, therefore, rabbis will inquire whether the parents of the bride or groom were ever divorced and whether that divorce was properly formalized by a religious bill of divorcement.

The proper attitude to take toward a spouse who seeks a religious decree is expressed in the rule of the Shulhan Arukh that no one should be forced to live with someone who is distasteful to him or her. If there is a divorce intended, it should be carried out properly in both civil and religious spheres, with a minimum of hostility.

Initiating Religious Divorce Proceedings.

When both parties consent, a *get* is relatively easy to procure. The grounds are most liberal; incompatibility alone is sufficient. The first step is to consult a rabbi, preferably one of the same orientation as the rabbi who performed the original marriage, if the first rabbi is not available. He may not refuse a divorce decree if it is obvious that only discord and degradation will result from the couple's continuing to live together. If he cannot bring the couple to a reconciliation, he will not obstruct the dissolution of their marriage. When there are problems in the situation (such as a spouse who cannot be found), he will determine how to proceed.

What Happens in Jewish Divorce Proceedings.

The formalities of the *get* procedure have been designed to slow down the process so that each party may give it serious thought, and to prevent the husband from impulsively divorcing his wife for a mere whim, which a superficial reading of the laws might suggest is possible.

A *bet din* (a rabbinical court consisting of three rabbis competent in the laws of marriage and divorce) is convened; there must be two witnesses. Both parties must testify three separate times that they are acting of their own free will and not under duress. The *get* is read aloud three times during the proceedings and handed ceremoniously to the wife. Once she accepts it into her hands, the decree is final.

The actual *get* is marked for identification and filed with the rabbi. The husband and wife each receive certificates (*p'tur*) attesting to the dissolution of their marriage according to Jewish law. Then both are free to marry again, although in Orthodox practice, a woman is expected to wait ninety-two days to remove any doubts as to the paternity of the child of the second marriage. The certificate should be safeguarded like any other important legal document.

Should it be impossible or undesirable for husband and wife to meet during the proceeding, the decree can be delivered through a proxy, who will act for the husband.

Unfortunately, the various branches of traditional Judaism do not recognize each other's divorces, and in Israel, where the laws of Orthodox Judaism are the state laws of marriage and divorce, only an Orthodox *get* suffices.

The State of Israel does recognize the civil law of other countries, thus leaving the country to marry is always a possibility, although burdensome. These marriages always remain questionable in the eyes of the Orthodox.

Resolving Serious Problems. Obviously, some marital situations can pose serious difficulties for the person seeking a *get*. Sometimes these can be resolved by consulting the rabbi of a more liberal denomination, or one who is a recognized expert in this special and complicated field of rabbinic law.

A religious ceremony is always possible in the Reform tradition, provided that the civil divorce papers are in order.

If the first marriage was not a religious ceremony, or the first spouse was not Jewish, no *get* is necessary.

79. *Divorce and the Social Scene*

Divorce is becoming more and more common, even among Jews, once known for their very low divorce rates. A recent survey of religious courts reveals that four out of ten Jewish marriages now end in divorce, even in the group observant enough to procure a *get*. Sooner or later most people have to deal with the social problems created by a divorce, whether as one of the couple, or as a parent, child, or friend.

THE CHILDREN

It is the children who suffer most when their parents decide to divorce, and their best interests should be the paramount concern. They should be told about the impending divorce before others know. Both parents must explain their decision to part and live separate lives in terms the children can understand. The living arrangements should be made clear in a caring way.

Unless they are so young that they do not really know the parent who leaves, children cannot help being ambivalent in their feelings toward mother and father, who are no longer an entity. It is devastating for a child to be asked to take sides, yet divorced parents often carry on a war for the affections and loyalty of their children. By demanding a unilateral devotion, the parent who has custody deprives the child of one parent, and in effect makes him an orphan. The parent with visitation rights often makes the child uneasy and unhappy by his questions about what the other parent is doing.

Unless some brutal or demeaning episodes have been the cause of the divorce, the parents should make an effort to be fair to each other about custody and visitation rights and to be fair to the child. They may not love each other any more and wish to go their separate ways, but a child cannot divorce his parents and needs to feel that he still belongs to both, and they to him, even though they now live apart.

Children caught up in a divorce need a great deal of reassurance that their parents will go on loving them afterward. After all, if daddy and mommy don't love each other any more, why should either of them continue to love him, a mere child? What is to stop them from abandoning him in turn? So goes the reasoning of a small child.

There may be other psychological problems of varying magnitude. There are many good counseling services available through community and religious organizations and the schools. When the emotional burdens of a divorce become crushing, neither parent nor child should try to carry them unaided.

CARRYING ON FAMILY TRADITIONS

If one can manage it, the times in Jewish life that are family occasions should be carried on together for as long as possible: the Passover Seder, bar/bat mitzvahs, and so on. If this is too strained, the child should at least be given the opportunity to share the holidays with each of the parents in turn, and coincidentally with the grandparents. Going to the two Seders at the homes of each set of grandparents in turn, attending a family Hanukkah or Purim party with the parent who does not have custody, for example, will help the child keep up his contacts with both sides of the family.

If there are religious differences between the parents, the one who does not have custody cannot enforce complete *kashrut* or Sabbath observance, for instance, on the parent who does, and he should not make the child feel guilty if the home in which the child must live is not totally kosher or Sabbath-observing any longer, or vice versa. The youngster will eventually become mature enough to understand that his parents have each gone their separate ways, and order their lives according to their own lights. The child must ultimately decide these matters of observance for himself.

SEPARATION

Couples who decide to separate on a trial basis before going through a divorce need no longer engage in the elaborate concealment subterfuges once common. Today's open attitude is much to be preferred; however, if there is any possibility of a reconciliation, especially when there are children, each partner should be careful to avoid spreading embittering recriminations and challenging friends and relatives to take sides. Such attitudes are always in poor taste. They can be acutely embarrassing if a reconciliation does come about.

WHEN THE DIVORCE BECOMES FINAL

Looked at constructively, a divorce offers release from a difficult, perhaps degrading way of life. It gives each partner a chance to start anew and hope for happiness with someone else. Even the so-called innocent party should finally see the wisdom of releasing a spouse who has come to love another person.

When the divorce becomes final, each spouse must, as it were, start life over and learn to "fly solo." The man, who is usually the one to leave the home, must set up a bachelor residence for himself and learn to keep house. The woman must now cope with all the ramifications of family life on her own.

Both must reorganize their personal lives. A new residence may be involved for each partner, should the original home be sold. The children must establish the routines of living with one parent and visiting with the other, and resettling themselves in a new community.

A woman has to organize her financial and legal affairs, and should seek expert counsel in these areas if she has never paid much attention to this side of her life before. She may have to get a job for the first time, or retrain herself for a better one. In addition, she must settle the details of daily living that indicate her new status.

A DIVORCÉE'S NAME

As soon as she is divorced, a woman must drop her ex-husband's name. Many women now resume their maiden names after a divorce. Others use their given names with the married name and style themselves "Ms." Others use "Mrs."—or no title.

Thus Mrs. Charles Solomon, after a divorce, would have a choice of names:

Mrs. or Ms. Elizabeth Solomon
Ms. Elizabeth Steinberg (her maiden name)
Elizabeth Steinberg Solomon

The resumption of the maiden name avoids confusion when the former husband remarries, especially if he lives in the same town.

A divorcée should order new stationery and phone listings, for she is no longer Mrs. Charles Solomon. If she decides to resume her maiden name, she may want to send a printed card to all those on her mailing list, including business associates, announcing:

The former Mrs. Charles Solomon will be known as
Elizabeth Steinberg.

A woman with children is not upset nowadays if she is called "Miss" or "Ms." instead of "Mrs." Even children can understand why their mother has dropped their father's name, if she explains her decision to them.

A couple who decided to use a hyphenated name when they were married would each drop the respective spouse's name. Thus Mr. and Mrs. Charles Steinberg-Solomon would go back to being Charles Solomon and Elizabeth Steinberg after a divorce. Neither one would want to retain the name of the person from whom he or she has parted.

A child's name would remain hyphenated, since both surnames are those of his parents.

REMOVING THE WEDDING RING

Most women take off their wedding rings as soon as the divorce is final nowadays, even when they have children. The engagement ring may still be worn, but it is transferred to the right hand, or may be made over into a pinkie ring. Although this can be a sad moment, these actions should be regarded as a therapeutic symbol of liberation from unhappiness.

Men should also remove their rings, although some continue to wear them for the "protection" they seem to offer against the legions of predatory females they imagine to be lying in wait for them as soon as they are free. It is, to put it mildly, rather dishonest.

A NEW OUTLOOK FOR WOMEN

A woman who has been married for some time often finds it difficult to take up again the lifestyle of a single person. However, making the effort to entertain and to date is important.

To function at her best socially, a newly single woman must overcome her reluctance to go out by herself. This is not easy, but reclusive living is not the answer. Having another single friend helps in "reentry" until one gains the poise and self-assurance to go to concerts, museums, theaters, or parties unescorted.

A woman on her own should get used to taking herself home in a cab or her own car, if there is no escort. She must learn how to travel about safely, and never to skip any of the security measures so necessary for personal protection and peace of mind. A thoughtful host will call a cab, or arrange for a ride home with another guest.

It is a mistake to associate exclusively with the couples who were one's friends before the divorce. Although this feels "safe," one finally comes to feel like the "odd number" and knows that the others are aware of the failure of the past marriage; moreover, every occasion brings to mind the time past, when the couple were together. However, one should not reject the efforts of friends to introduce an eligible date. Who knows? Some most successful matches have resulted from introductions.

Meeting new people can be a problem but there are many activities and organizations that can be helpful, among them Parents Without Partners (listed as PWP), synagogue, cultural, hobby, and political action groups. In New York City, the Mayor's Office of Volunteer Services maintains a list of activities besides the usual hospital and library services. Taking courses, getting a job, especially if one has never worked before, also help create a new, wider social circle.

Singles bars and dances are generally disappointing, occasionally humiliating, and sometimes downright dangerous. Although a woman may certainly enter a bar unescorted nowadays, unless it is known as a quiet social gathering place based on neighborhood or occupational acquaintance, she would be best advised to stay out of it.

THE NEWLY ELIGIBLE MALE

Theoretically, men have an easier time socially when they become single again. But the new bachelor has to face the same problems of feeling unloved and rejected, and in addition, usually has to cope with housekeeping on his own. Decorating, cleaning, and cooking are all new arts he must master, sometimes on a sharply reduced living standard when there is alimony and child support to pay.

It is easy for men to make casual acquaintances, since eligible men are very much in demand, especially in the older age brackets. Meaningful, relating friendships are more difficult to achieve. A man, too, is well-advised to fight his feelings of rejection and depression by seeking new interests and cultivating the people he meets in the course of his daily real-life activities.

DATING AND ENTERTAINING

Encountering Old Friends.   When you are out with a new companion, it may be embarrassing to meet old acquaintances who knew you when you were married to someone else. Some divorced people feel the impulse to turn and run or hide. This only feeds the gossip mill. It is best to handle the encounter frankly, by greeting the old friend and casually saying, in introducing your escort, something like: "Jane, you probably don't know that Peter and I were divorced [or separated] last spring. This is my friend Richard Blum."

Including the Children.   Some social engagements that can include the children, such as picnics or beach excursions, should be planned. Children, too, are often uprooted and lonely after their parents' divorce. If a move is involved, they will need active support in making new friendships and settling into new school situations. They, too, need to be able to offer hospitality to their friends.

Any new relationship that begins to be serious must also take the children into account. The new partner will become a stepparent, either full time, or during visits from children living with the ex-spouse. It is important that the children come to know and like the future stepparent.

Invitations to the Divorced.   Occasionally people sending out invitations to a large festivity, such as New Year's Day open house or a bar mitzvah reception, may not know that a couple has recently been separated or divorced.

The spouse remaining at home should respond to all invitations. When the occasion is a large reception that does not involve seating at a meal, one may accept for himself or herself, then phone or send a note to inform the host of the divorce, offering to forward the invitation to the spouse so that he or she may also consider attending.

When the party is more intimate, perhaps involving seating at a dinner, which would bring the two together in an undesirably close situation, one need not offer to forward the invitation, but may suggest instead that the hostess invite the other spouse separately.

A hostess who is a friend to both will invite the other spouse to some other party soon after. If she was close to only one, she need not invite the other.

THE RIGHTS OF EX-IN-LAWS

Unless a divorce proceeding has been so bitter and filled with hostility that the parent with custody of the child (usually the mother) feels she never again wants to see or hear from the ex-husband or his family, she should recognize that the child's grandparents have some rights and ongoing interest in the children.

The grandparents remain blood relatives of the children, even after a divorce. They may love them very dearly and want to see them, notwithstanding the quarrel between the parents. In the best arrangement, the visiting parent would take the children to see the grandparents from time to time, and perhaps have them spend part of a vacation period with them. As children grow up, it even becomes possible to send them alone to visit their grandparents, perhaps on a Jewish holiday.

When a grandparent dies, if the child has known him or her, he should be told about it, and allowed to go to the funeral or to pay a condolence call if he his old enough.

If there has been a friendly relationship between a divorced husband and wife, either one should pay a condolence call when the parent of the other dies, just as they would for a friend in mourning.

MEETINGS WITH AN EX-SPOUSE

Even when postdivorce relations are not the most amicable, there will be times when one must meet one's ex-spouse: bar mitzvahs and weddings of the children, for example. Since the happiness of the child is paramount on such a day, the parents should put the best face they can on such meetings. (See Chapters 43, 58, 69, 70.)

A line of civilized communications should be kept open. Children should send holiday and birthday cards to their father and let him know about their school achievements, graduations, and the like.

When the relationship between the divorced parents is very bad, they will avoid each other as much as possible, but every so often, especially if they still live in the same city, they may meet unexpectedly at some large social function. Neither ex-spouse should feel that he or she must give up going to a gala event because the other will be there. It is possible to attend and enjoy the function, while behaving as distantly to each other as nodding acquaintances.

A FORWARD LOOK

Jewish thinking encourages remarriage. It is not divorce, but the single state, that is regarded as undesirable and unhealthy. This philosophy is amply supported by fact, for U.S. Census statistics show that three out of four divorced persons marry again. Recalling these odds should be of some help in bleak hours.

FUNERALS AND MOURNING

Comfort ye, comfort ye ...

—ISAIAH 40:1

Death is an inevitable part of life. Jewish philosophy regards all men as equal in death, and proceeds always from the position that one's public behavior should not cause humiliation or embarrassment to others. This is the rationale behind the rules requiring austere simplicity in funeral procedures. Every respect must be accorded to the dead, as also to the living, but extravagance and ostentation are not recognized as means of showing this regard. In the Orthodox view, all Jews must be buried in the same kind of dress and in the same kind of coffin, both of the simplest.

80. Arranging an Orderly Estate

As a person matures and begins to manage his own affairs, he should give some thought to the final arrangements that will ultimately become the responsibility of his survivors. To help one's family, one should make a will, which should include funeral directions. If there is no will, one should at least discuss one's funeral and financial intentions with children, a spouse, or a close friend, or better still, leave a letter of instructions as a guide. A thoughtful person will also make provisions for a cemetery plot and prepare an accessible index of important papers.

Care should be taken to assure that someone knows the names of one's lawyer, insurance agent, and stock broker, and the location of the safe deposit boxes, bank accounts, securities, and the like. This list should also include social security numbers, pension numbers, and the names of any business, labor, or fraternal organizations that will provide death benefits.

Such steps taken to smooth the way for the living become a gracious, loving final gesture.

81. When a Death Occurs

NOTIFYING PEOPLE

A close friend or relative should be entrusted with the duty of making the funeral arrangements and notifying family and friends of the death. If there is no one else, one of the mourners may do this, provided he or she has the self-control in these first hours of grief.

The funeral director or burial society (*hevra kaddisha*) and the rabbi of one's congregation should be notified first, so that they may begin their preparations for the funeral immediately.

Close relatives and friends may be notified by telephone. Lengthy conversations should be avoided by the recipients of such calls, since many people have to be reached within a short time. In a large family, relatives who are informed may offer the kindness of calling others in their branch of the family to lighten the burden. It is permissible for the person who calls them to ask them to do this; he may also ask friends to inform others in the deceased person's profession, fraternal organizations, and the like.

Those who *must* be notified because they have a duty to mourn are the spouse of the deceased, parents, brothers, sisters, and children over the age of thirteen. Younger children who are mature enough to understand may be permitted to participate in mourning. (See Chapter 83.)

Informing people other than the mourners is discretionary, but since it is a mark of respect to have a well-attended funeral, every effort should be made to reach as many concerned people as possible.

The funeral director may be entrusted to place death notices in the newspapers, if they are desired.

LEGAL FORMALITIES

Obtaining a Death Certificate.   The attending physician prepares the death certificate, and the funeral director arranges to get the necessary copies, as none of the other funeral steps may proceed without it. In cases of sudden or accidental death, when no physician was present, the county medical examiner may have to be called. In such cases, it is best to call a physician first and let him decide how to proceed.

Autopsies.   Jewish tradition forbids autopsies, unless absolutely necessary for legal reasons. When a person dies in a hospital, there is often pressure to permit an autopsy. The family need not consent to this as a matter of course. If it is repugnant to the family, they may refuse permission, unless convinced it would help save other lives by advancing medical knowledge.

Calling a Lawyer.   The family attorney should be notified as soon as possible. There may be legal problems requiring his attention, and he is probably the custodian of important papers, including the will.

THE ROLE OF THE RABBI AND THE FUNERAL DIRECTOR

The rabbi will set the time of the funeral. He should be informed of the pertinent details of the deceased person's life so that he may make a suitable address during the service. It will be necessary to give him the Hebrew names of the deceased and the father of the deceased. If these are unknown (or perhaps were never given), the rabbi will make an appropriate choice.

Most synagogues have official funeral directors. One is not obligated to use them, but they are usually most to be trusted to carry out the arrangements according to the practices of their congregations.

If neither the person who died nor anyone in the immediate family is a member of a synagogue, a conveniently located funeral director should be selected. The funeral home will then provide someone to officiate at the funeral as part of its service. Since the home offers a wide range of funerals, it is important to keep in mind what is simple, seemly, and correct, and reject the proffers of unnecessary expensive "extras." One does this by requesting a traditional Orthodox funeral. Respect for the dead does not require the flouting of tradition or the extravagant diminution of a small estate. Given a choice of spending money on arid mourning display or on living memorials, one should always choose life.

82. *Traditional Funeral Arrangements*

ORTHODOX RITUALS

An Orthodox casket must be a plain wooden box (usually pine) constructed with wooden pegs, neither varnished nor carved. At the funeral it will be draped with a plain cover, supplied by the synagogue or funeral home, often embroidered with simple lettering and a *Magen David* (star of David) as decoration. It is permissible to use the American flag for a military funeral.

In traditional funerals the coffin is left closed, out of respect for the dead, who should be remembered as they were in life and not in the hour of their death. Thus there is no viewing of the body.

Embalming the body is forbidden. It is prepared for burial by ritual washing (*taharah*) carried out by the burial society of the synagogue or by the funeral home.

The body, whether male or female, is then dressed in a set of handmade, white linen grave clothes (*takhrikhim*), symbolizing purity and dignity. If a man owned a *kittel* (gown worn by the Orthodox on Yom Kippur and Passover), it is used for his burial. A *tallit* (prayer shawl) is placed over the shroud of a man, usually with one of the fringes cut. All jewelry is removed, except for the wedding ring, which may be left on.

No flowers are placed on the coffin or used in the chapel, since they are reminders of vanity and worldly pleasure. The money that might have been spent on them is usually donated to a charity in the deceased's name.

As a mark of respect, the body is not left unattended between the time of death and the time of burial. A watcher is provided by either the burial society or the funeral home. His function is to sit up with the body, reciting Psalms until the funeral begins.

Conservative practice generally conforms to this procedure. Reform ritual permits a more elaborate casket, flowers, and sometimes viewing of the body. Calling hours may be substituted for having a watcher sit with the body.

RITUALS OF FRATERNAL ORGANIZATIONS

Many organizations, such as the Masons, Knights of Pythias, and Shriners, have funeral rituals of their own. One should consult the rabbi before allowing the deceased's fraternal organizations to participate in the funeral. Some Orthodox and Conservative rabbis do not permit these observances; others have set rules for them.

TIME OF THE FUNERAL

Funerals may not be held on the Sabbath, Rosh Hashanah, Yom Kippur, or the major festival days, nor are they customary at night.

A funeral should be held as close to twenty-four hours after death as possible. On Friday (*erev Shabbat*) or the day immediately preceding the eve of a festival, the funeral is held as early in the day as possible, so as not to interfere with the necessary Sabbath or festival preparations.

If the family is widely dispersed, one may wait up to three days for the relatives to gather.

Some changes in the twenty-four-hour rule may be necessitated by all these factors. The choice of day and time made by the rabbi and funeral director will take all these elements into account.

Prompt burial is a mark of respect, as it is considered a humiliation to leave the dead unburied.

WHEN THE DEATH OCCURS FAR FROM HOME

The funeral usually takes place in the community in which the deceased lived. If a person dies away from home, some member of the family will have to go there to arrange to bring the body back and to attend to the required legal formalities.

Some popular retirement areas, inhabited as they are by many elderly people, have funeral directors prepared to handle all these arrangements for a fee. Check carefully to be sure that all the charges are understood before engaging such a service.

If one decides to hold the funeral away from the home community, one may have a memorial service at home after the funeral away.

FUNCTIONS OF THE FUNERAL HOME

The funeral home provides other assistance to the bereaved family by arranging for the transportation of the body from the hospital or home to the funeral chapel and to the cemetery, securing additional copies of the death certificate (as many as six are generally required for various legal purposes), arranging for the publication of any death notices desired by the family, providing a reception room and chapel (and rabbi, if necessary) for the services, arranging with the cemetery to have all in readiness for the burial, providing transportation to and from the cemetery for the family and other mourners as needed, and providing parking space for the cars of those attending the funeral. As many stools as the mourners will need at home for the *shivah* week, a seven-day memorial candle, and a *yahrzeit* calendar are also generally supplied by the funeral home.

DEATH NOTICES AND OBITUARIES

The death notice should set out, after the full name of the deceased (including the maiden name of a married woman), the date of death, names and relationships of the immediate family members (including the full names of married sisters and daughters), and the time and place of the funeral. The address where the family will sit *shivah* may be included, as well as a request that no flowers be sent, and the name of a charity to which the family wishes donations to be made. It is not necessary to give a cause of death. A death notice for a man might read:

RUBIN, George H. On February 13, 1978. Beloved husband of Beatrice (née Hanft), cherished father of Louise Weintraub and Eric, dear brother of Adele Isaacs, and adored uncle. Services Wednesday 1P. M. at Temple Sinai, Valley Road, Milltown, N.J. Memorial donations may be made to your favorite charity in lieu of flowers.

A death notice for a woman might read:

STEIN, Florence Berman, beloved wife of Bernard, devoted mother of Philip and Rose Frank, loving grandmother and great-grandmother. Services Thursday, February 16, 11:45 A.M., "The Riverside," 76th Street and Amsterdam Avenue.

Notices may be placed in the morning and evening papers of large cities, in daily or weekly local papers, and in Yiddish-language publications, as appropriate. (Yiddish publications will translate the material for you.) Some local radio stations carry death and obituary notices on the air once or twice a day. In most cases the publications or radio station will call back to verify details.

The family may phone the papers with an obituary. If the deceased was prominent in local affairs, business, the arts or professions, community service, or politics, the paper may have a reporter phone to request a biography.

THE FUNERAL SERVICE

Keri'ah. Just before the funeral service begins, the rabbi will take the mourners aside for the ceremonial rending of garments, an ancient expression of mourning. This is now done by making a small razor blade cut in some item of personal attire, usually a tie for men and a cardigan sweater or overblouse for women. Children are included.

Since one wears the slashed garment during the entire seven-day *shivah* period (some even do this for the thirty-day *sheloshim* period), it is best to select something that will be comfortable as well as not too expensive. The cut is sometimes made through a buttonhole (in a vest, for example), so that it may be darned later. However, most people discard this item of clothing when the mourning period is over.

Some follow the practice of wearing a slashed black ribbon pinned to the clothing, instead of slashing the actual garment. The wearing of a black armband, or all-black mourning clothes, is not a Jewish custom; it is regarded as an ostentatious sign of mourning, which is not permitted.

The Service. Services are generally held in the chapel of a funeral home nowadays, even if the person died at home.

Orthodox practice does not permit a funeral service in the sanctuary of a synagogue unless the deceased was an extraordinarily learned scholar; wealth and worldly distinction alone do not merit this honor.

Conservative and Reform congregations sometimes permit funerals in the sanctuary.

The rabbi reads from Psalms, delivers a eulogy, and recites the memorial prayer, *El Male Rahamim*. A close friend or relative may be asked to deliver the eulogy or read an appropriate tribute. The family may have a cantor chant the Psalms or other parts of the liturgy. After the memorial prayer, the family leaves the chapel first, following the coffin as it is carried out to the hearse for the burial service at the cemetery. All those who will accompany the mourners there form a cortege for the drive. The rabbi goes with the mourners to perform the graveside service.

THE BURIAL SERVICE

Serving as a pallbearer, accompanying the mourners to the cemetery, and participating in the actual burial are considered to be among the highest *mitzvot*—those of *hesed shel emet*, deeds of true loving kindness, for no recompense can ever be given for them, nor is it expected.

At the Graveside. At the cemetery the first Kaddish (memorial prayer) is recited; therefore a *minyan* (ten males over the age of thirteen) is necessary. Each male mourner drops a handful of earth into the grave, followed by all the men present who wish to participate in the *mitzvah* of burial by each dropping a spadeful of earth in turn. It is customary to remain until the coffin is covered. Some stay until the grave is filled.

Leaving the Cemetery. After leaving the gravesite, one washes one's hands at the cemetery gate, and also upon returning home. In traditional practice the necessary ritual washing materials (pitcher of water, basin, and hand towel) are set out at the door, so that the mourners can wash immediately upon entering, without going through the house.

COSTS OF THE FUNERAL

The costs of the funeral, grave plot, and tombstone are met out of the estate before any other bequests are paid. The will usually expressly provides this. Should there not be enough in the estate, the immediate family is responsible. Social Security, union, professional, and fraternal organizations should be checked for whatever financial benefits (including cemetery plots) they provide.

THE FIRST MEAL (SEUDAT HAVRA'AH)

A "meal of consolation," prepared by friends or neighbors, or if necessary, a caterer, is set out for the mourners upon their return to the home where they will observe the *shivah* period. It is customary to include hard-boiled eggs among the foods served, since they are regarded as a symbol of life, and of the unending circle of life and death. Both the foods and the manner of service should be simple. Serving liquor should be avoided; certainly the aspect of an "open bar" and convivial refreshment is reprehensible.

This is not a reception or an act of hospitality on the part of the mourners, but a gesture of consolation and sympathy offered them by others. They therefore must take no part in the arrangements, serving, greeting any guests, and the like. If they do not feel up to more than a token participation in the meal, they need do no more.

83. *Mourning*

The mourning period falls into two parts: *aninut* (the time between the death and the funeral) and *avelut* (formal mourning). During the brief *aninut* period the mourner may abandon himself to his grief. The *avelut* period is divided into two parts. First comes the ceremonial *shivah* (the first seven days after the funeral), and then *sheloshim* (the remainder of the thirty days after the funeral).

THE WEEK OF MOURNING (SHIVAH)

This period begins immediately upon the return from the cemetery and is referred to as "sitting *shivah*." The mourners sit on low wooden stools during the waking hours, generally for seven (in Hebrew, *shivah*) days after the funeral, hence the name. On the last day, one need sit only half a day.

Usually the immediate family gathers in one home, in which all will sit, but if there are small children to be cared for, or the family is very large, the various family members may sit in their own homes. The best choice is to remain together if at all possible. It is more comforting for the family, and easier for friends to call on them all at one time.

Although Orthodox tradition does not allow mourners to leave the house during the *shivah* period, Conservative and Reform practice permits mourners to return to their own homes to sleep.

A memorial candle that will burn for seven days is lit. In a traditional household the mirrors are covered or turned to the wall, since they are regarded as reminders of worldly vanity.

DUTIES OF THE MOURNER DURING SHIVAH

Orthodox Practice. During *shivah*, in Orthodox practice, a mourner may not leave the house, perform manual labor, conduct business, cohabit, perform any act of personal adornment, such as using perfumes or cosmetics, shaving, cutting the hair, bathing, or washing clothes. Leather shoes are not worn. A mourner need not greet visitors, nor is he obliged to talk with them if he feels unequal to this.

In general, during these first seven days the mourner may abandon himself to his grief and is not supposed to concern himself with any part of his normal worldly life. This includes the usual household duties of women.

The rabbinical interpretation of *shivah* is that three days are for weeping and the whole seven for lamenting.

Male mourners must recite Kaddish with a *minyan* (quorum of ten) every day. If there is no *minyan* in the house, the mourner may leave the house to go to synagogue for services. Friends often arrange to come to the house each morning and make up a *minyan* for the mourners. This is a great *mitzvah*.

Conservative and Reform Practice. Conservative practice usually follows these rules, with some modifications on the prohibition against leaving the house.

Reform custom shortens the *shivah* period to the first three days and does not require the rending of garments or the use of mourning stools. During the three days, however, the mourner is expected to refrain from work and entertainment and to remain at home unless he must leave to attend services. Kaddish is said with a *minyan* on the three days.

THE MONTH OF MOURNING (SHELOSHIM)

A period of modified mourning after *shivah* extends over the remainder of the thirty days after the funeral. During this time a mourner may not marry, attend places of festivity or entertainment (even of a religious nature), go on a business journey, or participate in social gatherings. Among the traditionally observant, one is also not supposed to cut one's hair, wear pressed garments, or shave, but if this will cause humiliation, business loss, or lower one's social or professional standing, one need not observe all of these restrictions of dress and appearance.

Men continue to say Kaddish at morning and evening prayers in a synagogue. Women may also say these prayers when the congregation permits it.

EFFECT OF SABBATH AND FESTIVALS ON THE MOURNING PERIOD

One is not permitted to mourn on the Sabbath, or to cause unhappiness to others on this day. Thus all outward signs of mourning stop for the Sabbath, even during the *shivah*, although one may continue any personal private observances. On a Friday one need sit no more than half the day, in order to allow time for Sabbath preparations. On the very short winter days, one must sit at least one hour. The *shivah* period resumes after sundown on Saturday.

Since the major festivals all last a week, their effect on *shivah* and *sheloshim* is more involved.

When a death occurs just before a festival, the entire *shivah* week is ended by the festival, provided one sits at least one hour before the festival begins.

If the *shivah* period ends on the eve of a festival, the beginning of the festival ends the *sheloshim* period. However, if the funeral occurred during the intermediate days of a festival week (*hol hamo'ed*) one observes both *shivah* and *sheloshim* after the festival week, counting the last day of the festival as one of the *shivah* days.

Except when mourning parents, all outward signs of mourning end after thirty days, and one resumes all normal activities.

CHILDREN AND A DEATH IN THE FAMILY

Should children sit *shivah*, attend the funeral of a relative, or go to the cemetery for the interment service? Many families tend to shield children from this experience of sorrow, especially if they are under the age of twelve or thirteen, but in the opinion of some psychiatrists and rabbis this may not be well-advised.

If the child is old enough to understand that someone near to him has died (about age five), he or she can be taken to the funeral service. Children of eight or older might even be taken to the cemetery. When the child is not permitted to attend, these experts feel, he may imagine dread "horrors" from which he must be protected. Seeing what really happens at a funeral or at the cemetery is probably far less frightening than the scenes he fantasizes when he is left behind.

Explaining Grief and Death. Exposure to the truth that adults grieve and cry, and that it is legitimate to feel sorrow and to express it, helps a child to cope with loss and deal with his own feelings. He may find relief for his own emotions in being permitted to mourn, and experience some consolation from the public words of praise about someone dear to him. There is emotional support in the knowledge that others share his grief.

When a child asks about death, it may be difficult to verbalize the truthful and uneuphemistic explanation—that according to Jewish thought it is the end of life for the body. However, one should avoid telling a child that the dead are "sleeping," thus possibly making the child afraid to go to sleep, or that they have "gone to heaven," implying that the body has gone to heaven, too.

Jewish tradition teaches that the soul of man continues to live in "the world to come." The details of this world are, indeed, a mystery, and as a truthful adult one should be prepared to answer that he does not, cannot know.

Return to School. Children over thirteen may return to school at the end of *shivah*. With younger children, the time becomes a matter of discretion. They must certainly show respect for a deceased parent, not to mention the grief they assuredly feel. Yet seven days of unrelieved mourning may be too much for some young children to bear. After the first three days a young child may be sent back to school if he or she wishes to go.

It may also be helpful for a child to remain out of school for the week, but to spend part of the time in the home of a friend or cousin, where his activities may be a little less constrained without his feeling guilty about his normal, healthy need to be a child.

THE YEAR OF MOURNING FOR PARENTS (*SAYING KADDISH*)

In traditional practice the rules of *sheloshim* are supposed to extend over a period of a year following the death of a parent. This is thought to be the time during which the soul is purged of its sins before being reunited with God. For the virtuous, the period is shortened to eleven months. Since one ascribes all virtues to a parent, one ends the mourning period at eleven months instead of twelve.

During the eleven months some modifications of the personal restrictions are permitted for business or professional reasons, but the duty of saying Kaddish every day always continues for observant men, as does the prohibition upon entering a "house of rejoicing" for both men and women.

Problems arising from the observance of these duties should be discussed with a rabbi. There are many solutions and modifications possible.

When the Prayer Is Said. The Kaddish prayer is a passage that occurs in many places in the liturgy. It is a text that extols the majesty, justice, and power of God, and the meaningfulness of life. Only one repetition of it is specifically called "the mourner's Kaddish"; it is the one that occurs just before the end of the morning and evening service, both weekdays and Sabbath.

In modern Orthodox and Conservative ritual, the rabbi will call upon mourners to rise for this prayer. If you are unfamiliar with the synagogue, it may be difficult to follow a more traditional service, where little English is used and the prayers are not formally announced. It is best to choose a synagogue where the ritual is partly in English if you are not familiar with the liturgy.

A transliteration and translation of the text will be found in most He-
brew-English prayerbooks at the appropriate place in the service.

Women and Kaddish.   Traditionally, saying Kaddish has always been
the duty of males. However, many Conservative and most Reform congregations now allow women to rise to say the mourner's Kaddish. Many
women find it a comfort to participate in this *mitzvah* at least once a week
at Sabbath services, especially when there are no male mourners in the family. A woman who feels that this is important to her may very properly inquire about a congregation that observes this custom, if her own synagogue
does not, and choose to attend services there while she is in mourning.

84. *Expressing Sympathy*

Consoling the mourner is a *mitzvah*. Although sometimes a painful duty, it
is always an act of true friendship, a loving gesture which, if neglected, can
never be made up for in any other way. Jewish custom provides a formalized series of actions and remarks that smooth the way at this difficult
juncture in life.

Sympathy may be expressed best by attending the funeral and making a
condolence call during the *shivah* period. If one is unable to do both, one or
the other visit suffices.

ATTENDING THE FUNERAL

It is important to be prompt at a funeral, as they are generally quite brief,
and start only a few minutes after the stated time. Although there are occasions when the mourners are secluded before and during the funeral, those
planning to attend should try to arrive early enough to exchange a few
words with the mourners if they are receiving.

Appropriate Dress.   Men and married women wear hats. The funeral
chapel usually provides yarmulkes (skullcaps) and black lace caps for those
who come without hats. It is not necessary to wear black. Dress should be
simple, conservative, and preferably in dark colors.

Upon entering the funeral home, callers should sign the register with their full names, so that the family, when they are less disturbed, may recollect who attended.

What to Say.   Mourners may not greet people, nor be greeted with the usual cordialities; in traditional practice one does not speak to a mourner, but waits for him to speak first. When attending a funeral, some repeat to themselves as they enter the blessing (always said upon hearing of a death):

Barukh Attah Adonai, Eloheynu Melekh Ha'olam, dayyan ha'emet.
Blessed art Thou, O Lord our God, King of the Universe, the true judge.

Kissing and embracing is permissible, if truly felt. Otherwise, as a purely social gesture, it is out of place.

The mourner may find it easiest merely to mention the name of the person approaching. This enables others to begin a conversation. Appropriate remarks to follow may include comments on how unfortunate it is to meet on such a sad occasion. One should not linger too long in conversation with the family at a crowded funeral, as each caller may wish to speak with them. If the mourners are obviously distraught, one should maintain a sympathetic silence. There is no need to force conversation at this time.

One may greet relatives and friends whom one meets at the funeral, but the conversation obviously is restrained.

Seating at the funeral service varies according to the practice of the chapel; some have segregated seating for men and women, some allow mixed seating. There will be ushers to guide people to the proper seats. The first row or two are always reserved for mourners and close relatives.

MAKING A CONDOLENCE CALL

When to Call.   After the funeral, close relatives may visit at any time during the *shivah* week. Friends usually wait until at least the third day, so that the keenest grief may pass. Most people tend to call in the evenings or on the Sunday of the week.

Conventional meal hours should be avoided, so as not to burden the family with guests at the table.

It is thoughtful to telephone ahead if one wishes to call at a less usual time, so as not to discommode the family, who may need some private time. Mourners need not hesitate to inform such a caller if the time is truly inconvenient. They have no duty of hospitality. Indeed, quite the opposite: expression of hospitality is not allowed during mourning. The duty is on the caller to be sincerely sympathetic and comforting.

Since the family does not sit *shivah* on the Sabbath, one does not pay a condolence call during the time from Friday afternoon to after dark on Saturday.

The Doorbell. In Orthodox households the door is usually left unlocked in a house of mourning, so that one need not ring the bell and require a member of the family to attend the door. If the door is open, one should knock and enter immediately. If it is locked, one must necessarily knock or ring.

What to Say. As at a funeral, in a traditional house of mourning one does not greet a mourner. One may repeat the *dayyan ha'emet* blessing to himself upon entering.

In some Orthodox circles there is no attempt at conversation unless the mourner initiates it. If he or she does not, it is customary merely to sit silently, sharing the mourner's grief and comforting him by your presence.

In most homes, however, conversation is acceptable, even desired, during a condolence call. Try to avoid trivial chatter. Instead, you may touch upon the virtues of the deceased, recollecting time spent together, and the like. It is better not to ask about the last illness and the details of the death, unless it is obvious that the mourner wishes to talk about these matters, in which case you listen sympathetically.

If you did not know the deceased personally, you may express sorrow for the great loss your friend has suffered and hope for the consolation offered by the passage of time.

You need not stay longer than for any courtesy call, about fifteen minutes, unless you know the family well and feel that a longer visit is sincerely desired. Upon leaving, say:

Hamakom yenahem $\begin{cases} otkha & \text{[masc. singular]} \\ otah & \text{[fem. singular]} \\ etkhem & \text{[plural]} \end{cases}$ *b'tokh avli t'Zion v'Yerushalayim.*

May the Lord comfort you and sustain you among the other mourners for Zion and Jerusalem.

In English you may say, "May God comfort you." It is also appropriate to express the wish that you will meet only at happier occasions in the future.

A *shivah* call is obviously not attendance at a party. Yet some homes become so filled with visitors at times that a festive air develops. Callers should not expect to be served food or drink, should be restrained in their conversation with other guests, and should not smoke without permission. One should always bear in mind that the purpose of the visit is to console and express sympathy, not to cause problems of hospitality for the family.

Shivah Gifts.   Elaborate gifts, plants, or flowers should not be brought to the home. With true thoughtfulness, one may bring a present of prepared food for the mourners.

The custom of sending elaborate food baskets or expensive, rich candies and cakes has begun to go out of favor, fortunately, to be replaced by a contribution to charity in the name of the deceased. If you desire to make such a contribution, you may ask the family for the name of the organization it favors. If no preference is expressed, a charity that is appropriate to the life of the deceased is a good choice.

Thoughtful Assistance.   Simple acts of thoughtfulness are sometimes the finest expression of sympathy. In a household where the women of the family are mourners, offering to do the marketing or the laundry, or care for a small child for a few hours, can mean more than any costly gift. A friend might also volunteer to answer the door and telephone for a few hours, receive telegrams, packages, and callers, or do any other household tasks that tax the family during the *shivah* period. Such gracious acts, freely offered, denote the true friend.

LETTERS AND CARDS OF SYMPATHY

If it is absolutely impossible to attend the funeral or to pay a *shivah* call, friends of the family should send letters of condolence. There is really no adequate substitute for a handwritten note which indicates that one cares enough to take a few minutes to write personally to a friend who is going through a difficult emotional time.

If commercial sympathy cards are used, a personal sentence or two should be added before the signature.

A condolence letter need not be more than two or three sentences long, if you did not know the deceased well. It should be written in blue or black ink on plain white or gray stationery. The letter should be addressed to the member of the family whom you know, or to the head of the family.

The contents should express sorrow at hearing the sad news, some brief words about the virtues of the deceased, and a closing wish for consolation. The other members of the bereaved family should be named in this closing. It is appropriate to include your spouse and children in the expression of sympathy.

If you had a close personal relationship with the deceased, the letter, of course, may be longer. It should dwell only on happily remembered incidents or the virtues and accomplishments of the deceased.

Grown children who do not live at home should write their own letters of condolence when there is a death in the family. It is a grace well worth training adolescents to perform. They should be reminded to write such letters when their own friends, employers, or teachers suffer a loss.

Colleagues and employers or supervisors who had a close working relationship with the deceased should also write letters or send a personalized card.

In these letters you may refer to a memorial donation you have made. When one spouse writes the letter for both:

Dear Joan,

　　Harry and I were so sorry to hear about the death of your mother. She was a wonderful person, gracious and loving, and in her passing you and your family have suffered a great loss.

　　May the memory of her many good qualities and the happy years you had together comfort you.

　　We are planning to make a donation to the Children's Hospital in memory of your mother. Harry and I send you our deepest sympathy.

　　　　　　　　　　　　　　　　　　Sincerely yours,
　　　　　　　　　　　　　　　　　　Alice Goldstein

Letter to a colleague who has lost a relative one did not know personally:

Dear Arthur:

　　It was sad to learn of your sister Ethel's death and I feel for you in your loss.

　　I never met Ethel, but if she was at all like you, she must have been a truly outstanding person. The staff joins me in the hope that you and your family will find consolation in happy memories of many good years together.

　　　　　　　　　　　　　　　　　　Sincerely yours,
　　　　　　　　　　　　　　　　　　Joseph B. Levy

Letter to a relative one knows well, when one could not attend the funeral (or make a condolence call):

Dear Aunt Bella:

　　It was sad to learn of Ted's sudden death. Unfortunately, Paul and I could not make the trip to Hartford on Wednesday for the funeral, but our hearts were with you and the whole family in this unhappy hour.

　　Ted was always so full of life, the leader in all our youthful adventures. It doesn't seem possible that he is gone! Paul and I shall always remember the day he introduced us to each other. His laughing face and cheerful wit are an unforgettable part of our college years. We shall truly miss him.

We are planning to drive out to Hartford to be with you and the family on Sunday. Meantime, we are making a contribution to the Cornell Scholarship Fund as a memorial to Ted.

> Your affectionate niece,
> Ann

HOW TO MAKE A MEMORIAL DONATION

To make a memorial contribution, phone or write a letter to the charitable organization selected, enclosing a check and the information that the donation is to be in memory of the person who has died. Give the name and address of the family so that the gift may be announced to them by the charity. The organization will also acknowledge the donation to you. The memorial gift should be made as promptly as possible after the funeral.

The amount of the gift depends on the means of the giver. Donations are often made in amounts that are multiples of eighteen, because the Hebrew number for eighteen also spells the word *hai*, meaning life.

There will necessarily be a lapse of time before the organization sends the gift announcement to the family. You may therefore send a personal note informing the family of the gift. Such a note might read:

Dear Harriet,

How sad that we had to meet on such a melancholy occasion after so many years!

I just wanted you to know that on behalf of Evelyn, the children, and myself I have made a donation to the Hadassah Israel Education Fund in memory of Benjamin. Hadassah will be sending you the certificate soon.

Education seems a fitting memorial to Benjamin, who spent so many years in this work.

May we meet again on happier occasions.

> Sincerely,
> David Martin

ACKNOWLEDGING EXPRESSIONS OF SYMPATHY

The family must acknowledge all personal letters of condolence, all memorial contributions, and all personal kindnesses shown them.

Many funeral directors and social stationers provide printed cards of thanks. These may be used, but a few personal words of gratitude and a signature should be added if the sender is thanking a relative or friend he knows. A completely personal note is to be preferred, if you are able to cope with this social duty at such a time.

Posting a card of thanks in your place of employment or placing such a notice in a newspaper is a dubious custom. It is certainly not wrong, but so impersonal that only an overwhelming flood of condolences, or real incapacitation because of grief, excuses the substitution of such a notice for the individual expression of gratitude.

85. *After the Mourning Period*

THE TOMBSTONE AND THE UNVEILING

Tombstones and Epitaphs. Tombstones and epitaphs have become very simple. Nowadays, many cemeteries allow only one large family marker in the plot, with smaller head- and footstones for each grave in the plot. Before making any decision on a tombstone, one should be very clear as to the cemetery restrictions.

In general, a tombstone should avoid ostentation. The inscription should carry the name in English (and in Hebrew, if one wishes), dates of birth and death, and a reference to relationships. Dates are given according to the English calendar, but Hebrew dates are often included as well. To keep the inscription short, one should refer to the deceased as, for example, "Beloved husband and devoted father," leaving out the names of the family members.

An epitaph may be included. It can be as brief as the mere chapter and verse citation of an appropriate biblical passage, or it may quote the first word or two of the passage in Hebrew or in English, as (for a woman) *"Eshet hayil,"* or "A woman of valor."

It is best to consult a rabbi if one has questions or desires suggestions for an epitaph. The community service departments of the Jewish Theological Seminary, Yeshiva University, or Hebrew Union College can also be helpful in these matters.

Unveiling the Tombstone. A tombstone may be set by the monument maker at any time during the first year, but in many communities it is not "unveiled"—that is, publicly dedicated—until the end of the year following the funeral, usually on a Sunday close to the anniversary of death (*yahrzeit*).

In some areas, where the winter weather can be very inclement, unveilings are held only in the spring and summer months. In such cases, it is best to plan the date with the rabbi.

Cards announcing the unveiling are usually supplied by the monument maker and may be sent to as many friends and relatives as one wishes to notify. The unveiling may, of course, be a completely private family matter.

Some people follow the custom of providing refreshments at the gravesite for those who attend. This is distasteful, at best, and, from a religious point of view, untenable, as a cemetery is considered ritually unclean. One washes the hands upon leaving the cemetery after an unveiling, just as after a funeral.

The unveiling is not a mourning occasion, however, as the soul is now presumed to have been purified and to be at one with God. One may very appropriately invite all who attend the unveiling to the house or to a restaurant for refreshment if one wishes to extend hospitality at this time. The occasion often makes for a quiet family reunion.

THE ANNIVERSARY OF A DEATH (YAHRZEIT)

Yahrzeit is an expression that refers to the anniversary of the death of a spouse or blood relative: parent, child, brother, or sister.

The date observed by Orthodox and Conservative Jews is the Hebrew one, which varies in the English dating from year to year. Reform practice generally keeps the English calendar date. (See Chapter 15.)

The observance begins on the eve of the date with the lighting of a twenty-four-hour memorial candle. One attends the evening and the following morning service in the synagogue and recites the mourner's Kaddish.

Some synagogues maintain a memorial register for members and publish in their bulletins and announce at Sabbath services the memorials of the week. It is customary to make a charitable donation in the form of a private pledge, which should be promptly fulfilled.

MEMORIAL PRAYERS (YIZKOR)

Yizkor is a special commemorative prayer for the dead added to the liturgy of Yom Kippur and to the festival prayers on Shemini Atzereth (last day of Sukkot), the last day of Passover, and the second day of Shavuot. (See Chapters 15, 16, 17, 18, 22.)

People who do not observe the holidays completely but come to the synagogue to say Yizkor should remain to the end of the entire service, out of courtesy to the congregation whose existence and functions have enabled them to fulfill a personal obligation, and also because the recitation becomes merely perfunctory in the absence of worship.

One makes a private pledge of charity as part of any memorial service. Money should not be carried in an Orthodox or Conservative synagogue, as each of these days is a solemn festival. Any pledge one makes should be promptly fulfilled. In a Reform temple there may be a collection, as Reform practice makes no restriction on handling money on holidays.

VISITING THE CEMETERY

Many people follow the traditional custom of visiting the graves of their parents or spouses annually. This is usually done before the High Holidays, but may take place any time the cemetery is open except during the thirty-day or eleven-month mourning periods.

Jewish cemeteries are closed after sunset each day and from sundown Friday till Sunday morning each week, and on every festival day.

On such a visit, memorial prayers are said at the grave and a small stone is placed on top of the tombstone to indicate that a visit has been made.

Charity. Sometimes you find a few elderly men who frequent the cemetery and offer to say the memorial prayer for visitors. If you are approached in this way, you should allow the man to say the prayers and give him a donation. He is offering a friendly assistance as a *mitzvah,* and since in the words of the prayer you will be pledging charity, this custom allows both parties to complete a religious duty.

The Remarried. A widow or widower who remarries is not customarily supposed to continue to visit the grave of the first spouse, but may do so if it will not disturb the new marriage relationship.

Children. It is appropriate to take children along to visit the graves of grandparents (or parents) if they are old enough to understand. It teaches them the duty of respect for the memory of the departed, most times before they are faced with the sad need to carry it out for their own parents.

REFERRING TO THE DECEASED

In traditional circles, especially the Yiddish-oriented, it is customary to add the expression *"alav hashalom"* (feminine: *aleha hashalom*) when one mentions the deceased's name, or the words "mother," "father," "grandfather," etc., referring to them. The words mean "May he [she] rest in peace." This is a respectful custom, but some carry it too far by inserting the phrase after every repetition of the name, peppering the conversation with pious interjections. Once or twice shows reverence; more than that in a single anecdote becomes comic.

An analogous remark is the expression *"zekher l'berakha"* ("of blessed memory") added after the name of a deceased rabbi, sage, or long-departed relative. This usage, too, should not be overdone.

RESUMING NORMAL SOCIAL LIFE

Excessive mourning is forbidden by Jewish tradition. Although the inner, private grief may endure much longer, all outward signs of mourning cease after thirty days, except in the case of the loss of a parent.

Most people feel that they are ready to resume some kind of sociability after three or four months. A widow or widower is expected to remarry (in Orthodox tradition, as soon as possible), and the resumption of dating and attendance at social affairs where one might make new friends is socially correct whenever one feels ready to do so. Nevertheless, there is a general feeling that one should not actually marry again until after the unveiling of the tombstone at the end of the year. The occasion seems to provide a logical termination to bereavement that makes remarriage psychologically possible. Certainly, waiting a year before making a permanent commitment cannot hurt a new relationship that is destined to be happy, and may prevent unfortunate alliances made in the emotional confusion of grief and loss.

Once a new relationship promises to become serious, a tactful person will put away pictures of the deceased spouse, take off a wedding ring if it is still being worn, and for a woman, move the old engagement ring to her right hand, or stop wearing it altogether for a while.

86. Some Special Problems

BURIAL IN ISRAEL

If it is known that the deceased wished to be buried in Israel, it can be arranged through funeral directors specializing in this service.

In such cases, a funeral service is held where the family lives, and the burial service and all formalities in Israel are supervised by the funeral director. The fees that will be incurred should be carefully checked ahead of time, to avoid unhappy problems after the funeral arrangements have been set in motion.

ATTENDING THE FUNERAL OF ONE OF ANOTHER FAITH

There used to be an Orthodox prohibition against entering a church; however, this reminder of the tragedies of the Middle Ages is not observed by most people nowadays. Thus Jews may in good conscience attend funerals held in a church, but should not perform any ritual that is forbidden by their own faith.

One follows the custom in standing and sitting during the service, for example, but one does not kneel, genuflect before the cross, nor pass before the open coffin to "pay last respects" to the dead. If you have any qualms about attending a church service, it is best not to go.

You may, instead, call at the funeral home during calling hours. In most cases, you may be able to avoid viewing the body, but tact may require that you do so sometimes, such as in cases where a relative leads you up to the coffin to see "how natural Uncle John looks." In such situations it is impossible to find a graceful way to refuse. Since the purpose of the visit is to console, there is no choice but to satisfy the mourner.

Although flowers may be sent to a non-Jewish funeral, many families now suggest that friends make charitable donations instead.

To attend church services, all women, even little girls, wear hats. Men remove their hats in church. Dress should be the same as that for a Jewish funeral.

LEAVING ONE'S BODY TO SCIENCE

Many people nowadays leave their bodies or some of their organs to science through "living wills" or simple checkmarks on driver's licenses that effect such bequests in the event of accidental death.

Jews who become interested in this idea should be aware that it is contrary to Orthodox and Conservative Jewish law, which prohibits mutilation of the body in any way after death. Before making a decision on a "living will," however worthy it may seem, one should discuss this matter with one's rabbi and with his immediate family, who will be affected by the decision.

CREMATION

Jewish attitudes toward cremation vary widely. Cremation was opposed in biblical times as being a punitive rite, reserved for burning the bodies of criminals, or as an undignified way of disposing of the bodies of animals. To some Orthodox rabbis, cremation even seems idolatrous, resembling the burning of sacrifices.

The great sage Maimonides held that burial in the earth should be considered a positive commandment ("dust thou art, to dust returneth . . ."). Thus the Orthodox forbid cremation, and do not even permit cremated remains to be buried in their cemeteries. Conservative rabbis actively resist the idea of cremation.

Reform congregations accept cremation as an alternative to earth burial, which they regard as an ancient custom, not a revealed truth.

Apart from religious attitudes, cremation presents many problems for the relatives of the deceased. Some states, for example, do not allow it unless specifically requested in a person's will. Many states also require the burial of the cremated remains, so that most of the expenses of earth burial still must be borne.

People who desire to be cremated after death would be best advised to investigate all these questions while they are still alive, and leave clear, written instructions for their families in a will or a letter, so that no unnecessary problems arise to complicate what should be a dignified end to life.

TRAVEL

Go forth out of thy country . . .

—GENESIS 12:1

Travel, once an exclusive pleasure of the leisure class, has become accessible to almost everyone as a result of the airplane, with its "magic carpet" transport over immense distances, the economical package tour, and the acceptance of low-cost student ways of travel living.

87. *The Jewish Traveler*

In Jewish terms, it has become almost commonplace to visit Israel, with attendant stopovers in such once-exotic destinations as Athens, Istanbul, or the ever-beckoning London, Paris, or Rome. Not only is there a virtually irresistible pull to witness the miracle of the Jewish state, but also the number of families with relatives or friends who have settled in Israel is constantly on the increase. The upsurge of Orthodox Jewish business and vacation travel has caused a concomitant development of special services for the observant traveler. No longer need one travel accompanied by his personal *shohet*, cook, and kitchen, as did Sir Moses Montefiore a century ago!

INITIAL BRIEFING

A wise traveler will make full use of the endless flow of informational material published by national tourist services, airlines, and tour operators. Once you have decided on a destination, study the guidebooks for that area carefully for specific data on climate, sights, customs, appropriate clothing, and suggestions for further reading on history and folklore.

Such general guides are not very often concerned with the specific needs of the Jewish traveler. However, several Jewish guidebooks are available. The most useful for practical data on overseas travel is probably the *Jewish Travel Guide*, published by the *Jewish Chronicle* of London. Its annually revised edition lists kosher and Jewish-style pensions and hotels, restaurants, Jewish organizations, and sights of interest, in great detail for the British Isles, and more briefly for other countries ranging from Afghanistan to Zambia. It rates the *kashrut* of all British and continental eating places, lists vegetarian hotels, private schools and camps for Jewish children, shipping lines serving kosher foods, and the addresses and phone numbers of the synagogues and Jewish organizations listed in each community. There is even a little map in Japanese to be shown to a Tokyo taxidriver if you wish to visit the synagogue, and the name and phone number of the one Jewish resident of Dakar, who understandably, is glad to meet Jewish travelers. In places where the Jewish community has disappeared, it lists the remaining Jewish relics worth visiting.

The library of YIVO in New York has this book and many more; other large metropolitan libraries and some synagogue libraries may have them as well.

There are some Jewish travel agents in New York City who specialize in meeting the needs of the observant traveler. Names, addresses, and phone numbers can be gleaned from the advertising in the Sunday travel pages of the *New York Times,* Anglo-Jewish weeklies, or the publications of many Jewish organizations.

PLANNING A JEWISH-ORIENTED TRIP

A Jewish tourist, making a long-awaited trip to a foreign country, will do well to exercise a little extra forethought and make up a personal itinerary of Jewish sights in the area to be visited. These are harder to seek out, but often at least as interesting as the succession of churches, shrines, and galleries filled with religious art that you are led to by guidebooks or "standard" tours.

Many Jewish fraternal organizations have well-organized travel departments. Their tours always include sites relevant to Jewish history and culture, and a good deal of thought is given to meeting the dietary needs of observant travelers—at the very least, to providing a list of kosher or vegetarian eating places and a guide to *parve* foods available in the area. The itineraries usually provide for Sabbaths at leisure.

Most classic travel sights have associations with Jewish history that are largely ignored by the typical guide's "canned" lecture. In seeking out meaningful experiences for the Jewish traveler and providing intelligent, perceptive lectures, Jewish organization tours rescue our culture and history from the conspiracy of silence and ignorance that work to keep it unknown and uncelebrated, even by Jews themselves. How many Jewish visitors, rightfully appreciative of the wonders of Venice, Rome, or Dubrovnik, have also seen the Ghetto Vecchio, the menorahs carved into the Arch of Titus, or the ancient synagogue of Dubrovnik?

Some organization-sponsored tours also feature people-to-people exchanges within foreign Jewish communities, and creative planning to provide for the special interests of their members.

Tour agents who specialize in Orthodox kosher travel have in recent years branched out to cruises and exotic resort destinations such as Hawaii and Puerto Rico. It is now possible, for example, to spend a *glatt-kosher* Pesah in some of the most luxurious resorts in the world. Most of these tours operate out of New York or Miami; others originate in London. A good travel agent in other cities should be able to locate such trips and make the arrangements for the Orthodox client.

SABBATH AND HOLIDAYS IN ISRAEL

Sabbaths and holidays are official state holidays in Israel. All shops are closed and public transportation does not operate from sundown of the evening before until sunset of the day after. In Jerusalem, and in the neighborhood of synagogues elsewhere, proper attire is expected in public places; there is also no smoking in public. If you must get about, you will probably find taxis operating.

CRUISE SHIPS

Kosher food is available on many of the cruise ships still running. It should, of course, be requested in advance. Some lines, notably Cunard, still maintain elaborate kosher kitchens in which all the food is freshly prepared; it is served in a separate dining area, usually in the first-class dining room, if the ship still keeps to class travel. The steward will consult with passengers at each sitting about the next meal's menu—all in all, a deluxe experience.

Other shipping lines accommodate their kosher passengers with frozen foods, but all is properly heated and served. In either case, the kosher menus are supplemented with every permissible neutral food and fresh fruits and vegetables from the regular fare.

If there are enough passengers who wish to worship together, Sabbath services can usually be held on board ship, in the chapel or in a small lounge. Ask the purser to arrange these. Even passengers who are not eating at the kosher table may wish to participate.

The usual synagogue decorum will prevail at such services. You may be called up for an *aliyah* if there is a *minyan,* and should, if necessary, review the blessings beforehand, both to be fluent and to be able to participate graciously. It is a special *mitzvah* to be part of a traveler's *minyan.*

CAMPING

A camping trip offers the observant family a splendid opportunity to combine *kashrut* with a vacation in novel places. There are freeze-dried and canned foods, some even packed under *glatt-kosher* supervision, to provide menu variety, in addition to *parve* foods available locally. Throwaway dishes and aluminum foil simplify cooking and serving.

Ushering in the Sabbath close to nature in a campground is a rare experience. In addition to the usual camping round of the United States and Canada, there are tropical campgrounds in the Virgin Islands (Cinnamon Bay), Jamaica (Strawberry Fields), and Puerto Rico. All necessary equipment may be rented; however, campers are advised to bring as much of their own food supply with them as possible, so the kosher camper would be exceptional only for his superabundance of paper plates. Reservations should be made long in advance, especially for popular vacation periods.

KOSHER RESORTS

In large Jewish communities there are generally some kosher resorts in vacation areas; some of them, like Grossinger's or the Concord in New York's Catskill Mountains, are self-contained communities with their own post offices and airports. They are visited by hundreds of non-Orthodox or non-Jewish guests in the course of a year, because their food and facilities are legendary. They have, as one guest remarked, "Indoor *everything*, in case it rains!" In addition to their accommodations for conferences, they offer complete religious services on Sabbaths and holidays (often with a cantor and an elaborate choir) and make a complete kitchen changeover for Passover.

The guest who is not Orthodox will encounter a number of differing customs. The menu will be strictly kosher, of course, which means there will be no mixing of milk and meat, no shellfish or pork. A skullcap is worn by men in the dining room at all times in some hotels, on Sabbaths only at others. In some, it is optional. Smoking is not allowed in public areas on the Sabbath. In some *glatt-kosher* (ultra-Orthodox) hotels, on Sabbaths and holidays the elevators may not run, or will be automatically programmed, as will be the lights in public areas. There may be no commercial entertainment on the eve of the Sabbath or holidays, and the swimming pool and other sports facilities may not be open. Discussion groups, outdoor walks, and *oneg* entertainments will abound. When in doubt about any of these observances, ask at the desk or watch others to determine what to do.

In some *glatt-kosher* resorts there is either no mixed swimming or a combination of segregated and mixed swimming hours. The times are usually posted, but it is best to ask if uncertain, before making a potentially embarrassing foray into a "forbidden" area.

Dress regulations with regard to swimming attire, shorts, tennis wear, and other abbreviated clothing should be carefully followed in every type of resort, but particularly so in ultra-Orthodox hotels, where "modesty" requires that such special garments be worn only in the immediate area of their use.

88. Solving Travel Problems

A traveler who is observant must make special arrangements for kashrut and Sabbath needs. Even those who are not so strict in their practice often find themselves longing for a familiar-tasting Jewish meal when far away from home, or wish to find a synagogue so that they can say memorial prayers on a *yahrzeit* or attend holiday services. There are a number of ways to meet these needs.

"AIRLINE DINNERS"

All airlines now provide frozen kosher meals in sealed packages, complete with cutlery and condiments (and in Amsterdam, a yarmulke, doily for the airline tray, and the text of grace before and after meals lettered on the box lid!).

Passengers desiring this special food must request it when making reservations. It is best to repeat the request when reconfirming or making payment. Vegetarian, low-cholesterol, diabetic, or salt-free diets may also be ordered at reservation time.

Despite all this advance preparation, it is prudent to pack some fruit and a bit of cheese in your carry-on luggage. It is not unusual for the meals to be delivered so frozen (because they are packed in dry ice) that the infrared warming ovens on jet liners cannot adequately defrost the food. The attendants do the best they can, but sometimes the food you carry with you may be all that is readily available during the flight except for some crackers, soft drinks, and other beverages.

If the kosher meal does remain frozen during the flight, do not abandon it. Wrap it in a few pages of the newspapers on board and take it along. It will thaw out in time for a late supper or the next day's lunch after debarking. And then take your pen in hand and complain to the airline passenger representative, giving date and flight number. If the name and address of the packagers are on the label, write to them as well. If enough travelers complain, the purveyors may finally be persuaded to deliver the meals warm, as the nonkosher food is, or make some other accommodation so that their food is truly edible.

The same kind of food is served on many cruise ships and in some hotels to accommodate the kosher traveler. They, of course, have adequate kitchens in which to heat the dishes properly and they are usually satisfactory, although hardly in the gourmet class.

KOSHER FOOD EN ROUTE

In many cities you can find kosher meals in unexpected places. Besides the usual kosher restaurants in a metropolis with a large Jewish community, there are Jewish student restaurants in university towns and communal eating places in pensions and student residences.

The food in such eating places is usually quite good, sometimes interestingly local in character, and the "regulars" are always happy to greet a visitor.

Sabbath meals must be prepaid; it is a good idea to phone ahead in any case to determine meal hours and be sure there will be additional servings prepared for visitors.

A KOSHER "SURVIVAL KIT"

There will be times when an impromptu picnic is the only alternative to fasting. To be prepared for such days, carry one of the army knives boasting can opener, bottle opener, and corkscrew blades. Even greater comfort (and economy) can be drawn from that corner of an overnight bag into which you have packed a mug for coffee, tea, or soup, a plastic plate, some plastic cutlery, a jar of instant coffee or tea, some dehydrated soups and other dried foods, and some device for heating water.

A family traveling with children often finds a separate "chow kit" invaluable when filled with enough utensils and convenience foods to serve all.

Purchasing some bread, cheese, tinned foods, fruit, and wine or other beverages in local markets can be an adventure in itself, the meal more tasty and restful than yet another overpriced, overstuffed restaurant "special." An ingenious traveler can adapt many of the suggestions in books on camping and backpacking.

Al fresco eating is acceptable at any park or roadside stop; as for your motel, hotel, or pension room, that is your castle. Be scrupulous about cleaning up after a meal and leaving the place as neat as you found it. Some European cities have very stiff penalties for littering, and Americans are notoriously careless in this respect. It is helpful to carry a paper or plastic litter bag, or failing that, to use a few sheets of newspaper to wrap up the litter until you find a waste can.

SABBATH OBSERVANCE

The first step to a pleasurable and restful Sabbath away from home is to arrange the itinerary so that there is no touring on a Friday night or Saturday. You might also attempt to arrange the Friday stop in a town where there is some Jewish life, so that you can arrange for prepaid Sabbath meals and attend synagogue services. If there is no Jewish hotel or boarding house, demi-pension arrangements or modified American plan with a request for fish or vegetarian meals will make it possible for you to rest and dine without handling money or traveling about for a meal. If a motel stop is planned, check to be sure there is a dining facility within walking distance.

Orthodox women who wish to light candles carry a set of small travel candlesticks and short candles which burn out in a brief time. Of course, you should never leave the candles unattended in a hotel room. In some situations it may be better to arrive at synagogue early and either light candles there or say the blessings over candles already lit.

The day may be most enjoyably spent walking through the city, visiting parks, zoos, or public gardens, or simply resting from the rigors of the tour schedule. For certain personalities, it helps to have a compelling reason to stop running about and take a nap instead.

FINDING A SYNAGOGUE

The word "synagogue" is fairly universal in one variant or another in most European countries, and usually inquiries of a concierge, tourist agency, or English-speaking "tourist" police yield the location and directions. You can also find the addresses of some synagogues before departing by inquiring of synagogue organizations or consulting guidebooks. The chief synagogues of Paris, London, and Rome are fairly well-known tourist attractions in themselves.

In the United States, the *Yellow Pages* of the telephone directory are helpful. Synagogues may sometimes be listed under "Churches," the Jewish Community Center under "Social Services." Local Jewish services are sometimes listed in the local Thursday evening or Friday newspapers on the church news page.

THE TOURIST IN SYNAGOGUE

It is a good idea to telephone ahead to determine the time of services, especially if you wish to observe a *yahrzeit*. In the summer, peak travel time, many synagogues operate on a very much curtailed schedule.

You may also wish to bring your own familiar *siddur* (prayerbook) along. Prayerbooks may be in short supply, and in foreign countries the books often have no translation, or one in the language of the country.

A donation in keeping with the pledge of the memorial prayer should be planned.

If you visit a synagogue when there are no services in progress and the caretaker has gone to any pains to open the building or show you about, you should give him a small donation as a kind of tip.

If you are traveling with a tour guide, do not hesitate to ask about synagogues and take time to go off to visit it or go to services. Chances are that you will be substituting a meaningful real-life experience for one more "sight-cum-souvenir shopping opportunity" and an overpriced "captive lunch."

Travelers intending to visit synagogues should pack appropriate clothing, including, for a woman, stockings even in warm weather. To avoid embarrassment, it is best to assume that the congregation is Orthodox in its tradition. In many areas, shorts on men or women are not acceptable at a religious site, no matter what the climate. (See Chapter 14, "Visiting a Synagogue.")

THE UNEXPECTED SIMHA

Occasionally when tourists visit a local synagogue, they find they have walked in on a congregational *simha*, such as a bar mitzvah or an *oyfruf*, or a Sabbath *kiddush*. If an invitation to the entire congregation is extended from the pulpit, or by a congregant to the visitor, he should by all means accept; to refuse might even be an affront, unless one has a clear and pressing reason to leave at once, such as a waiting tour bus.

Almost invariably, whether in Europe or the United States, the traveler is made very welcome; for some very small European communities it is a real event to have an American guest. If you can manage a *"shalom"* and a *"lehayim"* you will be equipped for the conversational amenities abroad.

Some knowledge of Hebrew or Yiddish also helps to keep communications open, as does the obvious desire of most foreigners to practice their English.

On leaving, be especially careful to thank the host and hostess and to felicitate rabbi, cantor, and honoree on the occasion. In foreign countries, *todah rabbah* (many thanks) and *yasher koakh* (congratulations) do very well. The appropriate greetings of the day are also in order. (See Chapter 3, "Greetings.")

Should you be invited to lunch or dinner after services, you may certainly accept if the host seems genuinely eager to have a guest. After the Sabbath you should send a thank-you note, and in Europe and Israel, flowers.

VISITING CHURCHES AND ANTIQUITIES

There is an ancient prohibition against entering a church which is still followed by the ultra-Orthodox. Observant *kohanim* (members of the priestly clan) also do not enter churches, since there are many graves inside the sanctuary. For others, who make a distinction between entering a church to pray and entering it as a tourist, such sightseeing is acceptable.

Church decorum, in general, is similar to that observed in synagogue, except that men remove their hats, and all women, not merely the married, are expected to cover their heads. A man may keep his yarmulke on, as long as he removes his street hat.

Abbreviated dress is not permitted; thus shorts, and strapless and halter tops, would not be acceptable. At the Vatican and in very strict Catholic churches, women are expected to wear dresses with sleeves, or cover their arms with a shawl or scarf. At one time women wearing pants were not admitted, but this now varies with church and denomination.

Museum visits are sometimes a problem to the Orthodox, because of the large number of nudes on display and the high percentage of pagan or Christian religious subject matter. A traveler to whom this will be offensive should study his guidebook or ask the tour guide about galleries of Jewish art he may see instead. He should seek out collections of porcelains, gems, antique furniture, and the like, or forego the museum visit altogether. Sometimes it is possible to substitute some other site of Jewish interest for some of the members of the tour.

In large areas of antiquity, such as the ruins of Pompeii, Delphi, or the Acropolis, it is possible to visit the area but avoid some of the sculptures and paintings.

A traveler on a once-in-a-lifetime trip, contemplating a thousands-of-years-old culture may allow himself some leeway; such decisions are an individual matter.

ASK!

Sometimes observant travelers suffer unnecessary discomfort by failing to make their special needs known. Never hesitate to ask whether meals may be prepaid, how certain foods are prepared, whether a "no-meat" menu can be arranged, where the synagogue is located, and so on. A courteous inquiry usually results in careful accommodation to the tourist's request. Often you discover Jewish hoteliers, restaurateurs, and merchants in unlikely places, or will be invited into the kitchens to select personally the food you consider permissible.

When far from Jewish haunts, it is sometimes simpler to state that you are a vegetarian than to attempt a difficult exposition of *kashrut*, especially when there are language problems. Most foreign countries are not as "meat-happy" as the United States and it is not difficult to arrange tasty and nourishing *parve* or dairy meals.

Enjoy your trip!

INDEX

Numbers in boldface refer to the page on which Hebrew and Yiddish words are defined.